DRIVEN
An Autobiography

DRIVEN

AN AUTOBIOGRAPHY

LARRY H. MILLER

with DOUG ROBINSON

DESERET
BOOK

Unless otherwise noted, all photos are courtesy of the Larry and Gail Miller family.

Library of Congress Cataloging-in-Publication Data

Miller, Larry H., 1944–2009.
 Driven : an autobiography / Larry H. Miller, with Doug Robinson.
   p. cm.
 Includes index.
 ISBN 978-1-60641-656-3 (hardbound : alk. paper)
 1. Miller, Larry H., 1944–2009. 2. Automobile dealers—Utah—Biography.
3. Businessmen—Utah—Biography. 4. Utah Jazz (Basketball team) 5. Mormons—
United States—Biography. I. Robinson, Doug, 1955– II. Title.
 HD9710.25.U62A3 2010
 381'.45629222092—dc22
 [B]   2010004202

Printed in the United States of America
Worzalla Publishing Co., Stevens Point, WI

10   9   8   7   6   5   4   3   2   1

CONTENTS

CONTENTS

CONTENTS

PREFACE

Where do I begin the story of this book?

Well, for starters, the book nearly died with Larry Miller.

Six times he almost died during the seven months we worked on it; five times he was resuscitated.

He was always eager to resume work on the book after each close call or medical crisis. He had something he wanted to share, and he was determined to finish this project just as he had finished so many others. But then he didn't come back that last time.

That might have been the end of it, but he didn't let me off that easily before he left.

The last time I saw Larry Miller was when I drove to his house to say good-bye. His wife, Gail, had called me on my cell phone while I was out for my daily run. She called to inform me of Larry's condition—she told me he was dying. "If you're going to see him," she said, "you'd better come today. The end is near." So I sprinted the last three blocks to my house, showered hurriedly, put on a dress shirt and slacks, and began driving north toward the Millers' residence at the other end of the valley.

As I drove, I thought about all that had transpired. Seven months earlier, Miller had asked me to help him write a book about his life. It was something we had discussed on and off for seven years, beginning shortly after I had written a lengthy profile about Miller for the *Deseret News*. Regrettably now, both of us were preoccupied with other things, and the book became something we would do "someday." People frequently asked him when he was going to write his life story, and his answer was always the same: "I don't know; I'm too busy living it." Then Miller was hospitalized for 59 days in the summer of 2008 with a heart attack and other serious health problems. After he was released from the hospital, he called me at home one day, and I knew why.

"We'd better do that book now," he said. "You never know."

We began meeting two or three times a week at his hilltop mansion. Little did we know that we were in a race against time. We talked and talked and talked. We talked at the kitchen table over Gail's homemade lunches. We talked in his home office. We talked in the hospital while he underwent dialysis. We talked while he lay in bed in the upstairs bedoom of his home until he fell asleep in the middle of a sentence. We talked through the late summer. We talked through the fall. We talked into the onset of winter.

We talked until he could talk no more—until, finally, he was forced to spend all his energy fighting for his life.

Gail greeted me at the door with an embrace and showed me to the living room, where we sat for a few minutes while she explained the latest medical crisis—there had been so many these past few months. Then she led me upstairs to the master bedroom. Larry was lying on the bed with the covers pulled up to his chest, his head propped up by a couple of pillows. He was staring at the ceiling through half-lidded eyes. His arms and hands were bruised purple.

PREFACE

It had been a long, weary fight. "Doug is here," Gail announced. I approached the bed. Larry was weak and spoke little, and then only in a whisper. I took his cold arm in my hand—his hands were too damaged to hold—and leaned over his face so that I could look down into his blue eyes.

"You never know," he whispered.

He remembered.

Here he was, exhausted, medicated, and dying, and he was being ironic. He was still sharp enough to recall, spontaneously, the words he had spoken to me seven months earlier.

I leaned close to his ear and expressed my admiration and love for him. "You're a keeper," he whispered generously.

I expressed my regret that we hadn't finished the book, and then he said the last words he would speak to me. "I don't want to drop it." He said it again: "I don't want to drop it."

I turned to Gail. "He means the book," she said, confirming what I thought.

I had written nearly half of the book and still had notes from our old interviews that would provide material for many more chapters, but there was much more we had wanted to discuss.

Seeing that Larry was weary and fighting sleep, I took my leave, casting one last look back at the man—a legendary figure in Utah history—before I reached the door.

I knew what I had to do; I had to honor his wish.

He died the next day, February 20, 2009. He was 64.

—Doug Robinson

FOREWORD

BY JOHN STOCKTON

Larry Miller became a fixture in my life in 1985 when he began the rescue of the Utah Jazz. He completed that task a few short years later. The move was bold and risky for him and his family, but his love for the Salt Lake City community and his desire to keep the Jazz in Utah trumped his fears. It became clear that there was a new sheriff in town as his unique ownership style found its way onto the court and into the locker room.

Without hesitation, Larry would tuck himself into his own Jazz uniform and actively defend us (the players), bumping and shoving, screening out during the warm-ups of home games. Occasionally he would charge like a rhino, snorting and puffing, into our locker room after unpalatable losses. He would roar his contempt for our effort and stomp back out the door. We had never encountered this type of intensity by an owner, and it took some getting used to. I surely did not know the blessing that had just graced my life. My respect for him, as well as a friendship, grew steadily as I came to know Larry over the next 25 years.

One of my first personal experiences with Larry took place when my contract with the Jazz came due. In an unorthodox manner, we each wrote a salary number we thought was appropriate on a piece of paper and handed it across his desk. Both papers contained the same number, and the deal was done. For the rest of my career, we renegotiated my contract face-to-face when it came due. Each time, I knew I had crossed swords with a pirate. His mind was so quick and attuned to numbers that he was calculating deferments and percentages of the cap, amortizations, and a lot more, before I could register what my salary might be. He could have buried me any time he wanted. Like a big brother letting me score once in a while, Larry treated me fairly and honorably.

Over the years we shared many conversations in his office or while driving around in his vintage antique cars. On one occasion, he even took time off to take me on an extended drive to see a sick child. Being the boss, he could have said, "Go!" Instead, he put his own valuable time aside, picked me up at home, and drove an hour each way to take me there. It was a remarkable trip for both of us and, I think, for the child. He showed the patience of a father with me when I asked questions about life, sports, or business and even tolerated some insubordination at times with grace.

I have watched Larry with such admiration as he has accepted his role as a hero, in a lot of ways, in the community. He never wavered or shied away from the resulting responsibility. Starting out in business as a "parts guy" without a college education, he became a giant. Publicly, he assembled an armada of car dealerships, providing jobs for thousands. He constructed our new arena, the Delta Center, on schedule and on budget, and seemed to know each worker by name. He built Jordan Commons, a local gathering place with restaurants, movie theaters, and office buildings. Miller Motorsports Park, a recent addition, was voted the best racecourse built in the last 20 years in the United States. He has at least five honorary doctorate degrees, and the list goes on and on.

More privately, his ability to build bridges gave people a boost in life and encouraged them to pass it on. He has provided educational opportunities for those who couldn't afford it. He taught classes at local universities and actively sought out people who needed his help. I asked him once, "How do you get so much done in a day?" He responded, "Well, I just do it!"

This is very true. Larry just did it! He directly or indirectly enriched all of our lives in the Utah Jazz and the Salt Lake community. His impact in athletics through the success and reputation of the Utah Jazz, the Salt Lake Bees, and Miller Motorsports Park can be felt nationwide and perhaps worldwide. Yet, his greatest accomplishments may be the helping hands, the lessons, the time and care he offered to those less fortunate than himself.

Larry Miller lived a fairy tale, a pauper who became a king. This king did not pool the resources of others to get richer and more powerful. Instead, he chose to be a servant king who used his resources and clout to enrich the lives of others. He was a good king and a good boss. He wouldn't ask someone to do something he wouldn't do himself.

Larry was a great man and great friend. I admire him and I am proud of him. I announced my retirement in 2003. Immediately, he insisted that we have a celebration of my career. I reluctantly accepted, only after he used his full weight to impress upon me that it was important to the people of Salt Lake City, the state of Utah, and Jazz fans everywhere. Amazingly, in a few short days, he orchestrated an event of epic proportions and no doubt cost. He didn't even charge for concessions (you might say he had to bribe people to come). Regardless of the details, it was an event that profoundly touched me, my family, and, hopefully, the fans, as was Larry's intention.

Over the years, Larry and I discussed the possibilities of him writing a book on all of the lessons he had learned and documented in his life. It cannot replace the conversations in person, but I am surely looking forward to reading about Larry's unique education. There will never be another Larry Miller. I miss him.

INTRODUCTION

By Doug Robinson

One afternoon, as Larry and I sat in his tenth-floor office, I saw a small airplane fly past the large window behind his desk, dragging a large SALT LAKE BEES banner that advertised Miller's Triple A baseball team. Miller, with his back to the window, was unaware of the plane, but over the next couple of hours I noticed it periodically as it circled lazily above the west side of the valley and passed by us repeatedly. My eyes kept coming back to that airplane while I listened to Larry. It was as if the pilot were trying to remind me that Miller's influence is everywhere in Utah. You can't escape it.

Looking out the west window, I could see his movie theaters and the Larry H. and Gail Miller Salt Lake Community College campus that he built with $50 million of his own money. And if I could have seen over the Oquirrh Mountains, I would have been able to see the Miller Motorsports Park as well.

1

INTRODUCTION

Looking out the north window through the telescope mounted there, I could see his basketball arena and TV station and more car dealerships lined up on State Street and his mansion on the hill.

Looking out the east window, and slightly north, I could see the University of Utah, where he paid for the stadium scoreboard and a chair in the English department.

Out the south window, beyond the mountains that block the view of Utah Valley, I would have seen more car dealerships stretching south, another movie theater, and the softball and baseball complex that he built at BYU.

Dan Jones and Associates, the redoubtable public-opinion pollster, once conducted a survey that revealed that 99 percent of people in the Salt Lake Valley had done business with one or more services provided by Larry H. Miller, whether it was patronizing his theaters or buying his cars or eating at his restaurants or attending his Jazz games—and that doesn't include tuning into his TV and radio stations.

Not bad for a man who was a D student in high school, attended college for only six weeks, and never took a business class in his life.

"I don't mean to sound boastful," he said during a wistful moment one afternoon, "but I have had an extraordinary life."

His story is a chapter out of a Horatio Alger book. After dropping out of college, he worked as a stock boy in an auto parts store and, through the sheer force of his personality, native intelligence, and work ethic, became the most successful entrepreneur in the history of Utah. Whether sitting in his hilltop mansion that overlooks the entire Salt Lake Valley or in his tenth-floor aerie atop the Jordan Commons office complex, he has literally risen above his working-class roots.

After working for various car dealerships in Colorado and Utah, Miller struck out on his own almost on a whim. To pass a dull afternoon during a vacation in Salt Lake City, he visited an old acquaintance in the car business, and by the end of the day he owned his first dealership, writing up terms of the deal on the back of a blank check. That was April 6, 1979. On May 1, 1979, he began operating Toyota of Murray in Murray, Utah, and he couldn't know what he was beginning. Upon his death nearly 30 years later, he owned movie theaters, auto dealerships, a motorsports park with a world-class racetrack, a movie production company, an advertising agency, ranches, restaurants, TV and radio stations, a real-estate development company, an NBA franchise, a professional baseball team, an NBA arena, sports apparel stores—nearly 90 companies in all, in six states, with 7,000 employees, all under the umbrella of The Larry H. Miller Group, which produces $3.2 billion in sales annually, ranking it among the 200 largest privately owned companies in the United States. (He also was the tenth-largest car dealer in the U.S., with 42 dealerships in six states.) All of this blossomed from a single car dealership with fewer than 30 employees.

He was a car man, and then he became all these other things—chiefly, an entrepreneur, an appellation he embraced. He became Utah's Great-Uncle Larry, the state's benefactor, advocate, and facilitator. For years, his auto dealerships televised a commercial that became famous in the state—"After all, you know this guy," the commercial concluded, but it turns out we really didn't know him at all. People thought of Miller as the car dealer and Jazz owner. That was only a small part of what he did. Gail heard a common refrain from those who attended Miller's funeral and heard speakers reveal the many layers of Miller's life: "I had no idea he did all those things."

He funded and took a hands-on role in a remarkable array of projects, including ventures related to LDS Church history (the Joseph Smith Papers), large and extensive scholarship programs, American history, historic building renovations, planetariums, hospitals, official government advisory roles, music, painting, architecture, horticulture, sculpture, opera, movies, teaching college classes, private and public philanthropy. This resulted in an eclectic circle of friends—governors, congressmen, Pulitzer-Prize–winning authors, artists, athletes, billionaires, church leaders, Russian professors, media personalities, religious and historical scholars, moviemakers, musicians, singers, schoolteachers, kids in the neighborhood, the proprietor of a local sandwich shop, and on and on it went. On the side, he wrote pages and pages of notes on his life and lessons learned, commissioned paintings and sculptures and documentaries, and collected artwork, poetry, and favorite literary passages, not to mention honorary doctorate degrees—the college dropout was awarded five of them ("almost one for every week of college I attended," he liked to joke).

Miller understood his role and embraced it, even though it proved burdensome at times. "Some days it absolutely blows me away the impact we have on this community," he once wrote in his notes. "There's nobody like us. Sometimes it feels like a heavy load. Sometimes it feels remarkable. Sometimes I think we've created a monster."

In his tribute at Miller's passing, *Deseret News* columnist Lee Benson wrote, "Everywhere you look, there's his imprint. Sports. Business. Charity. Education. Media. Architecture. Utah is a far different, and far better, place because of just one man." Perhaps only Brigham Young has done more for Utah than Larry H. Miller.

When Miller died, he was publicly praised and mourned by senators, congressmen, mayors, a former presidential candidate, the governor, the NBA commissioner, a billionaire industrialist, church leaders, community leaders, NBA players and coaches. Tributes to Miller were read on the floor of the U.S. Senate and House of Representatives. For days newspapers were filled with stories about Miller, starting with banner headlines that ran across the top of the page. Radio stations devoted entire programs to his memory. TV stations aired hour-long specials about Miller's life. Within minutes after the *Deseret News* posted news of Miller's death on the Internet, there were more than 100 comments posted by readers offering condolences and their personal tributes to Miller. A large billboard on I-15 was devoted to Miller's memory. For six hours, thousands lined up for the viewing at the basketball arena, many of them waiting more than two hours, and at the end of the line Gail embraced or shook the hand of every one of them. Scores of police and highway patrolmen led his hearse to the cemetery, where he was accorded a 21-gun salute because of his status as an Honorary Colonel in the Utah Highway Patrol.

It was a remarkable, perhaps unprecedented outpouring for a citizen and businessman who held no official title as a political or religious leader. That was his broad impact and appeal. A stranger approached me in the gym that week to say, "The thing that surprised me is the emotion I felt about his death. I didn't even know him."

In the end, even Larry's widow marveled at it all. "We never could go anywhere without people talking to him or thanking him," Gail said. "The thing that is surprising is that an ordinary man could do what he did and unite a community. Really, he was an ordinary man even though he did extraordinary things."

What struck me about Miller as we talked over the course of many months is that his entrepreneurial career wasn't fueled as much by money as it was by a sense of duty and community. He saw himself as a bridge builder—another appellation he embraced—someone who could organize efforts between people and organizations to make things happen. He didn't buy the Utah Jazz because it would be a great investment or an appreciating asset; he did it because he wanted the team to remain in Utah, convinced that the team was important to the economy of the city and that it would become a rallying point for the state he loved.

The cynic in you might scoff, but consider this: He went to great lengths and risked everything financially to keep the Jazz in Utah. Really it was a foolish financial gamble on his part every step of the way, to buy half the Jazz, then to buy the other half, then to build the arena, and, in the process, take on staggering personal debt. Among others, Jon Huntsman, the billionaire industrialist, advised against it. The team had never made a profit in any of its 11 years of existence. When Miller immediately made the team profitable and the value of NBA teams skyrocketed in the coming years, he passed up numerous opportunities to sell the team, though that not only would have erased his considerable debt but would have reaped for him millions of dollars in profit.

"Selling the Jazz," he once said, "would be like selling Canyonlands."

Miller will be remembered for many things, but when he was asked how he wanted to be remembered, he choked up and said, "I want to be remembered as a man who loved Utah." (Gail had the last five words of that statement inscribed on his headstone.) Miller frequently said he considered the Jazz his gift to Utah. He felt a sense of mission about keeping the Jazz in the state, and he believed he had the savvy to make it work when no one else dared to try. He convinced conservative, hard-nosed bankers to take that leap with him when they were determined not to, and he convinced them solely because he was Larry Miller. With no business plan and little collateral or cash, he persuaded them to invest millions in a basketball franchise that had been bleeding money every year since it opened its doors. Otherwise, the Jazz would have wound up in Miami or Minneapolis.

Miller was often asked why he didn't take his bridge-building skills to political office. His answer was simple: "I absolutely believe that I can be more effective in the private sector. If I were at the lowest-level political office for either party, it would negate substantially my ability to navigate society and do what I do. Half of the people wouldn't trust me."

As it was, everyone trusted and embraced him in the community. After all, you know this guy—or do you?

Did you know he was a marble champion and a Hall of Fame

fast-pitch softball player? Did you know he was a lousy student—and a National Merit Scholar? Did you know that this college drop-out taught college classes, for no pay? Did you know he didn't meet his real father until he was middle-aged? Did you know he had this strange habit of counting his steps wherever he walked? Did you know he committed the first crash on his new racetrack, and that it was something straight out of *The Dukes of Hazzard*? Did you know he was deeply religious and believed there was more than his own hard work that propelled him to success? Did you know that he worked six days a week, dawn to bedtime, for 20 years and missed his children's youth, and that it was his greatest regret?

Did you know that one of his great passions was his Shelby Cobra collection? Did you know he liked to drive around Salt Lake City on snowy nights looking for cars to pull out of snowbanks? Did you know he got kicked out of the house as a teenager and taken to detention by the police, and that it bothered him the rest of his life? Did you know he loved the same girl since junior high?

I thought I knew Larry well, but every time we talked, a new layer was peeled back. "Doug, you really don't know what you're in for," Gail warned me when we first began the project. She was right.

It helped that Miller had a strong sense of his own history. He filled boxes—now stored in a basement closet—with his monthly Day-Timers, in which he made daily notes about his life, dating back to 1976. At first, they were merely ways to keep track of his appointments, but beginning in the '80s, when he could see that life was going to present him with unique experiences, he turned them into mini-journals. He noted people he met and conversations and observations and transactions and even the most mundane matters—airplane flight numbers, departure times, doctor appointments, synopses of meetings and where they were held and how long they lasted. Many of them are what he called "thought starters" that he jotted on scraps of paper—a couple of spare details from an event that would trigger memories of the entire event.

He also kept all of his correspondence in file cabinets. One year's worth of letters fills an entire file cabinet. During our interviews, Miller referred to his Day-Timers to check dates and the accuracy of his recollections. He began hand-writing essays about his life on legal paper as early as 1980. After his death, stacks of these essays were found on his desk. He even wrote letters to Gail, though they shared the same house—not love letters (well, there were those, too), but letters about work, projects he was involved with at the time, family matters, and so forth. He used letters as a vehicle to track his history.

It was the same sense of history that drove him to work on this book. His illness wasn't the only thing that prompted him in 2008 to start telling his story for print. The project was also prompted by all that free time he had while recuperating, which forced him to relax in a way he had never allowed himself. "I had all that time to think about things, and about all the stories from my life that I wanted to tell my family and business associates," he told me in our first meeting. "No one knows how long he's got, so I better do it timely."

Initially, he wanted to share his story only with family, friends, and close business associates. As we talked, he came to feel that it might be something he wanted to share with the public, but only if he could still express some of his most personal feelings. In other words, he didn't want to change the content simply because he had broadened his audience. He was still going to talk unapologetically about emotional and spiritual experiences the way he would if he were addressing family members.

"A lot of people have asked me about doing a book," he said. "Maybe it will help them with business deals or decisions or in some other way in their lives."

And so we began the long process of discussing his life, meeting two or three times a week for several months, but it wasn't to be as simple as that. There were setbacks and long interruptions in which his poor health precluded interviews.

His problems were a continuation of what had begun earlier in the year. In June of 2008, Miller's body finally protested all the neglect, the long hours at the office, the stress, and the added burden of diabetes, which was exacerbated by erratic eating habits. His body finally organized a boycott to slow his pace. A heart attack was followed by kidney failure, gastrointestinal bleeding, and other problems associated with diabetes. This would trigger a domino effect: The gastrointestinal bleeding required ten liters of fluid to stabilize his condition, which caused the swelling in his feet, which caused the blisters on his feet, which turned into ulcers, which eventually led to the amputation of his legs below the knee. Meanwhile, he required surgery, eight pints of blood, and 59 days in the hospital— not to mention, he would tell you, prayers and divine intervention to get him into action again. Up to this point, he died four times— his heart stopped—but each time he was revived by doctors.

After Miller was released from the hospital, we began to meet in his house. Having recently turned his business empire over to his oldest son, Greg, in July 2008, Miller had decided to exile himself from his office to "give Greg some space" and to undergo his twice-daily physical therapy sessions at home. As part of the transition of the company leadership to Greg, Larry created an advisory board and participated in the first meeting via speakerphone. He ended the meeting by saying, "You collectively are representing my life's work, so don't screw it up."

Not that there was any pressure.

He was wheelchair-bound at the time and would be for the remainder of his life. His arms were tattooed with deep purple bruises from the IVs. He was so weakened that his early therapy consisted simply of standing for one minute at a time. On good days he walked the length of the main hall, 100 feet, with his therapist, Wade, and grandson Zane at his elbows and Gail following with the wheelchair. He created goals for himself: 100 feet, then 200 feet, then a lap of the hall. One day, when he felt strong enough, he asked Gail to drive him to the basketball arena so he could walk the entire length of the concourse. He had to stop a few times, but he made it. After that, his feet became so bad that he was never able to walk that far again.

In the early days of our interviews, he often rocked back and forth in his chair, with his arms crossed on his chest, as he shut his eyes deep in thought. "Pressure sores," he explained unbidden one day, as if he had read my wondering mind. "I'm rocking back and forth like this because I have pressure sores."

And then he would continue talking, often closing his eyes as if he were seeing the words and editing them before they arrived at his mouth. Gail was usually in the background, busy with household duties and meal preparations, but she liked to listen, too, I noticed. Gail has a calming influence on everyone near her, and during times of stress or crisis she is a rock, a great source of comfort for others. Her devotion to Larry and her family is heroic, as you will see. I was moved almost to tears as I watched her tend to Larry's needs over these months. I watched her get down on her hands and knees to clean, treat, and wrap her husband's diabetes-ravaged feet as Larry and I talked. I saw her hoisting his heavy wheelchair in and out of the car and helping lift and move Larry in and out of his chair with the aid of a slide board. I saw her test his blood-sugar levels routinely. I saw her harvest vegetables from her garden to make Larry's favorite lunches—or as close as she could get, after considering his diabetic diet, his kidney diet, and his heart diet.

The interviews continued as circumstances allowed. On one occasion I sat by his bedside in the hospital while he underwent dialysis to drain off excessive water weight his body had stored. As we talked, his blood could be seen coursing through tubes, and doctors were coming in and out of the room. On another occasion, we conducted the interview as he lay in his bed upstairs in his home until he fell asleep. I sat for another 45 minutes while he slept because Gail was running errands and I didn't want to leave him alone.

In typical Miller fashion, he did too much too soon, scheduling meetings in his home in pursuit of various projects. He wound up back in the hospital for nine days. In October, doctors discovered a bone infection in Miller's feet. When the infection didn't respond to antibiotic treatment, doctors removed two toes on his left foot and the great toe joint of his right foot, and then ordered six weeks of hyperbaric chamber treatment on an outpatient basis to speed healing. Then he was hospitalized again for other complications, and while he was there he died, again—his heart stopped, again. Doctors performed life-saving CPR with such rigor that they broke several ribs.

After a while, it seemed as if doctors were plugging holes in a leaky dam with their fingers and running out of fingers as they dealt with one health problem after another. Late in January, Miller developed a 104-degree fever, and the infection in his feet was oozing pus. The doctors told Gail to gather the children and grandchildren at the hospital; they didn't think he was going to make it. But he did, or at least he put off death for a short while. A couple of days later, on the evening of January 22, I received a phone call from Larry. "I have news, and it's not good," he said. His voice cracked, and my stomach dropped. "Tomorrow morning they're going to amputate both of my legs from the knee down." Doctors were trying to save his life, he explained, and as we continued to discuss things, I gently asked him about the long-term prognosis.

"They don't know," he said.

Remarkably, as the conversation closed he said, "I will call you, but it won't be tomorrow." He wasn't making an attempt at dark humor or understatement—who would expect a call at a time like this?—but it reminded me of how badly he wanted to get back to work and how badly he wanted to finish the book.

On February 12, doctors gave Miller more bad news. He had

contracted calciphylaxis, a rare disease that strikes a small percentage of those suffering renal failure or undergoing dialysis. The disease calcifies the blood, blocking the flow of oxygen. It is almost always fatal.

With continued dialysis, calciphylaxis patients can survive for several months. But after weighing his options for a couple of days, Miller told Gail that he would not undergo more dialysis. He couldn't face months of daily visits to the hospital and more tests and needles and procedures and rehab; if he couldn't resume his old, task-oriented life of projects and work and family, or even hope for such a thing in the future, well . . .

"He didn't want to live like that," Gail said. "His only concern was me. He didn't want to leave me alone, so I had to convince him I would be all right."

He passed away a week later in his own bed with his family by his side.

You could say Miller worked himself to death. He labored maniacally for most of his adult life—80 to 90 hours a week for decades—because he thought the way he could succeed was simply to outwork everyone. But it was more than that. He was passionate about everything he undertook. When he was involved in a project, he immersed himself in it; it dominated his thoughts around the clock. When he began to build the arena, he told Gail, "Basically, I'll be gone for three years." The pace he maintained at such times—and throughout most of his career—would have been physically and emotionally taxing for anyone, but especially for a man with Type 2 diabetes. There were days when he would rush out the door without eating breakfast, tossing a candy bar in the car; at the end of the day the candy bar would still be there because the thought of eating hadn't crossed his mind—he was just too busy.

Through it all, Miller, a demanding, sometimes hot-tempered, intense, hardworking, tough businessman, was a soft touch. He was famous for his tears. Did he ever hold a press conference in which he didn't cry, whether it was to announce Karl Malone's latest new contract or plans to build an arena? He got a huge charge out of helping people, although, with his visibility, the demands for help became more than he could handle. After realizing he couldn't help everyone, he picked his spots, but he was always genuinely looking for ways to help, paying off hospital bills and mortgages and car loans and solving problems for others.

Miller reminded me of a quote from Spencer W. Kimball, former President of The Church of Jesus Christ of Latter-day Saints, of which Miller was a devout member. President Kimball said, "Waste is unjustified, and especially the waste of time. . . . One must live, not only exist; he must do, not merely be; he must grow, not just vegetate" (*The Miracle of Forgiveness* [Bookcraft, 1969], 91).

That was Miller. He never wasted a minute. He loved work and had an immense capacity for it. As we discussed his life, I couldn't help but notice how often he used the word *fun* when he discussed his work. I recall the first time I arrived at his house to begin the interviews for this book. He had barely been released from his 59-day stay in the hospital and already he was sitting at the kitchen table with a group of men discussing business.

Miller was defined by his work ethic; his sense of wanting to achieve, contribute, and build; and the pure enjoyment he derived from a variety of projects to those ends. "Putting the company on autopilot and just running it the best it can isn't bad," he once wrote, "it just isn't any fun because you just do the same thing every day."

A perusal of Miller's journal entries reveals much about the way he thought and what he was at his core. "June 2007: The big questions: What manner of man do I want to be? 2) What is sufficient for my needs? 3) What do I do with the rest?" In 2008, he wrote, "Goals in life: Make the Utah Food Bank holler uncle because they couldn't take any more food; fill EnergySolutions Arena for the annual sing-along at Christmas." Another note from the summer of 2008: "I was lying in the hospital when, for some reason, these words came to me. 'Go about doing good until there's too much good in the world.' I decided right then I was going to use it as one of our company slogans. It's excellence for the sake of excellence. It just feels good being excellent, doing your best, learning everything you can about anything to which you apply yourself and then doing that thing well."

In the end, it all caught up with him and shortened his life—the obsessive work, the long hours, the drive, the intensity. Seeing him on his deathbed, I was reminded of the movie *Amadeus*, in which Mozart worked so hard to squeeze all the music out of his soul that he died utterly exhausted and spent.

Miller died completely at peace with death. He knew he had used his time on earth well, that he had worked hard and done so with integrity, that he had built a business empire that benefited many and left his community a better place through his efforts and never let his success change him. He had fought to overcome his weaknesses (especially his swearing and temper), found his faith, raised a big family that was thriving, secured that family's future, and put everything in order for his passing. He was grateful for all of it and said so. "I cannot comprehend why we have what we have," he wrote. "How lucky can a man be?"

Miller considered John Adams a kindred spirit after reading David McCullough's biography of the man. In Larry's copy of the book he marked a quote that Adams made late in his life: "I sleep well, appetite is good, work hard, conscience is neat and easy. Content to live and willing to die. Hoping to do a 'little good.'" That perfectly described Miller near the end. He also marked this passage written by McCullough: "Through all his life Adams would be happiest when there was clear purpose to his days." This was Miller, too, content only when he could work hard and accomplish things and be satisfied at the end, though wanting to do more. After Larry was gone, Gail was looking through a notebook in which her husband had collected his favorite stories and quotes. In the back of the notebook, there was a scrap of paper that appeared to have been torn from a larger sheet of paper. On it, Larry had written a note: "I have fought a good fight. I have finished my course. I have kept the faith. 2nd Timothy 4:7."

What was Miller really like? I am asked. He was intense, serious, and quirky. He had an amazing grasp of numbers and an uncanny memory. He was haunted by events of his childhood. He hated change. When he and Gail moved into their new home, Gail made sure the new bathroom and bedroom were set up exactly like those in the old house, with everything (Water Pic, clothing, notepad, medicine, toothbrush, clock) in the same place. When he left the house to go to work, where things were in constant flux, Gail explained, at home he needed constancy, a home base, order. He was an artist at heart who wanted to create and build, and he had an artist's temperament and emotions. He was sensitive and emotional, and privately he battled to conquer a hot temper. He was driven. He could outwork anyone and he was brilliant, and those two traits together made him a dynamo in whatever he did.

He was a great listener. You know how some people aren't really listening so much as they're waiting to say what they want to say? Larry listened intensely and sympathetically, trying to understand and get to know the person. It was the foundation on which he developed relationships. He made people feel like they were interesting and important; days or months later, he would remember something they had told him—a name, an event, something about their family—and he would ask about it. He was kind and interested, and he drew people in that way.

He was rich but frugal. He wanted to learn about everything that crossed his path and sought books and experts to teach him about everything from architecture to trees to sculpture to concrete. He knew something about everything, probably because he listened and made a conscious effort to learn. Clark Whitworth, who worked for Larry for years, once noted, "People loved his Thursday night radio show. He agreed to do the show to talk about the Jazz, but he didn't even have to talk sports. People would tell me, 'I really love to listen to that.' It was like a fireside chat. He could talk about anything, and he was knowledgeable, perceptive, insightful, and unguarded."

As I have reflected on Miller's life since his passing, I have often thought of the famous quote from Socrates: "The unexamined life is not worth living." Miller, intense and focused almost to a fault, examined his life constantly and it showed in our interviews. He had thought things through so much—his motives, lessons he had learned, his faults, his strengths, his weaknesses, his likes and dislikes, his feelings, events in his life, and so forth—that when we sat down for interviews it was as if he had rehearsed his lines. He knew exactly what he wanted to say and why and what it all meant.

Miller spent his last months working on this book, among other projects. As he discussed his thoughts and feelings and the events of his life with the famous Miller candor, he liked to say he had no secrets. He was always open and honest with his feelings, even when it was at his own expense. He told his story honestly. This is the man behind the man you saw on the front row at Jazz games (except on Sundays, of course). I can tell you this much: There is little difference between the public and private Miller.

He wanted to tell you his story. This is that story.

—DOUG ROBINSON

POSTSCRIPT FROM LARRY MILLER

One day a few years ago, Gail and I were driving home from Colorado when we began reflecting on our lives. Gail suggested that we make a list of the things we—and I do mean "we"—have done in our lives. Gail wrote the list on a notepad, and when we were finished, we were shocked. The list covered several pages; every few months for 20 years there had been a major business transaction or project.

INTRODUCTION

"No wonder we're tired," Gail said to me.

There are few great secrets to my professional success, just hard work and a conscious attempt to draw conclusions or lessons from things that happen to me and around me and to learn everything I can about my job and find a better way to do it. Whether something was a success or a failure, I tried to understand why that happened and learn from it. I worked 80 to 90 hours a week, year-round, for two decades, while Gail took care of the kids and made our house a home and supported me in everything I did, although I sometimes wonder how she managed it. I don't know why I was so driven, but when I look back at my boyhood that drive always seems to have been there, whether I was preparing for marble championships or softball games. Ultimately, though, my success came from a spiritual awakening as much as anything I did, and in time we will come to that.

The wonder of it is that it was all kind of a great big accident, or seemed to be. The Jazz, the 42 car dealerships, the movie theaters, the real-estate businesses and movie company and restaurants, the motor speedway, the Triple A baseball team, the Delta Center, the radio and TV stations, the advertising and finance firms, all of it—I never saw myself doing any of those things. I was a 41-year-old car dealer when I took my first step outside of the car business with the purchase of the Jazz. It's funny how life is like a river sometimes, and, if you do things a certain way, that river will just take you a certain direction and you ride it out and see where it takes you. People ask me if I set out with a plan. No way. The chain of events that began my entrepreneurial career was sparked by three failures: I dropped out of college, got laid off, and got demoted.

PART I

BEGINNINGS

CHAPTER 1

EPIPHANY

I can remember precisely the moment my life changed forever. I had an epiphany one morning, and nearly every detail of that moment is burned into the hard drive of my brain. It was March 1971, and I was at work, managing the parts department at a Toyota dealership in Colorado. I had just taken a 21-line Corolla crash parts order over the phone from a body shop, and I was checking to see what parts I had in stock when, like a bucket of cold water, it hit me.

Here I was, soon to be 27 years old, married, with two children and one on the way, and I was responsible for raising and supporting those children, providing food and shelter and college and housing and much more, while preparing for old age and retirement, and I realized I had nothing to fall back on. I had no college education, no special training. All I had was my energy and whatever talent I had been blessed with.

It scared me. The feeling was so overwhelming that I stopped what I was doing to ponder the matter.

I decided I had to be extremely good at something, and the thing I was best at was being a Toyota parts manager. That night I worked until 10:00. It was the start of my 90-hour-a-week work schedule. From that moment on, I began working from 7:30 in the morning until 9, 10, or 11 at night, six days a week. I did this for 20 years.

Reasoning that other dealers had the same parts and roughly the same prices to offer, I believed service and hustle were the things that would set me apart. I would simply outwork them. I would become so good that I could not be denied. I was obsessed with doing everything I could do and accomplishing as much as I could. It was difficult for me to go home with work undone. I wanted it to be done for the next day. A lot of people go through the motions with little sense of urgency; I had an extreme sense of urgency. A body shop would call and order 21 parts; I'd pull, pick, and price them in 15 or 20 minutes. If I could find only 19 parts, I was ticked off. If I was five minutes late, I was upset because I had created a system that wasn't more responsive. I became a student of everything—ordering systems, delivery systems, hiring practices, training practices, retention practices. I decided I had to be incredible in all facets so that I could control the outcome. I needed to become the best.

Well, I wasn't just good at delivering service and parts; I was world-class. I wanted parts delivered five minutes ago. I was a quarterback, running the two-minute offense. It produced results. When I started, the store was averaging $6,500 a month in parts sales, or $78,000 a year. In my first month on the job, sales jumped to $13,000 and increased every single month for 28 months. The parts department grew so big that the dealership didn't have room to store all the parts, so we bought houses around the dealerships and stored them there. In my second full year on the job, we became the first Toyota dealer in the U.S. to sell a million dollars' worth of parts in one year, an average of more than $83,000 a month—which was more than the dealership had done previously in an entire year. We were the highest volume Toyota parts dealer in the nation. We wound up selling parts in 39 states, including Alaska and Maine. We had a map on the ceiling of the parts department, and every time we'd sell parts to a new place, we'd put a pin in the map. Pretty soon that map was filled with pins. Because of my performance, I was promoted to general manager of the Toyota store dealership, and eventually operations manager over five dealerships.

I begin my story this way because it is a useful backdrop for any discussion of my life. It colors so much of what I did and so much of what happened to me. It was central to everything, whether it was working as a deliveryman or building a private business or growing into an entrepreneur or buying the Jazz or, I'm sorry to say, neglecting my family to do all of the above.

I worked and worked and worked, day after day, night after night, dawn to bedtime. I was driven to succeed, and the way I did that was the way I do everything—I overpower problems with work.

I had always been an unusually intense, single-minded person anyway, and the fear I experienced on that March morning in 1971 only added more fuel to that determination. This drive was evident even in my early years. When I was a boy, we played marbles. Not just playground marbles, but serious tournament marbles. I went to great lengths to practice and hone my skill. I hiked up Capitol Hill behind my house to the police rifle range and gathered brass shell casings of all sizes—hundreds of them. I arranged the shells upright in ten rows the width of my room, with the biggest shells—the 2½-inch 30.06 casings—placed in the back row some 30 feet away, and the smaller .22-caliber shells in the front row. Then I shot at the shells with marbles until I had knocked down all of them. It took accuracy and power to knock shells down from that distance, especially since the marble had to go over or through other shells to get to the big shells in the back row. I did this every day for three years. I won the school marble championship and finished second in the city championship.

One day while teaching an entrepreneurial class at BYU, I was telling students that whatever we learn through hard work and dedication will remain with us throughout our lives and benefit us in ways we can't foresee. To make my point, I pulled a marble out of my pocket and pointed to a young man sitting in the last row, on the fourth tier of a four-tiered classroom. I told him that even though I hadn't shot a marble in 30 years, I could hit him between the eyes. I flicked the marble with my thumb and it struck him between the eyes. It was a lucky shot, but I made my point.

The dedication to marbles seems to have been the earliest manifestation of my intensity and passion for success. I remember this: I decided as a very young kid that being mediocre is no fun. That drove me to do what I had to do to succeed. In my teens I turned that passion toward softball. I practiced pitching every day for years, even if it meant digging a foothold in snow and ice—but I will save that story for another chapter.

I don't know why I'm wired like this. I guess it's the thrill of success, the thrill of the hunt, the high of achievement and competition. Initially, after the epiphany, the insanely long hours that I worked were driven by fear, as I have mentioned, but then the success became intoxicating. Clearly, my motivation to work like that shifted from fear-driven to success-driven. And it was fun doing it. It was fun being as good at it as I was. Later, as an entrepreneur, I discovered that I could put together deals and financing that most people in my financial position at that time wouldn't have been able to do.

I thrived on work and on the details. Instead of delegating, as I should have, I dived into the minutia of every project we undertook. Even amid the great concerns about deadlines and costs and architectural issues when we were building the Delta Center, I was involved in every aspect of the project, even the window blinds and the type of concrete block we would use. I drove around town for hours trying to find a building that used a certain type of concrete block before finding it at the airport. I had to get security clearance just to look at that concrete. I worked for weeks to research what type of trees we should plant in front of the arena. I bought books on the subject; I consulted several horticulturists. I drove around town to see what various trees looked like when they were mature. (Ultimately, I chose to plant flowering pear trees in front of the arena because when they're planted a certain distance apart they grow together and form a canopy about 35 feet above the ground. The canopy provides shade in the summer and a beautiful treetop view for people looking out of the fifth floor of the arena.) I became an expert on trees.

What CEO of a billion-dollar company does this?

I was that intense about everything. We built dozens of buildings, and I was the one deciding the floor plan and the paint and the color of the carpet and so forth. I could have delegated these jobs to any of our thousands of employees, but I took pleasure in the details; I liked to make sure it was done right. I liked the sense of accomplishment and learning new things. Each time I took on a new project, I immersed myself in some new field and became expert at it. I can tell you the craziest things, such as how many Christmas lights it takes to decorate a tree in front of the arena or how many yards of concrete we poured to build that building.

In the arena project—initally named the Delta Center, but now known as EnergySolutions Arena—I attended daily meetings with architects and learned the trade as much as I could. I became pretty knowledgeable, too. During those meetings, I requested that certain things be done with the construction of the building, and architects would tell me they couldn't be done. I'd tell them, "If you look at your drawings and reconfigure your plans, I think you'll see that it can be done." The next day the architects would show up for another meeting and report, "You know what, you're right."

I liked that. I liked the simple enjoyment of learning, which I am sure is amusing to my former schoolteachers, whom I tortured daily with my class behavior and refusal to do homework.

People have asked me why I am like this, and how and why I have done the things I have done. It is probably some combination of genetics and the collected experiences of my formative years that made me yearn for success and achievement. Perhaps a couple of traumatic events, combined with the tenuousness and anxiety of my youth, have played a bigger role in shaping me than even I realize, because I have continually turned those things over in my mind all these years later and tried to make sense of them, and there I have failed.

CHAPTER 2

ON THIN ICE

One night during the summer of my 16th year I returned home to find my world turned upside down. It was late, close to 11:00 P.M., and I had walked home through the summer night on Capitol Hill as I often did after being out with friends. It was a typical evening, with a cool breeze stirring the maples overhead. I counted my steps as I walked, which remains one of my odd habits. As I approached our house, I saw three sacks on the porch and wondered what they contained. I walked up the stairs and onto the porch, peeked into the sacks, and was stunned by what I saw. They were filled with my clothes.

I was confused. What was going on?

I tried the front doorknob. Locked. I walked around to the side of the house to try the walk-out basement door. Locked.

The house was dark, but I knew my family was in there.

Slowly the realization of what had happened washed over me: I had been kicked out of the house.

But why?

I didn't know what to do, especially at this late hour. I was moving as if in a dream. I was too wounded to knock on the door and ask my parents what was going on. I did the only thing I could think to do: I picked up the three bags, hugging them to my chest, and walked down the hill to Gail's house. We had been dating for about a year now, and I spent a lot of time at her home. Her parents agreed to let me stay the night on their couch.

The next day I walked to the Haslams' house, which was three blocks from my own home. They had six boys, and I was a frequent visitor to their house. After I explained what had happened, they invited me to stay with them. At some point in the weeks that followed, Mr. Haslam—his name was Dale—sat me down to discuss the situation. He came off as a gruff man, but really he had a heart of gold. He made me feel welcome in his home, and I wound up living there for six months. I slept in a bunk bed on the back porch, which had been closed in.

During all that time, I never had any contact with my family, just three blocks away. I felt empty and displaced, but I did not have longings to return home, probably because of the tension that existed there. As Christmas approached, I finally began to experience some of those longings, so I called my mother and told her simply, "I think it's time to come home." Her response was cool. "You'll have to talk to your dad," she said. Two days before Christmas I moved back home. It was 1963.

In the years since then, Gail has interviewed my mother twice, with a tape recorder, to learn more about my family history. Both times she asked my mother why I was kicked out of the house. She could never adequately answer the question to my satisfaction. It's still an issue for me today. I think about it more than I should.

I look for answers and there are none—Dad is gone and Mom is unapproachable about it.

With only the retrospect and experience of an adult, I realize that my childhood was a walk across a sheet of ice, and I was never certain the world under my feet would support me. I did my best to survive, but little more. I was aware of the delicacy of my position and did my best simply to stay under the radar in those early years.

I wasn't always able to do this. Even before I was kicked out of the house, the police took me from my home on two different occasions, though no one ever could tell me what crime I was supposed to have committed. One evening a police officer knocked on our door. My mother answered and stepped aside as he entered the house. It was immediately clear that she had been expecting him. The cop, whose name was Willie, was cordial. "You're Larry Miller," he began. When I agreed, he said, "I need you to come with me." I was confused but taken in by his friendliness. I followed him as we walked to his car, which was parked on another street. We climbed into his blue Plymouth cop car, and he let it roll down the street before he popped the clutch to start it.

"That's a lazy man's way of starting the car," he said.

He drove me to the juvenile detention center, which is another name for *prison*. It had bars on the doors and windows. Inside the building, Officer Willie told me, "The word your parents are using about you is *incorrigible*. You're impossible to manage."

I ventured a question. "What have I done?"

This question hung in the air and died.

I was checked into the facility and assigned a room, and there I stayed for three days. I never went to court, and no one ever told me what I had done. My parents had simply called the cops and told them to haul me away. Most of what I remember about my stay there was that one of the "inmates" taught me how to start a fire with a pencil, tissue paper, and an electrical outlet.

Some time later—perhaps weeks, I don't know—this scenario

replayed itself, but before going into that, I must explain something about myself. I was resourceful and inventive at an early age. Using parts I salvaged from old telephones I found in a construction-site dumpster, I rigged up a private telephone line from my house to my buddies' house across the street—Denny and David Ashton's place. I did this by running a stretch of two-strand wire out my window, up through the Russian olive tree on the north side of the house, over our neighbors' roof and then across the street along some existing telephone lines and down into the Ashtons' house through the boys' bedroom window. One of the wires connected to earpieces and the other to mouthpieces, powered by a nine-volt battery and controlled by toggle switches. I also rigged up a buzzer—which I bought at an electronics store—to alert the Ashtons to my calls. When I wanted to call the Ashtons, I pushed a switch that rang the buzzer—one buzz for Denny, two buzzes for David. When they answered, I switched off the buzzer and switched on the phone so I could talk. It was a lot of fun, and it worked well, too, although years later our neighbors told us they could hear our conversations through their TV. I took it a step further by creating a switchboard from a masonite plate that I mounted next to my bed. It had several switches on it, which enabled me to turn on my radio, stereo, overhead light, desk lamp, tape recorder, and phone from my bed. The recorder allowed me to record my phone conversations—consider it an early form of an answering machine.

Anyway, I came home one evening and found a detective, a photographer, and two uniformed policemen waiting for me in my downstairs room. They had pulled my bed away from the wall and were taking photos and searching my room. I learned that the detective had come all the way from Denver to investigate my phone system. You would have thought I had stolen nuclear secrets. My parents—Mom, really—were convinced that I had done something criminal in building that phone line and that I had stolen the materials to make it. I was taken again to the juvenile detention center for several days. I don't believe I broke a law, and I was never charged with doing so. I have been bitter about it ever since. Whose parents call the police on them for something like that? Since then, Mom has bragged about how bright I must have been to build that phone system.

In some ways, I guess my childhood ended there. I had another epiphany of sorts: I realized while I was in detention that I did not feel compelled to regain my freedom to return home. Although I didn't like detention, home was not a much better alternative. I wasn't overly stressed that I was there, and the realization of this disturbed me.

I have wondered if the things I've accomplished over the years in my typically maniacal and driven style didn't come about as a result of my not wanting ever to lose control of my own destiny again. There have been many times in my life when I refused to leave any deal undone so that I would never again have to be subject to the whims of others, whether it was parents who wanted to jail me or a boss who wanted to fire me. I had experienced vulnerability, and I didn't like it.

What concerned me most while I was in detention was that I hadn't talked to Gail for a couple of days. Gail Saxton, my future wife, was my high school sweetheart and a source of great comfort for me even then. I needed her to know what had happened to me. I looked out the window of my room one afternoon through the heavy mesh screen. It was autumn and the ground was littered with yellow and red maple leaves. I saw a kid playing outside in the leaves, and I called to him. He walked closer to the window, and I told him that I needed a favor; I asked him to call Gail Saxton, and I gave him my name and her phone number. I learned later that he did as I asked.

These events led my mother and me to counseling, but we did this separately with different counselors. My counselor put me through a battery of inkblot tests and asked me typical questions about why I was unhappy. One day I decided to jerk his chain, so when he showed me some inkblots I told him, "I see a really unhappy boy sitting on a step wondering what he's going to do with his life." The doctor jumped all over it.

The irony was that I was not a bad kid. My friends got into trouble a few times, but I was seldom part of it. Once, while they were walking home near the capitol after a late movie, my buddies leveled a large glass greenhouse with rocks and bricks. I never did that kind of thing. I did have a temper, but I was never violent. I'd shout and slam doors, but I never hit anyone. I'd leave the house to cool down. The worse thing I did was to talk in school and ignore my homework. I was disruptive and fidgety in class, but that was as bad as I got. The bottom line is that I didn't deserve to be sent to juvenile hall. I have wracked my brain for 40 years trying to understand why my parents called the cops on me.

With all the undercurrents of my home life, I felt most comfortable when I was out of the house. My home was tense and contentious. There were always problems, and this has borne bitter fruit over the years. Talk about a dysfunctional family. It all comes from Mom's anger and the mind games she played with her kids.

All of this affected me in many profound and subtle ways. I was exceptionally bright, but I was a poor student who acted up in school. I was a good athlete who loved sports, especially baseball, but I never competed in high school sports. I tried sophomore football, but my mother harangued me about it every day and threw crying fits, saying I was going to get hurt. I decided it wasn't worth the aggravation.

I didn't feel I had any encouragement or instruction from my parents about how to function as an adult in the real world. I just floated around and tried to get by day to day. I had no confidence. Everything was a hassle at home. Everything upset somebody. So I just stayed out of their way as much as I could.

Instead of playing sports, I was a statistician for the West High

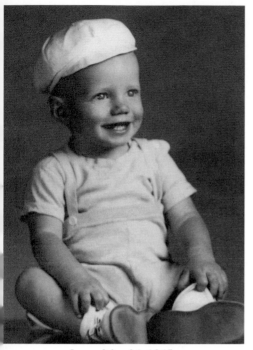

Larry, May 24, 1945.

Larry and his sister, Judy, December 1, 1946.

Larry's Sunday School class, May 1946. Larry is third from right on front row.

Grandpa William Horne, a major figure in Larry's life, with his family.
Left to right, standing: Wally, Shirley, Reid; seated: Lorille (Larry's mother),
Grandma Mary Horne, and Grandpa William Horne.

Grandpa Horne holding Larry.

Larry with his mother, winter 1945.

Larry's grandmother Etsa Talmage, another important influence in his life.

Frank and Lorille Miller on the day Larry and Judy were sealed to them in the Salt Lake Temple.

Frank and Lorille Miller, Larry's parents.

Gail Saxton with some of her siblings in front of their house in 1946.
Left to right: Kay, Lynn, Joy, Gail, Glen.

Gail and her siblings in 1953, together for the first time since 1947.
Left to right, back row: Joy, Lynn, Lory, Kay, Glen; front row: Richard (kneeling), Gail, Diane.

Larry on the front porch of his house, about 1953.

The Miller children, 1958. Clockwise from top left: Judy, Larry, Charlene, Tom.

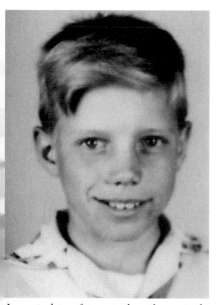

Larry in his safety patrol uniform, sixth grade, Lafayette Elementary School.

The "Capitol Hill Gang." This picture was taken in 1955 at the northeast corner of the Lafayette Elementary School playground with several of Larry's buddies who became lifelong friends. Front row, left to right: Terry Howick, Larry Miller, Eddie Nagasawa, Ernie Capel, Willie Radinger. Back row, left to right, Peter Hadreas, Ken Toone, Grant Cannon, (unknown), Rudd Warner.

Utah Drive-in Theatre baseball team, 1956. Front row: Jimmy Hunt,
Denny Ashton, Michael Versluis, Chuck Rawlins, Kerry Wilkins.
Back row: Mr. George Tucker (manager), Richard Jensen, Tim Coburn, Kelly Jensen,
Rodney Stone, Ron Westerman, David Ipson, Stephen Haslam, Larry Miller.

Pitcher Larry discusses strategy with his catcher, Richard Jensen.

Clockwise from top left: Judy, Larry, Tom, and Charlene Miller in 1957.

Larry (left) shows off a great day of fishing with scouting buddy Mark Eskelsen.

Capitol Hill Second Ward softball team, 1962. Left to right, front: Barry Olsen (batboy) in front of Ron Westerman, Stuart Cannon, Dennis Ashton, Grant Cannon, Peter Fairclough. Middle: Mike Fairclough, Stan Olsen, Larry Miller, James Hunt, Dennis Haslam. Back: Douglas Larsen, Steve Haslam, Ken Toone, Bishop R. Hulbert Keddington, Coach Glen Lloyd, Assistant Coach LeGrand Olsen.

Always ready for a good adventure, Larry and friends go on a SOCOTWA river trip in August 1959. Left to right, back row: Ron Westerman, Joe Keddington, Stan Olsen, Steve Haslam, Larry Miller, Dave Ipson; front row: Jerry Silver, Ken Toone, Clark Silver, Terry Toone, Rowland Francom, Grant Cannon.

Gail and Larry, constant companions, pose for a picture in front
of her house after school in 1960.

Gail's ninth-grade graduation from Horace Mann Jr. High School in May 1959.

Larry poses on the lawn of Gail's house, 1959.

Gail and Larry dated for six years before their marriage in 1965.

Sophomores at West High School, 1960.

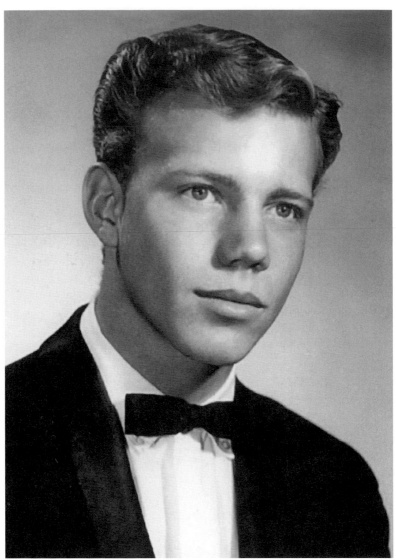

High school seniors . . .

And high school sweethearts.

Horace Mann Jr. High School, where Larry and Gail met in 1957.

Larry and Gail's first apartment, second from left, where they lived
for the first three years of their marriage.

The Miller siblings in 1966. Clockwise from left: Judy, Larry, Tom, Charlene.

Wedding day, March 25, 1965, Memorial House, Memory Grove, Salt Lake City, Utah.

basketball and baseball teams, which satisfied my fascination with numbers, and I played softball in Salt Lake County and LDS Church leagues.

I was alone even within the four walls of my house. My family went on summer vacation without me on a few occasions. At the time I didn't mind; it was almost a relief. At least I could stay home and play softball, and it undoubtedly saved me from some family confrontations. But I took a lot of it personally—I was very sensitive anyway. Years later, as an adult, I would look through old family memorabilia and see photos of places my family had visited on vacation—Seattle and San Francisco—that I never even knew they had visited.

There was an alienation of affection that was palpable. Sometimes it took on less subtle forms. As a child, if I was supposed to be home at 7:00, and I came home at 7:10, I would get 12 lashes. Sometimes it was with a belt. Other times they would send me out to the lilac bush in our yard to select a stick to hit me with. I cannot tell you how painful it was. They made me pull my pants down and they hit me on my bottom and thighs, with only my underwear to protect me.

Looking back now, I would say there were three things that kept me afloat during my teen years—Gail, softball, and a large cast of friends. They were the underpinnings of my life, and I don't know what I would have done without any of them.

POSTSCRIPT

Gail, whose association with Larry began in junior high, says this of his home life: "I remember him telling me that if he was not home on time for dinner, he didn't get to eat. It was as if they were saying, If you do what I say, you love me and you're worthy of my love. He told me that when he was a young boy he would go lie down by the dryer; the hum and the warmth of it was so comforting. He struggled with his relationship with his mother all his life. In the end, his mother was not aware that he was dying. He wouldn't let me call her. He didn't want to deal with her. He didn't have anything to say to her.

"*I think one of the reasons he worked so much was so he didn't have to deal with close personal relationships because they were too hard for him. Larry learned early to be task oriented because that's where he got his approval. At school and at work he found connections with coworkers and teachers that he didn't have with his parents, and then at the end of the workday he was able to distance himself from the demands of those relationships. He became married to his work. When he had children, he wanted to give them the best of everything. He believed his role was to provide what they needed. He didn't realize how important he was as a father and role model because he hadn't had parents who did that for him.*"

CHAPTER 3

FATHERS

I was warming up for a league softball game in St. George one evening in 1979 when a stranger approached me. I hardly noticed him because I am all business when I am getting ready for a game. But this caught my attention: "Hi, I'm your dad," the man said.

I was 35 years old, and I was just meeting my biological father for the first time that I could remember. Howard Hanley West married my mother, Mary Lorille Horne, in 1944. She was barely 17; he was 21. He reported to the war in the South Pacific, and when he returned they settled in Salt Lake. Apparently they were unhappy, and they divorced in 1946, when I was one and a half, and my mother was pregnant with my sister Judy. As part of the divorce settlement, Howard West made an informal agreement with my mother not to have contact with his children, and he honored that agreement.

I had heard from him only once in all those years before our meeting. He sent me a letter wishing me well on the occasion of my marriage to Gail, but I never responded. Then he showed up at that softball game. I was shocked. After introductions were completed and we had talked for a moment, he stood and watched me for a few minutes as I continued to warm up, still stunned, and then he excused himself.

"I just wanted you to know I was here," he said finally. "I don't want to break your concentration, but I'd love to talk to you after the game."

Later, Howard and his wife Evelyn met me and my family at the hotel. Howard was more than six feet tall, stocky and mostly bald, with a round, wrinkled face. He was 58 years old and had been married three times. He had had three children with his second wife, who also was from Salt Lake City, but none with his third wife, Evelyn. He owned a shoe shop—Anderson's Shoes—in a small town in Michigan. He had come to Utah to meet me and Judy. After our visit, we took photos of him and our families, and then we said good-bye, but through the years he continued to reach out to me.

He came again for the grand opening of the Delta Center and basked in the moment. He sat on a chair that was placed on top of a table in the concourse so he could see the crowd, and he introduced himself to everyone as my dad, which caused some confusion. I was uncomfortable with that because I had always introduced my stepdad, Frank Soren Miller, as my dad. People were asking me, "Which one's your dad?" I didn't like it—I was aware of it while it was happening—but I didn't want to take anything away from him; I wanted him to enjoy the moment. He was proud of me, and I took a strange pleasure in watching him experience part of my life. How many guys have sons who own NBA teams? Every NBA owner gets four tickets to his own team's road games, and over the years I gave those tickets to Howard for games in Detroit, Atlanta, and Minneapolis.

Howard West was a nice man. He never asked for anything. He was a former fast-pitch and slo-pitch softball player, and he liked to watch me play the game. Whenever we were playing in tournaments east of the Mississippi, he would show up. He always drove to these games. He showed up a few times when I didn't make the trip, and this irritated him, but he'd stay and watch the game anyway. He'd sit in the dugout with the team and ride the umps hard, and that created a few problems. The players liked him, though. Once, when we were playing in a tournament in Michigan, I accepted his invitation to stay overnight at his house. He invited me to stay the next night as well, but I declined. It was just too awkward for me.

It was clear from the start that he wanted a deeper relationship than I was comfortable with. From the very beginning, he wanted me to call him "Dad," but I couldn't. He always called me "son," but I called him Howard. He wanted an emotional connection, but I kept my guard up. It was a confusing relationship for me. My loyalty was with Frank Miller, the man I had always called "Dad," the man who fed and clothed me and put a roof over my head.

My mother married Frank in 1946. They produced two children of their own—Tom in 1951 and Charlene in 1953—and Frank adopted Judy and me from our mother's first marriage.

Frank—Dad—was a salt-of-the-earth guy—reliable, honest, hardworking. He was the inventory control clerk at the Phillips Petroleum plant. Phillips was the only employer he ever had after college. I remember he would only buy gas from Phillips. "They pay my salary," he would say. That's where I learned about loyalty.

He was a handsome man, six feet tall, with a trim, athletic build and a full head of fine, light brown hair that he swept back away from his face. When he was a kid he went to bed each night wearing a nylon stocking on his head to keep his hair in place. He said it "trained" his hair. He was always neatly groomed and fastidious in his appearance. His shoes were always shined and his clothes pressed. He was a dapper dresser, especially later in life when he liked to wear a blue-and-white striped sport coat with white pants.

He was a man of routine. My mother bought him an electric shaver for his birthday and a transistor radio for Christmas, and every morning for 14 years I could set my watch by the sound of his shaver and the early news report as he prepared to go to work. He left at 7:30 and returned home at 5:15.

Like so many others, my father was a product of the times. Born in 1921, he grew up during the Great Depression, and so he was frugal. He knew where every penny was going. He and my mother kept a white ledger book, and they recorded every expenditure at the kitchen table. They knew exactly how much money they had coming in and exactly how much was going out. They wasted nothing. My father liked to swim at the old Deseret Gym. For 25 cents, the gym provided you with a towel, a bar of soap, and a swimsuit. He brought home the used bars of soap and dropped them into a jar in the bathroom that was filled with water, and it was this solution that we used for shampoo.

He sold magazines to pay his way through the University of Utah, and later, after marrying my mom, he raised rabbits in the backyard to augment the family income.

I can remember eating in a restaurant only three times in all those years I lived at home, other than our annual hot-dog run. There was a lunch counter business on the ground floor where my father worked, and once a year they had a special day on which they sold hot dogs for ten cents and root beer for five cents. My dad waited for this event each year and took our family there for dinner when it came around.

Dad spent five of the first nine years of his life in a hospital, with tuberculosis. Doctors removed part of his hip, which left his left leg four inches shorter than his right. He didn't let this deter him in any way. He wore a lift in his shoe to even out his legs, and he was always active. He was a good tennis player and bowler—he bowled in a league—and he swam regularly. He loved to dance. In his later years, he took my mom dancing every week at the Rainbow Rendezvous, the Terrace Ballroom, or the Manhattan Club downtown.

He was not a warm man, but as I have learned about his life and become a father myself I have understood him better. He was raised by his mother and grandmother and had no male figures in his life. My father—and my mother, for that matter—did not know how to interact with me or help me in any significant way as parents. I'm sure I presented some difficulties for them, but I probably wasn't the first kid who didn't want to do homework and rebelled. I do remember that he watched me play softball—sometimes on weekends he would stay all day to watch our tournaments in the park.

In my youth, kids played a lot of marble games in the neighborhood and beyond; there were serious competitive tournaments in the city. One day my dad came outside to call me to dinner and found me playing marbles in the dirt in the alley behind our house. After watching me a moment, he asked, "Do you want to be good at this game?" When I said yes, he said, "I'll show you how to play at a different level, but it's going to be awkward and difficult at first and you're going to have to practice a lot to be good at it. If you're willing to do that, I'll show you." He showed me a new technique, with the marble seated on the knuckle of my thumb instead of the crook of my finger. It facilitated more power and accuracy, but it was difficult to master. I worked on it all that summer and became the school champion as a fourth grader and runner-up in the city championship as a sixth grader. But, as much as I reveled in those victories, what I remember equally is that it was one of those rare moments when my father took a real interest in me and worked with me. I remembered that moment, among other things, when Frank—my dad—died of Parkinson's disease in 2002. I believe he tried to be a good dad, and he was an even better grandfather.

CHAPTER 4

KEEPING THE FAITH

One afternoon, shortly before my 16th birthday, my mother said she needed to talk to me. She turned on her heels, and I followed her to my parents' room. I knew this was serious. The last time we had experienced such a scene, she had delivered traumatic news. I was six at the time, and for months I had been asking her and Dad if Santa Claus was real. I wanted him to be real in the worst way, but my friends kept telling me what I didn't want to believe. So finally one day my parents sat me down.

"Do you really want to know?" they asked. They repeated this question several times before finally telling me. It broke my heart.

This time it was only my mother who wanted to talk to me, but it reminded me of our Santa meeting. She sat on the bed and I sat on a chair in the room. She got right to the point in delivering another of the traumatic blows of my life that seemed to be her mission on earth.

40

"Your dad and I have decided that the things we have been teaching you all your life about the Church are not true," she said. "We're leaving the Church. We're going to have our names removed from the records of the Church. We want you and the other kids to do the same thing."

I was stunned, blown away. I have told you that my youth was a precarious walk across a sheet of ice that I was never certain would hold me, and now I had fallen through the ice and was gasping for air and grasping for solid ground. The foundation of my family life—our religious faith—had collapsed. My world as I knew it would never be the same.

I had always attended church regularly, along with my family. That meant three meetings on Sunday, plus youth meetings and activities during the week. Dad had married Mom in the Salt Lake Temple—Dad was inactive in the Church when they met, but she said she wouldn't marry him unless he married her in the temple. Judy and I were sealed to them as an eternal family. I can still remember the ceremony. I was four years old.

I rarely missed church in my youth. When I was a boy I attended what we Mormons call Primary on Wednesday afternoons, and I received certificates of commendation for regular attendance. Participating in church was an important part of my life. I didn't even think about it. It was just something we did, like eating. Almost all my friends shared the same faith. Almost everything I did revolved around the Church, including Church basketball and Church softball—both important parts of my young life—as well as the Church-sponsored Boy Scout program.

Years later, my mother told Gail during one of their interviews that leaving the Church made life much easier and happier for her. Well, if she thinks things got easier in my world, she wasn't paying attention. My world got turned upside down and was made much more difficult, and much of it goes back to that moment when she told me she was leaving the Church. I don't believe it made her life easier either.

She changed her set of friends. She became moody, irritable, and angry. She threw tantrums, one of them in the middle of a restaurant. She was unpredictable; she was a storm on the horizon and you never knew when it would break. She was the dominant personality in her marriage and in our house. She was the one who sent me packing and eventually to juvenile hall (it was not long after she left the Church that she threw me out of the house for the first time). It is revealing that my father, who had a mild disposition, never once discussed with me the decision to leave the Church.

To this day my mother has never really explained why she made such a drastic decision. As I have mused on this, I have speculated that she might have felt suppressed. She married my biological father just two days after her 17th birthday. She met Howard West at Normandy's skating rink and fell in love with him almost instantly because, as she told us, "He was so handsome." She told her father that if he forbade her marriage to Howard, she would get pregnant. She got her way—and wound up divorced from her husband two years later and eventually divorced from her church. In the ensuing years, she was unhappier than ever, and it was evident that her religious reversal had disturbed her so much that she lost the balance in her life. She had grown up with one belief system all her life and then dropped it.

The news of my mother's disaffection from the Church sent shock waves through our close-knit neighborhood. It was unheard of. The people in the Capitol Hill Second Ward—and that was pretty much everyone in our neighborhood—told me that Mom would come around, that things would get better. These people were a constant in my life during my formative years; I knew all of them. I went to church and school with their kids. They were my Sunday School teachers. They were my Scout leaders. I delivered the *Deseret News* to their doorsteps. They knew my parents. When

Mom left the Church, the neighbors consoled me by saying that she would come to her senses and that everything would turn out fine. I wanted to believe it, but it never happened.

Some 20 years later, long after I was grown and married, I visited two of the men who served as bishops of our ward during my youth to ask them why Mom left the Church—which tells you how much this has bothered me—but neither of them could explain it. I really wanted to know, and still do to this day. As nearly as my sister Judy and I have been able to determine, the seeds of Mom's rejection of the Church were planted when she went to therapy, which began as a result of her having sent me to juvenile hall and branded me as "incorrigible." The people who counseled her—there were two of them—were anti-LDS and made her feel uncertain of herself. I don't know why they had that much control over her.

I continued to attend church on my own, due partly to the extended family that was our neighborhood. Early in life, I fell in with a large circle of friends, and because no one ever moved out of our neighborhood, we remained friends throughout our youth. We palled around in various combinations from grade school through high school. My peers had their homes for sanctuary; I had my friends—the Capitol Hill gang, I have always called them, although the term *gang* had a far different meaning in those days. They included Steve and Denny Haslam, Grant Cannon, David Jex, Ken Toone, David Ipson, Ron Westerman, Craig Larsen, Ernie Capel, Denny and David Ashton, Stan Olsen, Mike Fairclough, and Ben Behunin.

Every Sunday morning, several of them would drop by the house, and we would walk down the hill to church. This continued after Mom left the faith. Every Sunday they would stand outside my house and shout, "Larry!" That was the way we did it in our neighborhood. You didn't knock on the door when you went to play with your friends; you just stood outside the house and shouted your friend's name.

BEGINNINGS

We lived at 548 Columbus Street in a small, square home that was shoehorned into one of the many tree-lined rows of homes running up Capitol Hill. Our house was a half block north and a half block west of the state capitol building and offered a panoramic view of the western half of the valley all the way to the Great Salt Lake. In the evenings, as I made my newspaper deliveries on Ensign Downs, I liked to study the valley below, especially in the fall when I could see the big flocks of geese way off in the distance, flying against the sunset.

It was a wonderful place and time in which to grow up. City Creek Canyon and the surrounding hills—not to mention the capitol and its grounds—were our playground. We hiked the side hills of the canyon through the sagebrush and tall grass, which turned brittle and gold as the summer wore on. We collected the tiny fossilized snails that were the ancient remains of prehistoric Lake Bonneville, which once filled the valley. Afterward, we'd stop to pick the cheatgrass out of our socks.

We fished in the cold stream that rolled down City Creek and didn't even use a fishing pole. We used our hands. We waded up the stream, feeling gently under the rocks and overhangs along the water's edge. There was a real art to it. If you touched the fish on its side, it was gone, but if you massaged its belly, it froze, which gave you time to slip your fingers into the gills and hoist it out of the water. We'd catch 50 or 60 trout a day, 10 to 12 inches long, and then turn them loose.

On the way home from school we routinely walked through the state capitol itself—through the doors on the south side of the building, across the lobby, then up the north stairs and out through the north door and up more stairs outside to a parking lot and a large lawn. We liked to play in the capitol building. We discovered a way to sneak into the capitol dome through a trapdoor in the ceiling of the men's bathroom, then up a long ladder that rose up through the middle of the dome, far from the security of a wall. It was a frightening climb. We sneaked in there when the building was open and stayed hidden until long after it closed. We probably had 25 hideouts in there, and we used them day and night. We also played ball games on the Capitol Hill grounds every Saturday, spring to fall, weather permitting. We wore base paths right into the lawn.

There were about 20 boys who were approximately the same age in our group. We walked to school together through all those years, first to Lafayette Elementary School, then to Horace Mann Junior High, and finally to West High School—the same schools Dad had attended. These friends were the constants of my young, inconstant universe, although I doubt they or I recognized it at the time. They were the solid ground under my feet when things were difficult at home, and they kept me going to church for their companionship and our shared beliefs after Mom pulled the religious foundation out from under me. They were my best friends, my family in many ways. There was only one person to whom I was closer.

CHAPTER 5

GAIL

G ail was shopping in a store one day recently when an acquaintance introduced her to a woman. After giving her the quick once-over, the woman said, "You don't look like you've got a million dollars."

That's Gail. She hasn't changed much, even if our bank account has. She's still the same woman who had to make her own clothes and to drop out of college to support her family. She's still the same woman who had nothing growing up.

She shops at Costco, hunts for sales, tends a garden, cans her own fruits and vegetables, and cooks for her family. She still irons our clothes, sometimes as many as 30 or 40 shirts in an afternoon. It takes several hours. People are always surprised to see her at the store. "You do your own shopping?" she's frequently asked. "Who else is going to do it?" she says. During one interview with a newspaper reporter, she wore sweatpants with a hole in them, which was duly noted in the article. Years later that same reporter was in our house and noted with delight that Gail was wearing a knit blouse with a tiny hole in it and Adidas sweatpants—and she had been out shopping in that outfit earlier in the day. Pretentious, she's not.

Money hasn't changed her, although there was a time when we worried it would change both of us. Gail's roots are deep in a different kind of life.

She was the sixth of nine children. She grew up in a house just down the hill from mine, less than four blocks away. Her family had little money. There were times they really didn't know where their next meal was going to come from. It was an exciting time when her dad came home with a bag of groceries. There were times when the family could afford just one lightbulb, so they moved it around the house as needed.

Gail says that she helped her family by never asking for anything. She never asked to go to girls camp in the summer because she knew her family couldn't afford it. She was a good seamstress and sewed all her own clothing, making new outfits or altering old ones. She made cute skirts and nice blouses. Sometimes she just improvised—she slipped cardboard into her shoes to cover the holes in the soles until the family had enough money to buy a new pair.

To earn spending money, Gail also made clothing for a friend and worked for a neighbor lady, babysitting her kids for 35 cents and cleaning her house for 50 cents an hour. There were times when she came home from work on Saturday with a check for four dollars, and her father would ask if he could have it to put gas in his car so he could go to work. During her senior year of high school, she took a part-time job as a long-distance telephone operator at Mountain Bell (a job she held through the first five years of our marriage). With money earned from that job, she bought a refrigerator and food for the family and a bedroom set for herself.

Her father, Joseph Herman Saxton, was another product of the Great Depression. His father had been a shoemaker and leather worker before immigrating to the United States from England. Joseph married Myrtle, an Idaho girl, in 1928, just in time for the Great Depression. They eked out an existence through the '30s. Like so many other men, Joseph couldn't find a job. In 1930, Myrtle was forced to take their baby and move in with her family in Wyoming. At one point, she received a letter from Joseph saying he had been laid off again and, after paying rent to the landlord, he had 11 cents to live on.

He was in a drugstore coffee shop in Salt Lake City one afternoon when he told a stranger, "If I had $200, I would start a shoe shop." The man gave him $200 and left the store. Joseph walked outside to thank the man, but he was gone.

Joseph opened a shoe store in the mid-'30s at 114 North Main Street. A few years later a fire destroyed all of the shoes he had repaired. He had to get ration tickets from the government to pay customers for their lost shoes. The landlord showed up every day with his hand held out, and Joseph would place a quarter in it. He finally had enough money to buy his own shop in the Avenues and maintained it for 17 years. After he sold the business, he bounced from job to job and struggled to make a living the rest of his life. He sold insurance, aluminum siding, draperies, and real estate, and the only real success he had was with the insurance business.

Gail, born in 1943, enrolled at the University of Utah after graduating from West High School, but her father had a stroke while on a family trip to California. Gail, who was the oldest of the three children still living at home, dropped out of school after one semester to help support the family. With her job at Mountain Bell, she became the primary provider for the family, which also received welfare assistance from the Church. Myrtle stayed in California for three months to be by her husband's side until he was well enough to return home, which meant Gail was charged with taking care of the house and the other two children, in addition to holding down a job.

GAIL

I met Gail for the first time when we were in seventh grade. I was just beginning junior high and wanted to meet some new friends. I asked my friend Stan McAllister a simple question: "Do you know any cute girls?"

He told me about a girl named Gail Saxton and gave me her phone number. That night I called her and delivered the boldest, most straightforward, here-I-am pickup line in the history of dating: "Hi, I'm Larry Miller, and I go to Horace Mann Junior High, and I heard you're cute."

As arranged, we met the next day before school at her locker. I still remember that she was wearing a red checkered skirt and a white oxford blouse and no makeup. She had dark, shoulder-length hair and a natural beauty—what I call a plain beauty—that didn't require lipstick or other makeup.

Nothing much came of our first meeting. We said hi occasionally in the hallway during the next two years. Midway through our ninth-grade year—January 30, 1959—we had our first date. We bumped into each other in the hall, and I invited her to go sleigh riding on the playground at Washington Elementary. We had no sleigh so we "sledded" down the hill on her coat, which worked surprisingly well. We had fun, and afterward I dusted the snow off her coat and walked her the half block to her home and we said goodnight. From then on, I stopped by her house every morning, and we would walk to school together. Usually I carried her books and we held hands.

We walked everywhere in those days. We walked to the movies. We walked to the capitol and looked at the displays they set up in the rotunda. We walked around Memory Grove Park in the canyon. We walked around the neighborhood. One of our favorite things to do was to walk to a small drugstore on 300 West. We'd get a 7-Up in a large glass and a bag of potato chips, and the cold and the saltiness—boy, was it good. It was only a quarter, but we didn't have many quarters, so we didn't do it often.

Neither of us asked our parents for money, or received any. We earned our own money. We would often have just barely enough to go to a movie. We'd be a penny or two short, and Gail would dig in her purse until she came up with just enough for two tickets. We'd chew gum for a treat.

When I was with Gail, I felt safe and comfortable, and I was aware of this even as a young man. It was in sharp contrast to my home life. She was a life preserver for me. She knew about my situation at home. She was the sounding board for everything—softball, friends, family, church, school. We had a lot of time to talk with all that walking.

I noticed early on that I didn't have to be someone I wasn't when we were together, and neither did she. If there was something to say, she would say it. I knew if she said something, it was what she believed and she wasn't trying to manipulate me. At that age, a lot of kids feel like they have to be something they're not. She was very comfortable with herself, a calming and serene presence, which is exactly what I needed.

Perhaps for those reasons, and against the backdrop of my home life, it isn't surprising that I was very possessive of Gail. I was clinging to the one sure thing in my life. We went together all through high school, but occasionally Gail dated other guys, and this was torture for me. Sometimes she did it when we had a falling-out, and sometimes we had a falling-out because she did it. I dated other girls three or four times, but usually it was because Gail had gone out with someone else and I wanted to get back at her. As I said, I was very possessive and easily angered. I did some weird things. She'd come home with a date, and I'd be waiting for her when they returned to her house.

You can imagine what her parents thought of me at moments like this. They weren't crazy about me anyway. I was drifting aimlessly, and they knew it. I didn't know what I was going to do with my life. Gail had the job with the phone company. I dropped out of college almost immediately and then went through a series of dead-end blue-collar jobs. Her parents didn't like me, and I didn't blame them. I wasn't the kind of kid a father and mother wanted their daughter to marry. They considered me a ne'er-do-well. It was hard to argue otherwise. They pestered Gail about me. "Why don't you date someone else?" they told her, and they complimented her when she did so. Even after we were married my mother-in-law didn't like me much, which was ironic because after we became successful she would sometimes introduce Gail as "Larry Miller's wife."

Perhaps the difference between Gail and me in those days was symbolized by the cars we owned. A year after she graduated from high school, Gail was able to buy a 1963 Ford Falcon Sprint convertible. I drove a two-tone 1952 Olds that I bought for $20 while in high school. My credit was so poor that I couldn't get a loan to buy a better car.

Gail and I continued to date for three years after high school. I had always thought we would get married—we had talked about it since we were 19—but, like so many other things in those days, I didn't do anything about it. I didn't seem to know how. Gail finally took matters in her own hands. "I've got a vacation coming on March 25th," she said one day. "It would be a good time to get married if you want to; if you don't, then we should split up." I said yes in about two seconds.

We married on March 25, 1965. Our ten-day honeymoon was a 3,000-mile drive along the West Coast, from Oregon to California, in Gail's Falcon convertible, which I had customized into a race car. It was fast and loud, which is probably why we were pulled over by police a couple of times along the way.

Not a lot changed with our marriage. We had changed addresses, but because we had dated for six years, there were not many adjustments to make. We had always just enjoyed each other's company. We liked to go for drives. We put 250,000 miles on her car. We drove to East Canyon or the Alpine Loop or Millcreek Canyon.

We drove to see the autumn leaves. We'd head off for one destination, and then we'd say, "Let's keep going," and we'd go to Wyoming or Moab. It was the time of our lives to do that kind of thing; for us life was very good.

I always use the term *we* when I refer to the things that I—we—have accomplished in business. Gail has had a difficult time with that. For a long time, she couldn't accept that this was a partnership in business as well as in marriage and that she had played a major role. She enabled me to do so much of what I did and never complained. I worked from 6:30 in the morning until about 10 at night for 20 years of our marriage to build our business. Other than the annual vacation we took, I had little interaction with the kids. They were asleep when I left and asleep when I got home. Gail was basically a single parent. She did the dishes, laundry, and shopping. She cleaned the house, cooked the meals, mowed the lawn, weeded the yard, fixed the broken screen door, repaired toys, planted flowers, painted the house, put up wallpaper, attended school events, disciplined the kids, met with their teachers, helped them with their homework, and drove them to their Little League games, which meant rushing four of our children to four different ballparks on the same day. I played league softball on Sunday, if not the entire weekend, and Gail brought the kids to the games just to be supportive, but it was a lot of work for her. She spent most of each game chasing our small children around the park.

Even when Gail wanted to do something as simple as having a family portrait taken, it was a logistical nightmare for her. She made the appointment, gathered the five kids, cleaned them up, got them dressed, piled them into the car, picked me up at the office, drove us to the photographer's studio, and then afterward dropped me off at the office to work into the night. I didn't even go home with them.

And yet, every morning, when I got up early for work, there was Gail ironing my shirt for the day. I asked her why she didn't iron them the previous day so she could sleep in—or iron several at a time. Her response was, "I want to see you off in the morning."

She did everything quietly, with no complaint. I couldn't have done what I did if she had been nagging me and not minding the home front. Our oldest son, Greg, likes to say she has the patience of Job. She needed it to live with me this long. I can't believe she put up with me all these years. Lots of times I didn't deserve it.

Gail is a born caretaker. She took care of her mother, Myrtle, for much of Myrtle's life until she died at 95. She shopped for her, did her laundry, and visited her regularly for 40 years. Gail was ward Relief Society president for four years and served as a counselor in several Relief Society presidencies before that. There are a lot of elderly ladies in our area, and some of them needed special care. She washed, cut, and curled their hair, changed their sheets, and did many other things for them.

When I was in the hospital, she eventually took charge and became my main care provider. It got to the point where the nurses deferred to her. She would show up in the morning for several hours, take a break to keep things in order at home, and then come again in the evening for a few more hours. I had pressure sores no one could fix. She took care of them in two weeks. She figured out which cream worked, one they had tried but quit using. After I got out of the hospital, she had to do all the work—getting me in and out of the wheelchair, loading and unloading the wheelchair in the car, helping me get in and out of the car. If there is a lasting image I have of her during that time, one that stirs my soul, it is thinking about all Gail has done for me these past few months while I have been sick. It was hard to not be able to do anything in return. It was difficult for me to constantly be the receiver, not the giver. It was a big adjustment, but she kept assuring me that I had done enough and that it was my turn to receive.

When Gail was growing up, she was the peacemaker in her house—she hated conflict and confrontation. That has never changed. She is soft-spoken and has a certain calmness about her that is immediately apparent.

She doesn't like to impose on anyone. I'll ask her if she wants to eat something when we're at the arena or a Bees game, or I'll ask her if she wants tickets to a concert or to the circus, and she'll say, "I hate to impose." I'll say, "Gail, you own the building; you own the team. If you want a hot dog, get one." She feels awkward imposing on employees. In many ways, she's still the unassuming girl who made her own clothes.

POSTSCRIPT

"He always said 'Gail and I' when he talked about the business, and that's the way it really was," says Gail. "Everything he does in business is in joint custody. I am his partner. This is an unusual arrangement in business, but he set it up this way because he had seen too many husbands use money as a weapon and a way to control their wives. We both own 100 percent of everything—if he dies, I own everything, and vice versa. That's just how he is. When we set up our first checking account he handed me the checkbook and said, 'Here it is; it's yours.' I had total control of the money. He never wrote a check on it. He had total faith and trust in me and knew I'd take care of things."

Looking back on their courtship, Gail notes, "If Larry wanted something, he pursued it till he got it, including me. That was hard sometimes. He'd be waiting for me when I got home from a date with someone else, or he'd show up at the door shortly after I was dropped off. He was insecure. He was just so intense in everything he did. He used to say, 'You are such a good conversationalist.' I didn't talk much; what I really did was listen. He wasn't getting that sort of attention at home.

"He was romantic and very outgoing, and we had a lot of fun together. He was also very sentimental. He kept everything from our dates in a box, including gum wrappers—we chewed a lot of gum in

those days—and movie ticket stubs. After he passed away, we looked at the contents of his wallet and there was his original business card from 1979—the day he started his own business—and a card I gave him in 1993 in which I told him to hang in there and that I loved him. He kept things that touched him. He kept everything the grandkids gave him—drawings or shoeboxes decorated with popsicle sticks. He cherished those things."

Since Larry's death, Gail has become more actively involved in leading the family business. Clark Whitworth, the company's CFO, says, "I wish Larry could see how good she is. She's a good businesswoman. She was trained by the best. Every night Larry would come home and talk to her about the business. Six weeks after Larry died, she called me and said, 'I'm not getting enough information. I used to get a daily download from Larry about what was happening. I need to know what's going on.' So once or twice a week she comes to the office and sits in on meetings and gives great input."

CHAPTER 6

THE BAD GOOD STUDENT

I graduated from West High School with a 1.77 cumulative grade point average. I barely graduated.

I was also a National Merit Scholar.

It makes no sense, I know.

I was a lousy student, but a bright one, too. I simply would not do the homework assignments. Nowadays they would probably say I had a raging case of attention deficit disorder. They'd probably be right. I fidgeted a lot, always moving in my seat or doing something with my hands. My mind wandered. I didn't pay attention in class. Even now, I'll be driving down a highway and see highway marker 105 and tell myself I want to see marker 106 and then miss it. I can't concentrate for that long. My mind is teeming with ideas or projects or better ways to do things.

Some teachers and administrators were perceptive enough to realize there was something more to the fidgety Miller kid. In third or fourth grade, I was called into a small room where a man was sitting at a table. He invited me to sit in the chair opposite him.

"Are you nervous?" he asked. "Your hands haven't stopped moving since you've been here."

I hadn't even noticed. The man proceeded. "We would like to give you a test. You don't have to take it."

"What kind of test is it?" I asked.

"An IQ test."

I took the test. It was the first of four or five IQ tests that I was given in school over the years, always alone in a room with some adult, separate from the class. I never learned the results, but when I was in the eighth grade, Norris Boyd, the principal at Horace Mann Junior High, called me into his office one day. "I have a proposal for you," he began. "Would you like to skip ninth grade and go to high school in the tenth grade?"

I thought about this for a couple of days and turned him down. As noted earlier, I had this wonderful group of friends in my grade, and to leave them would have taken me out of my comfort zone. But I appreciated the offer, and I appreciated that he had recognized my ability and wanted something more challenging for me.

It was certainly warranted. I was bored in school, and because of it I got into trouble. I was disruptive in class. I talked out of turn. I interrupted the teacher and talked to the other students. At the outset of my junior year in high school, I reported to Mr. (Rex) Snow's biology class, and almost the first thing he said to me was, "Your reputation precedes you, so I don't want you in class." Instead, he gave me a topic to study and write about and said he didn't want to see me again until the end of the term. It was his way of not dealing with me. He would give me a new topic at the start of each term. We wound up becoming friends. We talked about a lot of things, even theology. I earned his respect. He asked me to write a paper about time as the fourth dimension. He was teaching me to think.

My chemistry teacher, Mr. (Brad) Davis, greeted my arrival in his class the same way as Mr. Snow—"Mr. Miller, your reputation precedes you." He was smart. He used reverse psychology on me. He told me, "I don't think you can keep your mouth shut for a day." I said, "I'll not only keep it shut for a day, I'll keep it shut for a whole semester." It became a test of wills. He finally reached a point where he wanted me to participate in class. He would ask me questions, and I'd just shake my head. The only thing that could keep me quiet was my competitive streak. Just tell me I can't do something, and I'll do it. In that respect, I have never changed. That competitive streak is good up to a point, but I let people control me with it. I didn't, for instance, get all I could have out of chemistry. I would have been a better student if I had participated in class. It's important to make up your mind who you are and be yourself. That wasn't me.

Despite my reputation, I developed good relationships with many of my teachers—my Great-Aunt Mackey in first grade, Miss Issacson in second grade, Mrs. Peterson in third grade, Mr. Johnson in fourth grade, Mr. Wilkins in fifth grade, Mr. Johnson in sixth grade, Mr. Lundquist and Mr. Hughes in junior high, Mr. Neilsen and Mr. Winn and Mr. Snow in high school. There was something that made them like me. I stayed after school many times to talk to teachers about life or class topics. They saw something in me, even though I struggled to do homework and disrupted class.

During my senior year I was given another aptitude test and scored so high that I was named a National Merit Scholar—one of only two in Salt Lake City, the other being my friend David Jex. It was reported in the *Deseret News*. Besides prestige, it brought scholarship offers and interest from notable schools. I received letters from Northwestern and MIT, among others. They wanted me to visit their campuses.

When I was named a National Merit Scholar, that should have set off a flurry of activity. I never did one thing to pursue any of the opportunities that came with being a National Merit Scholar, though it could have made a huge difference in my life. But we'll never know, and things have worked out for me.

I was told all my life by adults—my parents, teachers, principals, and my Grandma Talmage—that I was bright and that I needed to go to college. But my parents never gave me any direction about how to do that, or explained anything as simple as registering for school or seminary or athletics or college. I didn't have anyone telling me, "Here's where you need to go, here's what you need to do." And I feared walking into the unknown. So I hung back and missed a lot of things, including high school sports. I guess I didn't feel inclined or was too overwhelmed by my home life or lacked confidence to figure things out on my own. I didn't play baseball beyond Little League. While the other kids' parents took them to register and helped them through the process, I had to find my own way and never bothered. I didn't even sign up for the military draft until it was almost too late. We were supposed to register when we turned 18. It was the law. I signed up two and a half years later. I would have been sent to Vietnam because of this, but I was deferred twice, the first time because I was married and they weren't taking married men, and the second time because Gail was pregnant with our first child. Although they were drafting married men by then, they were not taking married men with children.

My high school grades were so poor that I didn't even qualify to take a college admissions test. A family friend and neighbor named Frank Jex, who also was a psychology professor at the University of Utah, knew my situation and suspected there was more to me than that weak GPA. He arranged for me to take an entrance exam with a roomful of students at the U. A few days later, one of the school's counselors called and asked to meet with me. When I showed up for the meeting, the counselor was there with Mr. Jex.

"I need to talk to you about your entrance exam," the counselor began, and he proceeded to ask me questions. I didn't know what was going on. Finally, Mr. Jex, who had been quiet to this point, spoke up. "Larry," he said, "let me tell you what's going on here. We're looking at your grade point average in high school and the results of your entrance exam, and they don't match up. You scored in the 99th percentile on the test. The real question here is, did you have someone take the test for you?"

The question kind of hung there for a moment until Mr. Jex broke the silence again. "Did you take the test yourself?" When I said I did, he said, "Would you take the test again, by yourself, and supervised?"

I took the test again and produced the same score.

I was admitted to the University of Utah.

I dropped out six weeks later, proving two things: I had poor study habits and a short attention span.

Actually, I don't even think I withdrew from school—I just quit going.

Postscript

"Larry did learn a lot of basic values at home, such as work ethic, loyalty, caring for the underdog, and so forth," Gail says. "And he had an uncanny way of looking at things. He was always observing and learning. Even though he was a strong advocate for higher education for those who want it, and provides scholarships for hundreds of students, he would always tell our kids, 'All you really need to be a success in business is common sense and the ability to add, subtract, multiply, and divide.'"

CHAPTER 7

NUMBERS

During the brief time I attended the University of Utah, Mr. Jex asked me to participate in a class demonstration for his psychology students. He was trying to demonstrate the difference between a graduate student's mind and a freshman's mind—in other words, he wanted to show that a freshman's mind wasn't as developed as a grad student's. The graduate student and I were placed in front of the 70 or so students in the class and were given a variety of verbal tests. I held my own as we moved from one test to the next. Then, as a final challenge, we were given a test for numbers and memorization. The professor began by reading a five-digit number, and then we had to repeat it. The graduate student and I matched each other for a while, first with five-digit numbers, then six digits, then seven digits, and so forth until we reached twelve digits. At that point, the grad student couldn't do it and dropped out of the competition.

Mr. Jex was impressed even though I was killing the point he had planned to make about the superiority of grad students.

"How high can you go?" he asked, with the class looking on.

"I don't know," I shrugged. "I've never done this."

He resumed the number series—13 digits, 14 digits, 15, and finally 20, and I was able to repeat each one. Finally, he said, "Well, how many numbers can you do backwards?"

I shrugged again. We began again. He read a series of numbers and I repeated the series backwards. Again, we did this until we reached 20 digits. It blew the professor's mind. I've rarely told this story because people don't believe it's possible or it sounds boastful, but it really happened. Mr. Jex finally gave up. He concluded things by saying, almost in exasperation, "Well, this thing didn't go like I expected it to, but it was sure fun to watch."

I don't know what it is about numbers, but I have always loved them. Some might say I'm obsessed with them. My mind is always crunching numbers in some fashion. When I was a kid, to occupy my mind while I delivered newspapers or walked home, I added the digits of the license plates on cars that passed as I walked along the street. Utah's plates in those days consisted of four numbers and two letters. The benchmark for me was a score in the 30s. I didn't get many of those because they required 7s, 8s, and 9s. I tried to do this with every car on the road. I had to be fast if there was a lot of traffic. I could add them in a split second.

Since I was a kid, I have habitually counted the number of steps I take wherever I walk. Even now I am always counting steps—from my car to the office, walking around the house, walking the streets near my house for exercise, walking around Jordan Commons. I know, for instance, that it takes me 2,700 steps to walk a mile. During my daily walk near my home, it is 625 steps to a bush up the street, which is my turn-around point.

Even while counting my steps, I can still think and concentrate on a conversation with someone while maintaining the count. It's like an underlying current in the background. If I'm walking with someone I can hear everything they say and hold up my end of the conversation while still counting in my mind.

About 35 years ago I was driving back and forth between Denver and Salt Lake City frequently. I counted mile markers during those drives. It was a relief when I could listen to a basketball game on the radio so I didn't feel compelled to count mile markers. At such times I was calculating distances and traveling time. We would be on the way home from a 1,200-mile trip in the car with the family and I'd tell the kids what time we would reach home, and I'd be within a minute of my prediction. One day I was driving to an appointment with child psychologist Lynn Scoresby in Provo, and he called me on the phone. I told him, "I'll see you in 27 minutes." The fact that I picked such an odd number caused him to make a mental note of it. I arrived at his office in 27 minutes.

When I am discussing events in my life, I not only recall the dates they occurred but the day of the week as well. I purchased the Jazz on Tuesday, March 12. I moved to Denver on Monday morning, November 16, 1970. I bought my first dealership on April 6, 1979, and took possession on Tuesday, May 1. My first date with Gail was Friday, January 30, 1959. I have a mind for numbers. I can tell you that my parts store increased its sales 576 percent the first year, then 202 percent, then 200, then 201.

I guess my mind just has to be occupied, and I have a natural affinity for numbers. Even as a young man, I volunteered to be the statistician for the West High School basketball and baseball teams. I enjoyed the numbers. I created my own systems for keeping the stats. I still have those stats around the house somewhere. As owner of a professional basketball team, I created a new statistic for evaluating the productiveness of players—add points, rebounds, steals, blocks, and assists; subtract fouls, turnovers, and shots; then divide by minutes played. It's like a batting average, but for basketball players. I figure out a player's average in my head after every game.

BEGINNINGS

The job I enjoyed the most was being a counterman in a car parts store because it involved a lot of numbers and I was good at it. It's been more than 30 years since I worked as a counterman, and I can still tell you the stock number for almost any Toyota part. Just name the car and the part, and I'll give you the 10-digit number. The right front fender of a '71 Corolla is 53801–12070. The hood is 53301–12901. The grill is 53111–12070. The head gasket set for a 1600cc engine is 04112–26010. For a '71 Celica, the hood is 53301–14090. The filler panel between the hood and fender on a Land Cruiser from 1968 to 1974 is 53304–60010. The vibration damper is 13407–60011. The connecting rods are 13201–60010. I could take a Corolla, Celica, or Land Cruiser from that era and build a vehicle a piece at a time with the numbers.

I live in a world of numbers, and I seem to have a penchant for remembering and processing them. In my business we borrow a lot of money—$3.5 billion a year. Each year we make presentations to the seven lenders that we do business with. For these presentations we put together a packet that consists of 12 to 15 pages filled with numbers. It includes numbers for sales, profitability, costs, and so forth, all listed by department. That includes numbers for 42 car dealerships, 70 movie screens in five complexes, two restaurants, 34 Fanzz stores, two radio stations, a TV station, an advertising agency, the arena, the Jazz, and so on, all summarized on paper. Though none of these banks individually is financing all aspects of our organization, we show them the entire organization so they have a full understanding of what we're doing. Anyway, everyone around the table is handed this packet, which contains these 12 to 15 pages that are jammed with thousands of numbers. I sit at the table and conduct the meeting without looking at the pages, and while I'm talking I recite numbers without ever looking at the paper. And usually I hear others in room saying things like, "How does he do that?" They love it, but this is more than entertainment. It shows that I am not just a figurehead in the business, that I'm involved and know what's going on.

People ask me if I have a photographic memory. I know that when I see things on paper, they're emblazoned on my brain. Or if I hear something like a radio or TV commercial and I wasn't paying attention, but then I catch something near the end of it and want to know what it was about, I can replay it in my mind. I can recall the sounds of the voice and what was said. I also store numbers in digit patterns, usually in groups of threes. It's scary how many phone numbers I remember. It's hundreds. But I do seem to retain information on a need-to-know basis. We had a phone number for ten years, and then we moved and got a new number, and a week later I couldn't remember the old number. If I don't need it, it's like I reject it so I don't have useless junk floating around in my mind.

I recall a time when my memory served me well in a court of law. In the mid-1970s there was a growing demand for stretched-cab Toyota pickups. They weren't being produced at the factory at the time, so various body shops began vying to do the job through the Toyota dealership where I served as general manager. Eventually, a man showed up at my office and convinced me he was qualified for the job. He was an engineer. He showed me his blueprints, and we put his stretched truck on a hoist so he could show me the quality of his work.

Now fast-forward a few years. One of those stretched-cab trucks that we sold was involved in a wreck. As the truck rolled, the 16-inch panel that had been added to stretch the truck broke open and the driver's arm protruded through the opening and was severely injured.

A suit was filed. I was called as a witness, and while I was on the witness stand I was grilled by the attorney for the plaintiff. Eventually, he asked me if I had bothered to determine if the truck was structurally sound. I recounted how we had hoisted the truck and that the man was an engineer who showed me blueprints and welds and specifications and the metal used for the extension. I recalled that we had talked for an hour. The attorney challenged me. "You can't possibly remember that from five years ago," he scoffed.

So I replied, "Well, let me tell you some more. We took the truck for a ride up the freeway to see if it had vibrations and to see if the extended cab was solid. It was fine. We parked it in the third stall from the left in front of the store and opened the tailgate and looked at the finish inside. It had blue shag carpet and Rossignol skis and boots in it." The lawyer challenged me again. "I don't believe you remember that," he said. Well, they had a Toyota parts box in the courtroom as evidence. Inside was the roof of the truck. The attorney turned to me and said, "Okay, you can convince me if you can tell me the parts number on that roof." I calmly and confidently replied, "It's 58301–89101." The judge asked the bailiff to check the number, and I was right. The lawyer was speechless and took his seat. It was a *My Cousin Vinny* kind of moment.

People ask me how I learned to crunch numbers in the business world if I never had a business class and went to college for only a few weeks. The answer is: No one ever told me. I never learned math above addition, subtraction, multiplication, and division. I never had a financial statement explained to me. When you look at it, it looks complex; it's not. It's a series of hundreds of numbers, maybe thousands. We produce it monthly. They all tell you something. You just need to understand what it is, how it fits in year-to-date and month-to-date. If there's a complexity there, it's in the mass of numbers; it's not that difficult to understand what each number means.

POSTSCRIPT

Denny Haslam, who knew Larry for 50 years—first as a boyhood pal and later as his lawyer and president of the Utah Jazz—saw Miller's gift with numbers during thousands of business meetings. "I don't believe he had a photographic memory in the truest sense of the word," he says. "What he had was a remarkable gift of analysis. He could look at hundreds of numbers and tell you what they mean."

Miller's CFO, Clark Whitworth, notes, "Larry liked to say, 'I never had a business class, but I can add, subtract, multiply, and divide, and if you can do that and bring some common sense you'll succeed.' He didn't need college, but not everyone is like him. I would tell him that. He would assume others would succeed because he could see it so clearly, and he couldn't see why they didn't see it. He would get frustrated with people he was helping with their businesses because even after he explained things they just couldn't do what he could do."

PART II

FINDING MY WAY

CHAPTER 8

FINDING MY WAY

A BYU professor named Keith Hunt once told me that almost all entrepreneurs become entrepreneurs because they failed at other things and didn't know what else to do. That certainly seems to have been my story.

After dropping out of college, I had no idea what I wanted to do, and so I wandered aimlessly through a series of odd jobs that taught me what I didn't want to do. I worked in a book bindery, framed houses, mixed and carried mortar, drove delivery trucks, picked strawberries. Gail says that when we were dating I wasn't interested in doing anything with myself. My options were college, a Church mission, the military, marriage, and a career. I chose to do nothing about any of them.

In high school, I worked construction for my Uncle Reid Horne, and during the school year I worked at Mountain States Bindery. I continued both jobs after my graduation.

I was a hod carrier for my uncle's construction company. It's the lowest, worst form of labor in construction. It requires you to mix mortar and haul brick and block for the masons, as well as construct the scaffolding. It's hard physical labor. At the end of the day my hair was white with mortar dust and my shoulders and back ached. I built powerful muscles in my shoulders and forearms. Using brick tongs, I was able to lift 42 pounds of bricks with each arm and place them on four-foot scaffolding all day.

The bindery was less intensive labor. I trimmed books after they were sewn together, and I helped make the covers and attach them to books. During the yearbook season, I could work as many hours as I chose. I'm not proud to say that in high school I frequently called in sick or invented some excuse not to go to work.

None of these jobs held much interest for me, but a pattern began to emerge that would prove significant. I discovered that I had a knack for creating work systems that produced stunning results, and this has served me well throughout my professional career.

One of the jobs we undertook at the bindery was packaging a recording of the Book of Mormon, which consisted of 25 long-playing records. We laid the back cover flat on the table, pushed two Chicago screws up through it, laid each of the individual record sleeves onto the screws through pre-drilled holes, attached the top cover with a thumbscrew, then fit the entire collection of records into a box. The company bid the job by figuring that we could assemble ten of these record sets every hour, but in reality the people hired to do this were completing only six per hour. I thought about this job and devised a scheme. I was granted permission from my boss to set up one of those large wooden spools that are used to hold cable. I used a lift truck to make room for the spool and then laid the spool on its side on the floor. I made 25 stacks of records around the spool—a stack of the No. 1 records, a stack of the No. 2 records, and so on—and I laid out a stack of back covers and a stack of front covers, as well as a pile of screws and boxes. Within two days, while working midnight to 8:00 in the morning so I wouldn't get in anyone's way, I completed an average of 61 boxed sets per hour. My employers were thrilled. A job that previously had been the task of a half dozen people was now turned over to me alone.

As I look back now, I realize I was practicing time and motion studies, although I didn't know it at the time. It was simply a manifestation of my personality, and it would become the hallmark of my labor style. I was making efficient use of my time. This was evident on my next job, as well.

In the summer of '64, I worked for Aarons Coverall and Towel Service, driving a truck, making deliveries and pickups. I was paid $15 a day and drove my route six days a week. Usually a driver would start at 8:00 in the morning and return at 6:00 in the evening. I looked for ways to improve my speed so I could finish early, but without cutting corners—in other words, if I was supposed to pick up ten coveralls and only eight were there, I would take the time to find the other two; or if I was supposed to place my delivery at a certain location and something was in the way, I would take the time to move things and put the delivery where it was supposed to be. And the other thing I was determined to do was to be friendly and develop good relations with my customers. I learned all the shortcuts and side streets to increase my speed. The other thing I did was to get in and get out—I went straight to work and straight back out. I was always in motion. I didn't take breaks, and I didn't stand around shooting the breeze. I maintained customer relations while on the move. I became so efficient that, instead of finishing at 6:00 or 6:30, I was finishing before noon, which was my goal because that's when customers would lock up for their lunch break. My boss thought I was skipping customers or not courting good customer relations, so he visited customers on my route and they told him, "He's the best you've ever had." Then he followed me around for a couple of days to see what I was doing. It was another time and motion study.

I needed to make more money, so that summer I went back to work for my Uncle Reid's construction business. A few months later Uncle Reid announced that he had no other work for his crews, and we were all laid off.

I was shocked. I hadn't seen it coming. In retrospect, it was the best thing that could have happened to me because it led me to the automobile business and, ultimately, a career.

I had begun to hang around the drag-racing scene on Saturdays while I was in high school, mostly at the Bonneville Raceway. I worked on the crews that helped keep the cars running. There is a constant need for parts and repairs, and I made many visits to a small mom-and-pop store on State Street called American Auto Parts. When I was laid off from my construction job, I was only a few blocks from the parts store, so that's where I went. I didn't go there to look for a job; I just didn't know what else to do with myself. It was just a social call. The husband and wife who owned and operated the store asked me if I needed help. I told them I had been laid off, and only then did I think to ask, "Do you happen to have a job?" They said they needed an experienced counterman.

"I learn really fast," I told them. "If you give me the job, you won't be sorry."

They gave me the job for $1.10 per hour, and I began by stocking the bins with parts, making deliveries, and sweeping the floor. It got busy in the evenings and on weekends, and on Friday night I observed the heavy customer traffic in the store and listened to what was happening. They had a rack of catalogues that provided numbers for each part indicating where the parts were stored on the shelf. On Saturday morning there were four countermen, and each one had four or five people in line and the phones were ringing. I couldn't stand it. I answered the phone and helped customers the rest of the day. I had to ask the other countermen where things were, and they usually had to look things up in the catalog to find them.

What I realized was that if you memorized the number system of the parts, rather than look them up in a catalog, you would be able to find things quickly and help more customers more efficiently. The other guys were spending too much time looking in the catalog. Instead of having my nose buried in a catalog, I decided I would interact with people. The second thing I realized was that if I took the time to study the catalogs, there were patterns that could make it easy to memorize parts numbers.

So I began to memorize the parts numbers and their locations. Once again, I was practicing time and motion systems. I would go to bed each night and see catalog pages in my head listing fuel pumps and filters and gaskets, and I couldn't shake it. It was stuck in my brain like a song, and I had trouble falling asleep.

The Saturday crowd was always coming to the store trying to find a way to connect various types of copper and steel lines on fuel, brake, and hydraulic systems—say, a Chevy fuel pump to a Ford fuel line. It was very difficult and frustrating for them to hook up all these parts from different car manufacturers. They were always needing custom fittings, elbows, sleeves, compression fittings, flare nuts, that kind of thing. That's when I decided to sit down and understand the different types of threads, connecting systems, elbows, and compression unions so that I could properly serve these customers. It was fun solving their problems. We had a brass fitting rack with 15 rows of drawers in it, and each of the drawers was subdivided. They contained hundreds of different parts. One day, when things were slow, I got a stool and sat in front of this rack and memorized the parts and their locations. I could see a pattern of where this stuff was. It paid off. When people came in with grease up to their elbows and frustration on their faces and asked if I knew how they could connect certain parts, I was able to say, "Yeah, you take this, connect one of these and this to that, you need an elbow here, a compression fitting here, and you've got it." They thought I was brilliant, and I had a lot of fun.

I was soon working seven days a week, every hour they were open, for four months. I was doing this so I could learn. It took me only a few days to realize I liked being a counterman. It was not about cars but about the numbers. I had been infatuated with numbers all my life, and now I was surrounded by them.

Within a year I was doing the hiring, firing, scheduling, and ordering of parts. The owners, who had been working bell to bell, had enough confidence in me that, for the first time, they felt they could go home early or come in late. I was running the operation for them, and I was handling most of the customers. I felt it was only fair that I should be rewarded for this. I was making $1.45 an hour by now, and I felt I deserved a raise. The store had a policy in which employees were given a nickel raise every 90 days. The problem was, there were people who had been there longer than I, and they were making more money than I was but not doing as much.

One day, to prove a point to the owners, I started answering every phone call and helping every customer at the counter that I could, and I did this easily. After doing a little research, I discovered that I was waiting on 65 percent of the customers by myself, which meant all the other employees combined were handling only 35 percent. I pointed this out to the owners. I told them that Gail and I were about to get married, and I needed a 25-cent raise. After discussing it, my employers called me into their office at the end of the day and denied my raise, explaining that it would violate their raise policy. I was dejected. I believed raises should be based on performance, not tenure, plus they were technically in violation of the law because they didn't pay overtime. I was working 83 hours a week.

I was upset about this. That night I had dinner with my Grandpa Horne, my mother's father, and he taught me a great lesson. My family had lived with Grandpa until I was four and, as I got older, he knew about my strife at home. He had a special way of stepping in occasionally with some wise counsel. We had a special relationship. He called me "Laddie." He was a Mormon bishop for 26 years, as well as a traveling salesman. He used to take me on long drives with him while he was working, and he used these opportunities to teach me and talk to me. As I got older, he was my moral compass, especially after my mother left the Church. He was a wise, kind man and one of the greatest influences on my life. Years later he performed our marriage ceremony, and later gave Greg a blessing when he was a sick baby. Anyway, once a month he took me to dinner, and he often invited Gail along as well. After I was denied the raise, he picked me up for dinner and immediately asked, "What's wrong?" I told him, "Nothing," but he persisted. "Yes, there is; I can tell," he said. I told him about being rejected for the raise and how much work I was doing for the store. He sat silent for a long time thinking about this before he replied, "So what do you intend to do about it?"

"No matter how hard I work," I explained, "I can't perform well enough to accelerate my pay, and I'm getting married."

He repeated his question: "Okay, what do you intend to do about it?"

"I guess I'll only give them a $1.45 job if they're only going to pay me $1.45."

He thought about this for a few moments, and then he said, "You could do exactly that and still perform at such a high level that you would outperform your coworkers. So they would never know you were giving less than you had. But you would know, and frankly, you would be the only guy to be hurt by your underperformance. So, as your grandpa, I am going to promise you that as long as you continue to take their paycheck, if you work as hard as you can and learn all that you can in that business, someday it will pay off many times over."

I didn't realize then how profound his counsel would prove to be in my life. For some reason, while I was normally hardheaded and ignored advice—preferring, it seems, to learn the hard way—I took Grandpa's counsel to heart on this occasion. It really made an impression on me. It was one of the great lessons in my life, and I have given my best effort in everything I have done since then. Grandpa was right. It wasn't about beating my employers and their policies; it was about me and doing my best because it was the right thing to do.

I stayed a few more months at the parts store, but I wanted more and I had to move on.

CHAPTER 9

UNKEPT PROMISES

I f you're paying attention to the lessons that situations present, you can learn a great deal. Usually, when some setback or challenge occurs in your life, you're upset about it, and you're aware of it, but when the situation is resolved most people don't examine it to learn from it. I was taught a valuable lesson when I was in my twenties and still searching for a job I could call home, but I'm not sure I would have noted the lesson if it hadn't happened repeatedly. The lesson was taught to me this way: I was cheated by five different employers, just to make sure I was paying attention. The lesson was this: Treat your employees well, and it will pay off in many ways.

After leaving American Auto Parts, I briefly worked in construction again, framing houses, and then I found my first job with a car dealership through a newspaper ad. Bountiful Motors was looking for an experienced parts man. I was hired for $300 a month with this promise: "If you work out, we'll pay you $350 the second month." When I opened my check for the second month, it was for $300. This upset me. I had "worked out," as they put it, and when I asked management they didn't disagree. They denied ever having made such a promise. They refused to pay me the extra $50.

I was working alone one Saturday morning when a man came to the parts department with grease on his hands and coveralls. He was looking for a part for his '61 Mercury Meteor. It was an obscure part that was difficult to find. He stood at the counter and watched me as I searched the catalog over and over trying to find the part. Finally, after 20 minutes, I found the part in an unexpected place in the catalog and had to place a special order for it. The customer was impressed that I had persisted in looking for a part that cost only $3, and he was even more impressed when I called days later to tell him the part had arrived. Some parts guys wait for the customer to call to see if their part is in.

"I've got guys who wouldn't take the time you did to do this," the man said. "I want to hire you."

He promised to pay me $425 a month to work for his paint and body shop, which was called Paint and Piston. Grandpa Horne's lesson—work hard—had borne fruit. I worked there for a year and liked it, but once again I needed more money. One of our customers owned a gas station called Gresh and Jerry's Chevron. He offered $450 a month and said I would only have to work 40 hours a week, Monday through Friday. This appealed to me because it would allow me to spend more time with Gail. So I went to work for Gresh and Jerry's, doing light mechanical work, pumping gas, and managing parts inventory. Almost instantly I found myself working six days a week, 12 hours a day, and not being paid overtime.

One day the general manager of the Peck and Shaw GMC-Toyota car dealership tracked me down at Gresh and Jerry's. He had called several parts shops looking for a parts guy to hire, and my name was the first one that was mentioned more than once. He offered me a job, but I turned him down. I was tired of changing jobs and didn't want to return to a dealership after my experience at Bountiful Motors. He persisted and convinced me to visit him at his office on a Friday afternoon. He explained that he had a one-man parts operation he wanted me to oversee, serving a half dozen techs in the shop. I turned it down again. He showed me the parts department, which was in complete disarray, with everything piled haphazardly in boxes. Nothing was on shelves; there was no order to it at all. I saw it as enough of a challenge that it intrigued me, so I took the job.

I quit my job at Gresh and Jerry's that night, reminding my employer that he had reneged on our agreement that I would only work a 40-hour week.

"You need to change that if you want to keep people," I told him.

Peck and Shaw was turning one parts department into two—one for GMC and one for Toyota—at different locations, and it was left to me and a man named Harold Taylor to choose which one each of us would manage. I deferred to Harold and his seniority, but because he didn't have a preference, I chose Toyota even though it would mean opening a new parts department at a new location. To my way of thinking, Toyota had a superior, more logical numbering system, and I thought that would make life easier.

I started serving body shops with our Toyota parts. We got into the wholesale parts business with independent service shops and body shops. We did direct mailers to our service customers to let them know we had a new service department and that we wanted their business. The business grew rapidly, and because of this I was asked to spend a month fixing Peck and Shaw's GMC parts store as well. I was developing a good reputation. When Peck and Shaw bought an old dealership in downtown Salt Lake City, they called on me again. The dealership was big—and sick. I was asked to report to a meeting at the new dealership. With more than 100 employees from the parts, service, and body shop departments looking on, the general manager announced, "This is Larry Miller, and effective immediately he's our parts and service director at this dealership. Anything he says goes, and we'll back him." With that, he walked out of the room.

I was 25 years old, and I had never managed more than 20 employees. I said, "Fellas, all I know is I've been told these operations are sick, and I'm no genius, but I know how to work hard and we're going to fix it. I hope you'll obey the simple rules and work hard, and I'll do everything I can to make your jobs easier."

The problems were immense. There was no organized inventory control system; the parts department was in disarray, with parts all over the place; and the mechanics bickered, which meant a loss of productivity because of the time that wastes. Employees hid out in the service and parts department, and the paint and metal guys didn't do much. They were slow getting jobs done. And the place was dirty and dingy. To make matters worse, we had such a shortage of parking that we had to park customer cars illegally on the street. We made a deal with the police: They would write tickets once a day for our illegally parked cars and bring them to me and we would pay the tickets.

Meanwhile, the fixed operations were losing $40,000 a month when I took over. They became profitable in just five months. I was making $450 a month, and I thought that was a lot of money.

By this time my reputation had spread throughout the parts community and I received a visit from the owner of Main Motors, which sold snowmobiles, motorcycles, trucks, and trailers. He invited me to come meet with him at his store. I wasn't really interested in the job; I was happy where I was and I was tired of changing jobs. He called me four times and each time I said no, but finally I agreed to meet with him just to get him off my back. Gail was working from 5:00 to 11:00 P.M. with the phone company, so I was tending our son, Greg, at the time. I made an appointment to see the man that evening, and I took Greg with me. I was waiting with my very active two-year-old in the showroom, and the time for the appointment passed. I sat there for two hours trying to keep Greg happy while I waited. A salesman kept telling me that the owner was aware that I was waiting and would be with me in a minute. Finally, he showed up and showed me around the store. I didn't like what I saw. The parts department was a mess. There was no order to it. We retired to the owner's office and began to negotiate. I was angry that he had kept me waiting and I wasn't impressed with the operation. I didn't want this job.

He then asked me how much I was making. I said $500—which was a $50 exaggeration, but I thought if I told him that amount he wouldn't hire me. To my surprise, he offered me $550 if I would come to work for him in two weeks. After we talked some more, he said he would pay me $600 if I would come to work for him in one week. I agreed. Finally, he said, "As long as we're going for it, I'll pay you $650 if you come Monday."

He promised to pay me $650 a month, plus 10 percent of the net profit of the parts department. They were not making a profit when I was hired, but I got the department turned around and made it profitable in the first week. My department was doing well, but the overall store was struggling. I worked there for some time before I realized I wasn't being compensated properly for my performance and for the profitability of my department, as we had agreed. The owner told me repeatedly that the parts department was not making a profit and refused to let me see the financial statement, but I knew that parts and service were doing well. By accident one day I saw the company's financial statement, and it verified what I had suspected. My department was turning a profit, and they weren't rewarding me for it. After I confronted the owner, he still refused to pay me what I was owed. Once again, my employer didn't honor his agreement—he wouldn't pay me 10 percent of the net profit.

Any employer with any brains should have treated me fairly and helped me to do my job—after all, I was making money for them—but that wasn't the case. As I discovered so often early in my career, businesses often don't take care of their employees or provide them proper support. The overall dealership was still losing money, and cutbacks were ordered. We were already shorthanded in the parts department by two or three countermen, which created a lot of pressure and stress because of the new business we had generated. To make matters worse, instead of giving us more countermen, they fired three of them. I was furious. I told my boss, "You can't do this. I can't believe you're impeding my ability to make this department profitable for you. In service, nothing happens if you don't have parts guys." He told me that parts guys were a dime a dozen. I took a dime out of my pocket and slammed it on his desk and told him to get a dozen, and I quit on the spot.

As fate would have it, I was being courted by a national-class softball team in Colorado that was sponsored by Hegsted Volkswagen of Denver. They wanted me to pitch for their team and promised to arrange job interviews in the area. The Burt Chevrolet-Toyota dealership in Englewood, Colorado, hired me to be their Toyota parts manager for $1,000 a month, plus 10 percent of the net profit. I accepted the job, but after returning home to prepare for the move I reconciled with my boss at Main Motors, so I called the Burt dealership to tell them I wasn't coming. Then, after the reconciliation, I found that with all his promises, things still didn't change, and I decided to leave. On November 16, 1970, after working another long day, I came home realizing I couldn't do it anymore. I asked Gail to pack me a lunch because I was going to drive to Colorado that night. I was too embarrassed to call the Burt dealership in Colorado to say I had changed my mind a second time; I thought it would be better if I just showed up. I drove all night and was there when they opened the next morning. I was hired on the spot, but once again things didn't work out as promised.

We moved the family to Colorado and lived in the "Lucky U" Motel for two weeks while we looked for a house to buy. Gail, who was pregnant with our third child, had quit her job to be a stay-at-home mom on the promise that we would make enough money that we could afford for her to do this. I had been promised by my new employer $1,000 a month. As usual, I took over a parts department that was a complete mess. To get parts, mechanics had to sift through stacks on the floor. I got things organized quickly.

But when I opened my first check, I discovered that I had been paid half of what had been promised. I complained to the owner that they had agreed to pay me $1,000 to be their Toyota parts manager. The executives discussed this among themselves for a few hours and then told me that they already had a guy who would be parts manager for both Toyota and Chevrolet; they had hired me as the Toyota parts manager, but they were paying me as a counterman until a new store was built, which was under way but wouldn't be finished for a year.

Well, that wasn't what they had told me when I interviewed for the job. I gave them my two weeks' notice. In the last hour on the last day of that two-week period, my boss called me into his office and asked me if I was serious about leaving. I made it clear that I was. He had a proposal for me: They were going to move to a new Toyota store in a year and wanted me to be both the parts and service director for $2,000 a month. Well, I knew they had promised the service job to someone else, but they didn't know I knew it. I told them, "I'm not going to do it because I know you promised that job to another guy, plus I've seen how you guys do business and I know you'll do what suits you. So we'll part company." Then they had the nerve to ask me to stay until I had finished organizing their parts department, which I did.

I didn't really learn much the first couple of times I was mistreated by employers, but the third and fourth time it happened, it really sank in. I remember thinking that if I ever got my shot at being a general manager or owner, I would treat my employees better than that, because I know how it feels to work hard and do a good job and then have my employer fail to live up to promises, even though I had helped make him profitable. Those lessons served me very well when I became an employer. We honor our commitments. We let our employees know that we appreciate them. We know they are the reason we got where we are today, and we acknowledge it. I write notes to employees who have done a good job, or surprise a department with bonuses or celebrations. I try to be aware of what's going on in the lives of our employees. I reward performance. I try to create situations that will help them do their jobs. I like to tell our employees, "Once you get in here, it's hard to get out." We take care of them. That's why we don't lose many people.

These lessons were further ingrained in my mind after I had the opposite experience with my next employer. On March 8, 1971, I was hired by the Chuck Stevinson Toyota dealership in Lakewood, Colorado. It was a familiar story: Their parts department was a disaster. They had already fixed the other departments—new cars, used cars, and service—but the parts department was the last piece of the puzzle, and they wanted me to fix it. There were 1,083 Toyota dealerships in the country at the time; the Stevinson dealership ranked 961st in parts sales. Their monthly sales record was $9,091; they averaged $6,500 a month. It was a one-man operation with no delivery service and no solicitation of business. In my second full year on the job, we were making more money in one month than they had in the entire previous year. We went from 961st in the nation in parts sales to first in 28 months. We set monthly records every month. We not only became the first Toyota parts department to reach $1 million in annual sales, but we reached $2 million before anyone else reached $1 million, and we became the first to reach $3 million as well.

When I took over the job, Gene, my immediate boss, told me, "We're going to hand you the ball, and if you stumble, we'll talk about it." Well, I ran with it. Most parts managers are limited to their primary market, within 10 to 15 miles of where they work.

I developed a national wholesale business. We did some creative things. During the gas crunch in the '70s, people were eager to buy locking gas caps because gas was being stolen straight from their cars. We did some research and discovered that only two companies made locking gas caps, so we bought their entire stock. Any store or individual who wanted to buy a locking gas cap had to call us. At the time, air conditioners were not standard equipment on some cars, but they were a dealer-installed option. There was a shortage of them in the Texas-Louisiana Toyota district. We called Toyota's master depot in Torrance, California, and ordered every AC in their stock. We had semitrailers packed with them. We didn't even unload them. We just sent them on to Louisiana and Texas and made a nice profit.

As Chuck Stevinson bought more stores, he was taking guys out of my stores to put them in his other stores around Colorado. I had hired and trained them as novices, and they had become not just adequate but sensational, and I rewarded them for it. I called them all together and gave them each an expensive watch. I was so proud of them and what they had become. Three of those five work for me to this day.

I worked tirelessly. I was driven to excel. As I mentioned earlier, I was working 14 to 15 hours a day, six days a week. I also hired a good staff and solicited business from body shops and independent mechanics. I had a Watts line installed and sent out mailers so that if Toyota dealers around the country couldn't find the part they needed locally, they could get it from us. This gave me visibility in Toyotadom. I was making a name with the regional and national Toyota organization. My bosses recognized something in me.

In late 1973, Gene Osborne, who was part owner along with Chuck Stevinson, called me into his office and told me, "We want to prepare you for more than just being parts manager. Start getting ready; find your replacement. We're going to promote you to general manager." I was surprised. Such promotions don't happen to parts managers; they happen to people in the sales department.

Because of the oil embargo in 1974, which slowed the economy, my promotion was delayed a year. In the fall of '74, Gene told me again to start learning how to be a general manager. The plan called for me to begin following Gene around for a few days beginning January 21 to learn his job, but on December 15 Gene called me into his office and said, "I've got some things to do at the Chevrolet store if you need me. Just answer my phone and open my mail and conduct sales meetings and call me if you have a problem." He never came back. It took me a long time to realize that it was by design. He had decided that the best way for me to learn was simply to throw me into the job. I called Gene often in the beginning, but one day I was sitting at a stoplight in Denver when it occurred to me that in every situation I faced I was always wondering how my mentor Gene would do it. I decided I couldn't worry about how Gene would do it anymore; I was going to do it how Larry would do it.

It was the dawn of a new era for me. I took the entrepreneurial ideas I'd had in the parts department and ran with them, without being shackled by preconceived notions of what could and could not be done. The year I took over, the store made $368,000; I tripled the profit in my first full year on the job. Toyota was starting to get on a roll in the U.S. en route to becoming the giant it is today. At the end of 1977, Gene and Chuck came to me and said, "We want you to run all five of our dealerships. We're going to make you operations manager." Gene took me to national dealer conventions where they show the new models just so I would gain some experience. The other dealers would ask Gene, "What the heck are you guys doing in parts?" Gene would put his arm around me and say, "I just got me a helluva horse to ride."

After about a decade of wandering from one job and one

employer to another, uncertain about what I wanted to do or for whom I wanted to work, I had found a home.

POSTSCRIPT

Larry's intense competitiveness found a home in the business world, and he wasn't above doing the equivalent of an end-zone dance following some of his bigger scores. As general manager of Stevinson Toyota, when his dealership overtook local archrival Douglas Toyota in monthly car sales, Larry made sure his rivals knew it. He ordered a marble headstone with the inscription: "Here lies Douglas Toyota, who gave it their best effort but failed." He and his staff delivered it personally to the doorstep of Douglas Toyota in a hearse with a bouquet of flowers.

"They were not happy," recalls Dan Ware, who has worked with and for Miller for more than 30 years. "They were miffed. It was not a friendly rivalry. They were the enemy. It illustrated Larry's single-mindedness."

A representative from another local rival called Miller almost monthly to ask him how he was consistently beating them in parts sales each month. Miller simply said he didn't know, but after the fifth or sixth call, he finally told the man (in more colorful language than we'll use here), "Okay, I'll tell you. I come to work every day with the sole purpose of beating you guys."

CHAPTER 10

TITHING AND REACTIVATION

My reconversion to the church of my youth was a long road, but it might have begun with the simple words of a child. One day, five-year-old Greg asked his mom, "Where does God live?" It occurred to her in that moment that we had neglected to give Greg and the other children any formal religious training.

I was immersed in work and had little time for church. I had remained active through high school even after my mom announced that she was leaving the Church, but gradually my church attendance faded. I attended church just enough to be eligible to play on Church softball teams, but by the time I was 22 I didn't even do that because I had moved on to play in the more competitive Metro League. My friends left town to serve Church missions when they turned 19. So many of them were gone that it made it difficult to put together a wedding line for my marriage to Gail. For her part, Gail worked for the telephone company on Sundays, and her activity waned as well.

Then Greg asked his question: "Where does God live?"

Gail and the kids began to attend church after that, without me—I was too busy. "How is Larry doing?" the bishop would ask Gail. When Gail said I was fine, he would say, "Tell him he'll do even better if he comes to church." When the home teachers made their monthly visits to our home, I would stay in the other room.

Eventually, I realized what I needed to do, but I was reluctant to jump in there. I don't know why. I always believed the Church was true. I never spoke against it, or anything like that. I was working hard in those days and doing well professionally after years of struggle. Sunday was my day to relax or play softball. Our team played 70 to 90 games a year and was ranked in the top ten nationally. We traveled around the country and qualified for the national and world tournaments every year. In addition, our car dealership had a close relationship with the Denver Broncos and their players. I had season tickets through the dealership and attended many of their games on Sunday.

But a seed had been planted by Greg's question, and it began to grow, slowly. I was starting to think about church and religion and did so for the next four years without doing much about it. I went to church on Easter and Christmas and that was about it. Then one night in 1975 Gail convinced me to attend a Relief Society dinner at the ward. After the dinner I saw our elders quorum president, Steve Carpenter, and his wife, Marie, in the kitchen washing dishes. There were probably 600 items to wash by hand—dishes, silverware, pots, pans, and glasses. Everyone else had left the building. I couldn't leave the Carpenters like that, so Gail and I helped them.

We washed dishes all night. As I washed dishes, I watched the sun come up the next morning. Steve and I talked for eight hours. You don't do things like that without developing a bond, and that night created a bond that was pretty powerful. He told me, "Your life would be better if you came to church. You need the priesthood in your home."

This stuck in my mind, but I didn't do anything about it until the next visit from my home teacher, Larry Hunter. I was no longer hiding in the other room when he showed up, and, following his visit, he said something as he was leaving the house that sounded like something straight out of a Church movie or magazine: "How would you like to go to priesthood meeting with me in the morning?" I didn't relish the idea of driving six miles to church in 10-below weather at 7:30 A.M.—I wanted to sleep in—but he caught me off guard with his question, so I agreed to go. It was one of the pivotal experiences in my reactivation. Larry taught the lesson in the elders quorum class that morning. It was about the 2,000 stripling warriors, a well-known story from the Book of Mormon. It became my favorite story in all the scriptures. I came home really excited and wanted to talk about it with the family.

Steve Carpenter had been urging me for a year to meet with the bishop about being ordained an elder. The interview consists of answering a series of questions to determine your worthiness to hold this priesthood—do you obey the Word of Wisdom (abstain from cigarettes, alcohol, drugs, etc.), do you attend your church meetings, do you keep the law of chastity, and so forth. I continually put off the interview, but, flush with the excitement I had experienced on Sunday, I told the bishop I would meet with him now, with this proviso: I wouldn't answer the questions, but I might ask questions of my own if I didn't understand something. I wanted to know what I would be committing to if I became an elder. I already knew about the straightforward stuff regarding morality and the Word of Wisdom and supporting the leaders of the Church. I was worried there might be some questions that would blindside me, but there weren't any. I had cleared the first hurdle, but nothing really came of it for a time except that it was one more step, and it prepared me for things that were about to happen.

TITHING AND REACTIVATION

After the interview, I continued to attend church most of the time while also playing softball on Sunday. Then a series of intense things started to happen. After asking me to serve as ward volleyball coach, they upped the ante and called me to be the assistant teachers quorum adviser. My job, it was explained, would be to arrange a meaningful activity for the teachers quorum, which is composed of 14- and 15-year-old boys, every Wednesday night. My profession provided me with many resources that enabled me to do fun things with those boys—we attended Broncos and Nuggets games, made videos, baked cakes, and we had good participation. I agreed to do all this, but I told the bishop, "Don't call on me to pray or teach lessons, because I don't know what I'd be teaching, and I don't want to teach stuff I don't know." For six years I remained noncommittal toward church. I put off invitations for my priesthood ordination. It finally took some strange events to force the issue.

In 1977, my softball team qualified for the world tournament in Sun City, Arizona. Most of the guys flew there, but I liked to drive, so a teammate named Jerry Scavarda and I packed my station wagon floor to ceiling with the team's equipment and set out for Arizona. After we won our first game, I went to bed that night with an excruciating toothache. I tried medication, but it didn't even put a dent in the pain. After a fitful night, I got out of bed at 6:00 A.M. and drove the streets in search of a dentist. I drove on Grant Avenue through metro Phoenix wondering how I was going to find a dentist in a strange town, especially at this hour. Following a strong prompting, I made a U-turn and drove back about a mile. For reasons I can't quite explain, I pulled into a shopping center and there was a dental office. I entered the office at 7:55 A.M. and noticed there were already a man and a woman in the waiting room. I explained my problem to the receptionist and told her I was from out of town. She took me straight back to see the dentist, ahead of the other people in the waiting room. The dentist discovered a

93

chunk of food wedged between my gum and tooth. He picked it out and released all the pressure, which provided tremendous relief.

Now, what is the likelihood of making a U-turn and finding a dentist at 7:55 A.M. and having him take me straight back to his office immediately?

"How much do I owe you?" I asked the dentist,

He ignored the question. "You're LDS, aren't you?" he said.

I have no idea how he knew this. I told him yes. "So am I," he said, "and today is my last day here. I'm moving to San Diego. Let's call this one brother helping another."

He refused payment.

Later in the day, after our team was eliminated from the tournament, Jerry and I started driving back to Utah. When we reached the Four Corners area, we found ourselves driving on a highway that stretched out forever in an endless ribbon across the desert. Miles ahead on the horizon we could see two white specks on the side of the road.

"Know what those are?" I asked Jerry.

"My eyes aren't good enough," he said.

"Neither are mine, but those are Mormon missionaries."

"How do you know that?" he asked.

"Just do."

I don't know how I recognized them from that distance, but as we got closer, I could see they were missionaries walking on the side of the road, miles from nowhere in the blistering heat of the day. I pulled the car over and asked them if they needed a ride. We reorganized the equipment that was stuffed into the car to make room for these young men, and they squeezed into the backseat. They thanked us for the ride. They explained that they weren't allowed to hitchhike, but they were glad for the ride because they were going to meet some people to baptize them later that day. We drove on for another ten miles and reached the missionaries' destination just as another car loaded with Navajo Indians stopped at a stop sign on a dirt road that bisected the highway. They were sitting in a red 1949 Chevy pickup, with the parents in the front seat and the kids piled into the back.

What were the odds of me both recognizing those missionaries from miles away and then delivering them to their destination at precisely the same time as those Navajos arrived at the agreed-upon meeting place?

After dropping off the missionaries, we continued our journey and reached Denver at about 3:00 A.M., passing under the yellow lights that illuminated I-25. As Jerry slept in the other seat, I mused on the events of the day, wondering what it all meant. To me it was obvious: Somebody was saying, "Look, I've been talking to you for six years, and you are a really slow learner. So I gave you a gift today to get your attention and get you back on track." I decided it was time to quit messing around.

A few months later, I was asked to be the teachers quorum adviser. I tried to think of reasons they shouldn't ask me to do this. I told them that I didn't want to give up softball, that it meant a lot to me and I'd miss probably 13 Sundays a year to play ball. The bishop said, "Would you give me 35 Sundays?" We were negotiating now. It was like buying a car. I paused. The bishop, Lowell Madsen, broke the silence.

"I have to tell you that I have a selfish motive," he said. "My son Mark is about to become a teacher, and I want you to be his adviser."

It was one of the great compliments of my life. It was hard to say no to that. I accepted the calling.

A few weeks later I was sitting in my office at about 10:00 one night when the phone rang. It was Bishop Madsen. That morning, I had been thinking that it was time to resolve this old issue of priesthood ordination. As I left the house, I had told Gail, "I have put this thing off long enough." And now the bishop was calling and telling me, "We need to meet." I said, "You're right."

We met an hour later at his home. After exchanging pleasantries, he got to the point: "I've finally figured out what your problem is," he began. "You expect yourself to be perfect before you can be ordained, not merely worthy." I knew immediately he was right and said so. "By the way," I asked, "why did you call me today?" I figured Gail had called him, based on what I had told her as I left the house that morning.

"I've been thinking about calling you for a couple of weeks," he said. "And the prompting to call you was so strong last night that I got up at 3:00 A.M. and wrote in my Day-Timer to call Larry Miller." He told me that later that morning, as his son Mark rushed out the door to go to school—Mark was among the boys I worked with in the teachers quorum—he turned to his father and said, out of the blue, "Are you going to call Larry today, Dad?"

"I figured I was supposed to call you today," the bishop concluded.

So here we were, sitting in his house late at night, and he turned serious, even stern. "I'm going to ask you the worthiness questions, and this time I want answers." So I answered all the questions, and there was only one question that I answered negatively: "Do you pay tithing?" I said no.

The bishop asked why.

"I don't know," I said. "I can afford it; I just don't."

So the bishop asked me if I would start paying tithing, and I agreed.

Then he asked if there were any other problems we should discuss.

"I swear—a lot," I said.

"Do you take the name of the Lord in vain?"

"No."

"Why do you swear?"

"It's better than hitting people," I said.

The bishop laughed. "Will you quit swearing?"

When I quickly agreed to his request, the bishop said, "You said that readily."

"Well, I don't swear in front of women," I explained, "so I guess I can control myself at other times, too."

The bishop concluded the meeting by asking again, "Will you quit swearing and will you pay tithing?"

I said yes. I went home—I remember the date: December 28, 1978—and I told Gail, "Starting the fifth of January, I want you to take our gross income and pay tithing on it and don't ever ask me about it again."

A lot of things broke loose after that. If you asked me what the turning points of my life were, I would say marrying Gail and paying tithing. Ever since I made that decision to pay tithing, the Church has been the guiding force in my life—in business, family, everything. I have undergone a curious change since then as well. When I was younger, going to church was a duty. I did it because of social and family pressure. That all changed. Church became an enjoyable refuge for me and a place to learn. I love going to church, sitting there listening to the songs, the lessons, and the testimonies. It feels like a safe, comfortable place, and I have found something to be true that I have always preached to my employees: You can learn something in every meeting if you're teachable and have the right attitude and are humble.

The Church and its teachings have been a guide to me in my business dealings. We do millions of transactions each year, so I can't guarantee that they are all done right, but most of them are. We teach this constantly in our meetings. We talk about ethics. I tell employees that during their careers they will see people who take shortcuts and cheat, and it might be a temptation for them. But in reality they will emerge more successful if they do things with integrity. I ask them: Is it worth the accomplishment if you have to cheat to get there? Does your golf score mean anything if you pick up the ball for any putt that's outside of six feet? We're not keeping a daily scorecard the way we do in golf, but maybe we should. In the end, at least in my estimation, God does not care if you were a millionaire or a janitor or a CEO or a street sweeper; what He cares about is how you conducted yourself and how you fared as a father, husband, and friend.

POSTSCRIPT

"The one thing Larry always did is live by the Spirit," says Gail. "He'd get out of bed and get on his knees and have long silent prayers. He would tell me about them. The burden he was carrying was so heavy that he felt he couldn't do it alone. And he felt a great responsibility about his role in the community and toward all those people who worked for him and their families. He prayed for guidance as to what he should do and what decisions he should make."

In the notebook in which he kept his favorite sayings, he included a short list of favorite quotes he liked to consider relating to his faith:

Are we mortal beings having a spiritual experience, or are we spiritual beings having a mortal experience?

When the student is prepared, the teacher will appear.

Children are the messengers we send to a time we'll never see.

When obedience ceases to be an irritant and becomes our quest, in that moment God will endow us with power.

If we were charged with being followers of Jesus Christ, would there be enough evidence to convict us?

CHAPTER 11

ON MY OWN

Six weeks after I began to pay tithing to my church, my world collapsed. Chuck Stevinson, the owner of the five dealerships over which I was operations manager, called and asked me to meet him at a Denny's restaurant, immediately.

It certainly sounded ominous. Within minutes I was sitting with Chuck at Denny's. He ordered coffee, and I ordered a milk shake. He turned over a place mat so that he had a clean sheet of paper on which to write. He drew an organizational chart of his real-estate and car businesses. He indicated that he was overseeing the real-estate business himself. That brought us to the automobile side of his holdings. Chuck had eight sons, and he wanted them to follow in his footsteps on the automotive side. The bottom line: He was going to put his sons in charge of his automobile dealerships, and I was being demoted to general manager of one store, with no cut in pay. He wanted me to mentor some of his sons.

"What do you think?" he asked when he was finished.

I knew it was pointless to debate his plan. It was pointless to remind him that he had told me several times that he would add more stores as soon as I was ready, which indicated I was part of his future plans. Or that we had grown from two dealerships to five since I had worked for him. I was blindsided by this. I thought I was going to be doing this the rest of my career, but in reality he had planned to give the business to his sons and never told me.

"They're your stores; do what you want to do," I replied.

But I was churning inside. I realized that the demotion would dead-end my career. It closed off my horizons. I quickly realized that running one store was no longer enough for me. We left before I got my milk shake, and as soon as I walked into my office the phone was ringing. It was Gene, who was my supervisor and Chuck's partner in the automotive business. He had found out about my demotion just moments before Chuck had met with me.

"What are you going to do?" he asked.

"Right now I'm numb," I said. "I need to go home and think about it."

I met with Gene the next day. I told him I was looking for a job.

"I was afraid of that," Gene said.

I got a little testy. "Well, what would you do if you were me?"

"I'd do what you're doing."

I had no plan for my next move. After eight years of working for Stevinson, I knew it was time to move on. What happened next was a major turning point in my life. Sometimes we must take a step back before we can move forward in a way we never would have imagined.

Our family had planned to leave on vacation in a couple of weeks—our children were on a year-round school schedule and had a break at that time. We had rented a houseboat at Lake Powell. We packed up and drove to southern Utah, with my future murkier than the waters of Lake Powell. After spending a few days at the lake, we drove to Salt Lake City to visit family and friends.

One afternoon Greg and I were stuck at my mother's house with nothing to do while the rest of the family was shopping. We decided to kill the afternoon by going for a drive. Eventually, we wound up at the Toyota of Murray dealership to visit a longtime business acquaintance named Hugh Gardner.

I took Gardner to lunch at a small Mexican restaurant, and Greg tagged along. After we finished eating, we stood up to leave, and I asked, half in jest, "When are you going to sell me your dealership?" It was an old gag between us, a ritual we had practiced for years. Gardner always turned me down, and we would laugh about it. This time I was stunned when Gardner replied, "How about today?"

"Are you serious?" I asked.

"Yep, if we can put it together."

We got in our cars and returned to the dealership and began negotiations immediately. We haggled over the value of the assets and real estate. We wrote the terms of the deal on the bottom half of a check stub.

I was 35 years old, and I had worked for car dealers most of my adult professional life, and just like that, on April 6, 1979, I bought a car dealership for $3.5 million.

"What would you say if I told you I spent a million dollars today?" I told Gail that night.

"I didn't know we had a million," she said.

Actually, we had only $88,000 in the bank. It's ironic now, but no banks would loan me money. Utah banks wouldn't give me a loan because I lived in Colorado and my money was in Colorado banks, and Colorado banks wouldn't give me a loan because it was for a Utah business. To help finance the deal, I called my uncle Reid Horne to be my partner, and he borrowed $200,000 from a bank to help finance the transaction. He had seen what I had done at

Stevinson, so it wasn't much of a leap of faith for him. I put down $20,000 in earnest money and signed over two of my Shelby Cobras as collateral. Because I had no credit, I couldn't get a conventional loan, but the sellers were motivated and I took out three notes with them, due in ten years. We were leveraged to our eyeballs. If you go by the book, you're not supposed to be leveraged more than 1:1 (debt to cash), although banks and manufacturers might go 2:1. I was about 40:1!

Gail was nervous, but she never expressed it or nagged me. I was willing to take the risk and so was she. I was betting on myself. This dealership was underperforming badly, and I knew I could take a store, especially a Toyota store, and crank it up.

Hugh and his partner Tony thought they were going to outsmart us by selling most of the cars off the lot to their friends at cost before we took possession of the business. We had expected something like that, and we knew their inventory was low anyway. Toyotas were hard to get at the time because they were selling so fast. I had enough clout with the Toyota people from my Denver days that I was able to arrange a new shipment of cars and store them at the railroad yard until we took over the dealership. We opened on May 1 and sold 172 new cars the first month at a dealership that had been averaging 30 per month. We never looked back after that.

Consider this: On January 5, I paid tithing for the first time. On February 17, I was demoted. On April 6, I bought a car dealership. By May 31, I had sold 172 cars and was off and running in the car business. People might say this was a coincidence, but how many coincidences need to occur before they're not considered coincidences? When I began paying my tithing, that was absolutely the beginning. Then I was demoted and it forced me out of a situation where I thought I would be indefinitely. There were forces at work that sent me back to Utah.

We endured hard times when the economy turned sour in the early '80s. There were a lot of business failures in '80 and '81. We had just barely gotten going when the downturn came. We didn't even have enough to pay our bills sometimes. I returned home one evening and told Gail that we hadn't made enough money to pay ourselves that month; we had just enough to pay everyone else. We almost didn't survive. We came within days and hours of making it. Gail, who had experienced lean times when she was a teenager, knew how to manage meager resources. She would wait until the last minute to pay a bill, and she wouldn't pay all the bills at once, or she would pay only part of them. She was pretty nervous that first year, especially because we were responsible for employees and their families. Gail tells people now that she had complete trust in whatever I said I could do; she didn't worry about me taking risks. But she did wonder how long it was going to continue like this and if she needed to take a job again. I would deposit my paycheck each month and tell her to determine what she needed for the household and then write a check to the company for the difference. I was funding the business with my personal earnings as much as possible to avoid unnecessary debt. We felt a lot of stress about being in business for ourselves. Everything depended on us, including other people. It was a scary time.

In the midst of the economic downturn, another problem arose. Uncle Reid—my partner for two and a half years—had incurred serious financial problems through a series of misguided business ventures. This threatened the business and me. I wound up borrowing $700,000 at an exorbitant rate to buy him out.

This was another of those defining moments in my life. Now I had no partner; I truly was on my own, to sink or swim with my own abilities and finances, and I was faced with the challenge of considerable debt.

We survived the debt and the lean times—the economy took a turn for the better in '83 and '84. We gained traction in our car dealerships. We emerged from trying times, and it looked like we were going to make it.

And then I had a dream one night that was so remarkable in its clarity that it has stuck with me all these years later. It was actually the third or fourth time I had had this same dream, but this one made an indelible impression on me. I dreamed I was in a high-ceilinged room with open skylights, and there was a knock at the door. I took a white package wrapped with white ribbon that lay on a table and gave it to someone at the door. Moments later, there was another knock. This time there were more white packages on the table. I took them to the person at the door. The scene repeated itself over and over, and each time I gave away a box I discovered it had been replaced by many more boxes on the table until eventually they filled the entire room. In the dream, I asked Gail, "Where are these coming from?" She said, "The only thing I can figure is they're coming through the skylights."

I had never told Gail about the previous dreams, but this time I did. After I recounted the dream for her, Gail asked, "What did you learn from the dream?"

"It teaches me the promise of tithing made in the scriptures."

If nothing else, it solidified things for me. I believe the dream was about paying tithing, which is not just a Mormon belief, of course, but something that is mentioned in the Bible as well.

I have been so fortunate in my life, and not just in a material way. I have been able to do so many wonderful things and meet so many people. I've been able to build and create things and work with NBA owners and players, governors, church leaders, congressmen, people in the community, artists, musicians, and doctors. When I think about these things, I wonder, *Why me?* I set out to be a parts salesman. It has been a wonderful life that has exceeded all my expectations.

POSTSCRIPT

In 1980, on their 15th wedding anniversary, Larry and Gail were sealed to each other and their children in the Salt Lake Temple, which, in the Mormon faith, means they are united forever and not merely for time on earth. Before the ceremony, the temple sealer said, "I feel impressed to tell you that your name will be known in this valley by thousands, perhaps tens of thousands." As Gail tells it, "We had been in business one year. We owned only three dealerships at the time, and Larry didn't do his own advertising then so his face was not recognizable to the public. This was years before we bought the Jazz. We were just a struggling young couple. We looked at each other and wondered, 'What is he talking about?' After Larry died, I received an e-mail from a lady who had been there in the temple with us. She wrote, 'Do you remember what was said in the temple that day?'"

CHAPTER 12

ENTREPRENEUR

Just four months after opening my first store, I received a call from Erwin Ashenfelter, who was the assistant zone manager for Toyota in Denver. "Have you thought about buying a second dealership?" he asked. "There's one available, but you've got to move fast. You need to know it's really sick. It's in Spokane, and it's the number-six volume store in the country. The owner got into financial trouble. This is a fire sale."

I was still trying to get the store in Murray going, but I couldn't pass up the opportunity in Spokane. I had to convince banks in Washington—which had a moratorium on new financing—to loan us money purely on my reputation. We needed cars immediately, but we didn't have a dealer code, so Toyota couldn't ship them to the store in Spokane. I called national headquarters in Torrance, California, and told them to ship the cars to our store in Murray and bill us there, and then I shipped the cars to Spokane to get around the dealer code challenge. This was the entrepreneur in me. They said, "We've never done it that way." I told them to find a way. They also balked because I had no flooring line (financing to buy the cars), so I told them I would pay cash. I bought the dealership, and after that more opportunities continued to present themselves, and I couldn't resist the good ones.

I had never anticipated buying a second car dealership; little did I know that one day I would own more than 40 of them, along with many other businesses. Such things never occurred to me. I was not thinking big in those days, but I discovered I was a natural at putting together deals and finding a way to make things work. I could see the big picture. Where others saw nothing, I could see something, whether it was finding a way to finance and purchase arenas and NBA basketball franchises or another car dealership or related businesses. I discovered I had a knack for entrepreneurship.

Entrepreneurs start new businesses or revitalize existing businesses. Most new businesses fail; an entrepreneur looks for opportunities—potential—in these businesses where others don't see it, and he makes them work. The entrepreneur turns "nothing" into something very significant. He assembles the resources to make it happen.

In retrospect, my skills in those early years as an entrepreneur were—if you'll excuse the boast—incredible. I didn't think in terms of "if I could"; it was "I will." I'd just keep trying ways till I got it done, and that proved useful when it came time to buy the Jazz and build an arena.

Shortly after I bought the second dealership, another opportunity presented itself. I had a friend who lived in Salt Lake City who was a factory rep. These reps are constantly visiting dealerships as part of their jobs. They see dealers who are making millions when they're making only sixty grand, and they want to do it but don't know how. This friend got some money from his mother and bought a dealership in Moscow, Idaho, and immediately started

losing money. He was in over his head. I had been his adviser, talking to him on the phone at length about the business. But talking
about it on the phone and running the business are not the same.
He couldn't implement the things we discussed. To take him off the
hook, I bought the dealership from him.

By then I had decided I wanted to buy another dealership in
Phoenix. I was playing in a softball tournament in that city in
August of 1980, and while I was in the stands watching a game,
my broker approached me and asked if I wanted to buy a Phoenix
dealership called West Side Toyota. I met the owner the next day.

"How should we structure this deal?" he began.

"What do you think it's worth?" I countered.

"Seven million dollars."

"Okay," I said, "what does that get me?"

"Everything."

"No, what does it get me in parts, real estate, used vehicles—
what are the assets?"

"I don't know," he said. "We just want $7 million."

"Well, I've got to know how much it's making and how much
blue sky is in your number."

"Blue sky" is what you pay for the right to find out what you can
make potentially with the business. Nothing is assured; he might be
doing great with it and you could go in the toilet. But you've got to
know enough to evaluate what you can do with the business you're
thinking about buying. Finding out what you can do with that business is blue sky. We evaluated it and determined the blue sky was
$4.5 million and the assets $2.5 million.

Anyway, I told him I didn't have $7 million and that I was hop-
ing he could lease me the property for a few years and let me get my
bearings. He got very indignant. "Look," he said, "this is a Toyota
franchise in a Sunbelt city. This store will be sold before the day is
over. I've got guys coming in limos and private jets to buy this."

I was more than a little offended, so I said, "When these

high-budget guys get in their limos and fly home and you've still got this store to sell, call me." He responded, "Don't let the door hit you on the way out."

Three weeks later I got a call from this guy, and he acted like we were long-lost buddies. He asked if I were still willing to make the same offer, and I said yes.

This transaction taught me a principle I've employed many times since then—establish what something is worth to you, whether you're buying a hubcap or a large dealership, and then stick with it. If you get in a bidding situation you can let emotion carry you way past limits of good sense. I made what I thought was a fair offer for both the buyer and the seller, and I didn't let the guy pressure me into inflating what value I put on it.

I continued to put together deals to purchase new businesses. Some people wonder how a car guy got into so many seemingly unrelated businesses, but actually they are related businesses. In the business world, it's called vertical integration. Rather than hire others to do our advertising, we started our own advertising agency. Rather than hire out our printing needs, we formed a printing company. Instead of sending our car customers to another company for service contracts and collecting only a commission, we started Landcar Agency and sold our own service contracts. We started our own car insurance company as well. We started a real-estate company to hold properties for our dealerships to do business on. After buying the Jazz and building the arena, we started a catering business and a booking agency for concerts and events, as well as radio and TV stations to broadcast games. At one time we owned nearly 90 companies.

I loved those early years of my entrepreneurial career. I miss them. I had to be creative to put together deals to finance our many ventures simply because I couldn't get traditional financing in those days. Today, it's not nearly as much fun. By the 1990s my reputation made financing and borrowing money as easy as a phone call. It was almost too easy. It was boring. The early days demanded all my energy and skills as an entrepreneur.

In the business sense, I am a classic entrepreneur. I am constantly on the lookout for ideas and ways to make them happen. Over the years I found that I became less interested in overseeing the day-to-day operations of the company and more focused on bringing ideas to life and building things. It's the way my mind works. I love interacting with architects and contractors. It is not unusual for me to have 10 to 15 building projects going at once. In the mid-'90s, with the company growing so big, I divided our business in half—one side was sports and entertainment and the other side was automotive. I put a chief operating officer over each division. This took a huge load from my shoulders. I was able to do the things I enjoy and that I believe I am good at—expansion, land acquisition, the entrepreneurial.

This is the way my entrepreneurial mind works. It is very flighty. My attention span is short. I can concentrate on a project and write something that will take a half hour. I have all these things I get involved with that are floating around in my head, little bubbles or balloons. There are lots of them, and once I put something in there it stays and it's floating and moving and it will stay until I deal with it. If I follow up on it, I can snip it and it's gone and it stays gone.

In my experience, an entrepreneur is someone who understands certain principles:

1. Hard work.
2. Risk and reward.
3. Supply and demand.
4. How to feel a marketplace.
5. Overcoming fear of failure. Risk may cause failure, but success cannot come without it.
6. The principle of goal setting.
7. Having a vision of a project and being willing to go forward with it even when no one else shares the vision.

8. Knowing it can indeed be lonely at the top, but going there anyway.
9. The relationship between freedom and free enterprise.
10. The place he lives and works should be better when he left than when he came because he was there.

POSTSCRIPT

"His mind never stopped," says Gail. "It was always creating and formulating ideas. Once we were out for a drive and he saw an empty building and said, 'We ought to buy that and hire people to make quilts in there and give them to the homeless.' This would not only create quilts for the homeless but provide jobs. The only reason he didn't do it is because it turned out you can't make quilts as cheaply as you can buy them. But that's how his mind worked. Often it involved things that would help people who needed assistance or jobs. He often talked about wanting to build housing for the homeless."

Miller relished taking an idea, especially one that would benefit the community, and seeing it become a reality. He dreamed big and built big and only did things first class. He spent millions of dollars over budget just to re-create Salt Lake City circa 1877 inside his Jordan Commons theaters. He didn't just build a building or two as he was asked to do for Salt Lake Community College; he spent $50 million and created an entire campus. It was the artist in him. He was driven to create and to create something grand. Sometimes it got him into trouble. Although the vast majority of his businesses were hugely profitable, some of his ideas were financial disasters. His Mayan-themed restaurant of the same name, which featured cliff divers and waterfalls and robotic animals that could talk to the guests (and cost $25,000 each), lost millions every year until it was sold shortly after Larry passed on CEO duties to Greg. The Work and the Glory movies lost millions, and the racetrack has struggled financially. The old-fashioned gas station on State Street—where he wanted to have attendants gas up cars and clean windshields and so forth for customers *the way they used to—also loses money. He had an artistic bent that sometimes superseded his business sensibilities. Some of his projects weren't motivated by money, but by nostalgia, art, philanthropy, or all of the above. Larry acted on a simple romantic notion of the past to build the old-fashioned gas station—"Wouldn't it be fun to go back to the olden days?" he said to Gail.*

"He was a creator," says Gail. "That's what he did. It was much more fun for him to create than to run a business."

Says Greg of his father's projects: "Cost was an object, but he had this soft area. If he had a good idea or it seemed unique, he'd try to make it work. He was fully aware of what was happening, with the exception of the racetrack, which got away from him."

Miller's skills as an entrepreneur led him to the next stage of his life . . .

PART III

THE JAZZ

CHAPTER 13

THE JAZZ

I t began with an unsolicited letter. It ended with Jerry Buss—the owner of the Los Angeles Lakers—shouting down another owner in support of my bid to win approval from the other NBA team owners. And in between, it was a race against the clock, one that had me crashing bankers' meetings and dashing around town leading a fast break to secure loans to buy the Utah Jazz literally at the last minute.

Not that my bid to buy the Jazz wasn't asking the impossible. All I wanted was an $8 million loan—more than two times my net worth at the time—from wary, conservative bankers to buy a professional basketball franchise that had never shown a profit in its 11 years of existence. Plus, I had no cash to put down and no business plan to show how I would make this financially strapped team profitable. All I had to offer was my word and reputation.

Most fans don't realize how close they came to losing the team that has become such an intregal part of Utah. The answer is, they were within minutes, and this is no exaggeration.

It was a lonely path I followed for a long time to keep the team in town. Nobody—and I mean nobody—wanted to go down that path in the beginning. I look back on that time with great satisfaction because it called into play all my skills as a budding entrepreneur, someone who could put together creative deals and make things happen with very little in the way of assets. At the time, it was a worrisome, time-consuming, risky campaign to save the Jazz, but I became convinced the Jazz were worth saving, and this became my mission. From a personal point of view, I risked everything—my car dealerships, my small fortune, my entire career—to do it.

I had never considered owning a professional sports franchise, and little did I think that was where I was headed when I opened a letter from the Utah Jazz in February of 1985. It was a prospectus the franchise mailed to 40 businessmen. As I read through the prospectus I realized its purpose: They were seeking $200,000 investments from ten people to recapitalize the team for $2 million through limited partnerships to keep the team in Utah.

The Jazz were having financial problems and always had. They became an NBA franchise in New Orleans in 1974 and then moved to Utah in 1979. They had lost $17 million in 11 years. Even in their best year, the Jazz had lost $1 million.

Sam Battistone, the team's owner, struggled to make the payroll. That's why they traded Dominique Wilkins, the team's number-one draft pick in 1982, for three players and cash. The Jazz simply needed the money. At the end of nearly every season, they made a public plea for financial help from the community. Each spring brought the next chapter in the continuing saga of "Will They Stay or Will They Go?"

They had tried several Band-Aid fixes—public stock offerings, a partnership with Dr. Gerald Bagley, limited partnerships. In 1984, they tried to sell the team to Adnan Khashoggi, the extravagant

Saudi Arabian billionaire arms dealer and investor who two years later would appear on the cover of *Time* magazine with the headline, "Those Shadowy Arms Traders." He agreed to buy half of the Jazz for $8 million. All he had to do was win approval from the NBA. The NBA checks the backgrounds of potential owners to determine if they can handle it financially and to ensure that they have had no criminal dealings. Khashoggi refused to produce records of his international business dealings. The NBA denied the deal and, indeed, in the coming years Khashoggi would be tied to a couple of major scandals, including Iran-Contra, and was arrested (and later acquitted).

Nothing had worked to help the Jazz's financial problems, and the vultures were circling. Every year another group tried to buy the Jazz and move them to a new city—Santa Ana, Anaheim, Memphis, St. Louis. In 1985, there were at least nine suitors for the Jazz.

After reading the letter from the Jazz management that day in my office, I wondered why they had sent it to me. I didn't have $200,000 in cash to throw at a basketball team—my money was being used to service debt at my five car dealerships, and I was scratching and clawing to make it. I was worth less than $4 million at the time. That's pocket change for an NBA owner.

I didn't think much more about the letter until March 10, when I received a call from a secretary in the Jazz's front office. She wanted to know if I had received the prospectus and asked what I thought about it.

"I'm interested in helping the Jazz stay in Utah, but I don't think limited partnerships are the answer," I told her.

Within ten minutes, Dave Checketts, general manager of the Jazz, was sitting in my office. He hadn't called ahead; he simply showed up. "Let's talk about this," he said.

I told him there was nothing to talk about, that I didn't have

$200,000, but I was adamant that limited partnerships weren't the answer to the Jazz's problems.

"What if something more comprehensive were done to fix this?" he asked.

By now, our impromptu meeting had stretched to an hour as we talked about the Jazz's financial situation. I ventured a question of my own: "If we were to do something more radical, what would it be?"

"I am authorized to sell half the team for $8 million and no less," Checketts replied.

I balked at that price. Originally, the Jazz had been bought in New Orleans by 11 investors for $6.25 million, which they borrowed from a New Orleans bank. They had kept the interest current, but they had done nothing to reduce the principal. During the Jazz's five years in New Orleans, those investors went to Battistone one by one and asked him to buy out their shares, which he did.

I focused on the debt of the team, not on the financial condition of its operations, which was a mistake. I told Checketts I would take away the debt, which meant I would buy the team for $6.25 million, but Checketts, under orders, held firm on the price. It was only later that I learned that they needed $1.75 million to recapitalize the operational side of the franchise. It proved to be a good thing for me that they held firm on the full price, because I would have had to come up with that money anyway after I bought the team. But I didn't know this and I stuck to my offer of $6.25 million, not understanding why they wouldn't budge from their price. I should have looked at the operational side of the business and realized they needed the $1.75 million just to get back to zero.

Two days after my meeting with Checketts, I met with Battistone. We hit it off pretty well, but both of us held our ground—$6.25 million and $8 million respectively—and our negotiations stalled for a couple of weeks. During this meeting I learned that Battistone was having similar discussions with other prospective buyers besides me. During the next three weeks, Battistone and Checketts met with these other interested parties and invited me to come along. It was a strange position to be in—I was on both sides of the table. On the one hand, I was trying to buy the team, and on the other hand I was helping to sell the team. During this time I was meeting with them almost daily, a total of 30 times or more. It was almost nonstop for three weeks. All of my time was being spent on the Jazz, and I was neglecting my dealerships. I didn't even make time to eat. I'd throw a candy bar in the glove box of my car for lunch, and it would still be there at the end of the day. I was just running from one meeting to the next and making one phone call after another. It was one of the most intense times of my life.

By this time I was really wrestling with the notion of buying the Jazz. I knew that we had to keep them in Utah somehow. This was important to me. Early on, my interest was mostly a ploy; some high-powered guys in the community had looked into buying the Jazz but had passed. I thought that if I manifested confidence in this transaction and showed interest, the others would want to step in and buy it. They didn't, which they probably regret now. It was surprising to me. I was hoping someone else would buy that other half of the team or help me. I didn't care if I was the owner—it was all about keeping the Jazz here. But it became clear that if anyone locally was going to buy the team, it would have to be me. Was this something I should and could do?

I was turning all these things over in my mind nearly every waking hour trying to make a decision. I can remember sitting at our kitchen counter one afternoon trying to decide whether to pursue the Jazz. I asked Gail to write down some numbers that I recited for her. After looking over the numbers, I told Gail, "I think we can do this."

One afternoon I visited Gordon B. Hinckley, a member of the First Presidency of the LDS Church at the time, to seek his advice in this matter. He asked me some very perceptive rhetorical questions that helped solidify things for me, and then he acknowledged the potential for good in the millions of tiny impressions that would be made by the posting of Jazz scores and the mentions of the team in the news. He knew that keeping the team in the state would be beneficial for Utah and, by extension, for the image of the Church in Utah.

Shortly after my visit with President Hinckley, Gail and I were driving on I-15—I can remember we were near 4500 South—when suddenly I announced, "The Jazz can't leave. We have to do everything we can to keep them here." Gail was a little shocked because my declaration came out of nowhere. I had kicked it around, done my homework, and so from then on it was a go.

By now I was spending considerable time with Sam every day, and when I wasn't with him he was very accessible—he always returned my phone calls immediately. But then suddenly he dropped out of sight, and nobody knew where he was. This went on for three days before I finally got a call from him. After apologizing, he said, "I have been with a guy who is trying to buy the team, and we've been negotiating at his beach house in Newport Beach for three days. His people are wining and dining me. They made an offer, and I need to know if you can come to a meeting this morning at 10:00." So here I was again, caught in the middle—a potential buyer participating in a meeting with another buyer. I sat on one side of the table with Checketts, Battistone, and his attorney, Frank Suitter. On the other side of the table sat Sydney Schlenker, a big, heavyset man with curly, disheveled, salt-and-pepper hair. Sydney, a playwright who lived in Denver, had just sold a TV station in Houston for $90 million and was searching for investment opportunities. He was embarking on an ambitious scheme: He wanted to build a new TV station in Miami and then, to provide programming for that station, he would buy two basketball teams for which he would own exclusive TV rights—he would fully fund a new men's basketball team for the University of Miami, Florida, and buy an NBA team to bring to Miami. He wanted the Jazz to fill the latter role.

I didn't know any of this when I walked into the meeting. I was introduced to everyone in the room and was told that Sydney had made Sam a cash offer of $18 million—$9 million now and $9 million when the team moved to Miami in two years, following completion of a new arena there.

This immediately created a big problem: How many fans are going to buy Jazz tickets once they know the team is going to move in two years? Sydney said he was willing to deal with that problem, but he didn't leave it at that. He went on to say that if he was willing to run the risk of losing fans and money during those two lame-duck years in Utah, then he had the right to make changes. When Sam asked what changes he planned to make, Sydney said he was going to get rid of Adrian Dantley, the Jazz's best player, and Frank Layden, the coach.

I was a fly on the wall during these discussions, and I watched as things got heated. I had never seen Sam yell, and it was something to behold. You have to understand that Sam's wife, Nan, thought Adrian Dantley walked on water. You also have to understand that when Sam brought the team to Utah the first guy he hired was Frank Layden, and Frank did everything to make it work. He was coach and PR man. He worked his tail off, and his humor, affability, and energy did much to help the franchise gain a foothold in Utah. He once drove 90 minutes to Logan just to speak to a group of eight people. He did everything he could to help the team. To his credit, Sam recognized this and he was loyal to Frank. He was also loyal to Dantley because he liked how he played. So when Sydney said he was going to get rid of these two men, Sam started shouting, and things got pretty lively. The veins in Sydney's neck were standing out, and he was pounding on the table. Finally, Sydney said, "Okay, then I'll pay you $20 million cash right now and take over the team immediately." I knew this was the moment of truth, and in the middle of all the screaming, I made a time-out signal with my hands, but to no avail, so finally I screamed, "Time-out!"

I asked Checketts, Battistone, and Suitter to meet with me in the hall. "Let me ask you a question," I said to Sam once outside the room. "If I will pay you $8 million for half the team, will you keep it here?"

"Yes," he said. But then he qualified it. "Here's the problem: The NBA's Board of Governors meets in nine days, on April 12, to approve transactions. You have until April 11 at 5:00 P.M. to raise your $8 million."

In other words, if there was going to be an ownership change that year, it had to be approved by that deadline or wait another year, and the Jazz could not wait another year. The team needed the money now.

The reason Battistone agreed to accept my offer, which was considerably less than Sydney's offer, was because, again to his credit, he wanted the Jazz to remain in Utah. He also didn't want to undertake the financial risks inherent in a lame-duck franchise waiting for Sydney to finish his arena.

After we agreed to this deal in the hall, Sam returned to the meeting and explained my offer to Sydney. "He's a little undercapitalized, but I am giving him until April 11 to raise the money," Sam told him. "If he can do it, I will sell to him. If you leave your offer on the table, I'll sell to you if he can't raise the money."

That very minute I set out to raise the $8 million. I went to four banks—Zions, First Security, American Savings and Loan, and FMA/Moore Financial (which was owned by Boise-based Moore Financial). I asked each of them for $2 million, but I suggested to Zions and First Security that I might need $4 million from each of them as a backup plan because I was less certain the other two banks would grant me the loans. They both said they would consider the request for $2 million. They really stood their ground and convinced me that that was all the money I could expect from them.

I met with Zions Bank in the Kennecott Building on the morning of Day 1 of my nine-day countdown. I walked into the room and faced 18 Zions officials, including Roy Simmons, chairman of the board for Zions Bancorporation. All eyes were on me. They knew why I was there. I felt like I was walking a gauntlet when I walked between those bank officers to reach Roy's desk.

"What can we do for you?" he asked.

"I'm here to borrow some money to save the Jazz."

"Do you have a business plan to turn them around?" Simmons asked. He knew the team had lost $17 million in 11 years and never less than a million dollars in any given year.

"That's what I do as an entrepreneur," I said.

Then he warmed me up for his next question. "I've told these gentlemen I would ask this question. We may base our answer on your response."

This made me nervous. I had no idea what was coming and was uncertain how quickly I could pull together a good answer with all these eyes on me and so much at stake.

"With all the history the Jazz have had as a losing proposition on one hand, and your success as a businessman in your ventures on the other hand, we have two different perceptions—one of a successful Larry Miller and one of a crazy Larry Miller for attempting this. Which perception is right?"

"Only history will tell," I replied. I felt like it was a simple reply, perhaps too simple, but it was the first thing that came to my mind. Simmons put his hands behind his head and laughed.

"Was the answer funny?" I ventured.

"No," he said, "but I had suggested to the people in this room that I would ask the question, and I couldn't think of an answer you could give me that would garner my support, but you just gave me one."

I don't really believe my answer had anything to do with it. I think in his heart he wanted to help me. He took a brief call from his wife—who called to say she had a flat tire—and then resumed.

"We'll commit the $2 million to you," he said. "We'll do it early to encourage the others to come along."

So by the end of the morning on Day 1 of my nine-day count-down, I had $2 million of the $8 million I needed to buy the team. I left that meeting and walked one block to First Security, but they were still gathering information and weren't ready to commit to anything yet. I met next with American Savings and Loan, which was reeling at the time because of the savings and loan scandal that had beset such institutions nationwide, and then with FMA/Moore Financial. By the end of Day 1, I had met with the four targeted financial institutions.

I called them every day to see where things stood and to ask if there was anything more I could do to hasten the process. By the third day, First Security also committed to $2 million, which meant I now had half the money. I was feeling good, but American Savings was dragging its feet, and I wasn't getting any answers from FMA/Moore Financial.

I could understand their reluctance. The Jazz looked like the *Titanic,* and I was still a fledgling businessman. I had no time to work up a business plan on how I proposed to turn this team around. I didn't even know who to ask about a business plan. Obviously, Sam didn't have one. Anyway, I had to save the team first before I could implement a business plan.

The week wore on. On Day 7, American Savings called to say that, between the acquisition we had proposed and the condition of savings and loans institutions throughout the country, they rejected our loan request.

I turned to FMA/Moore again, trying to get a decision from them. I repeatedly called Rich Jackson, an FMA/Moore official I had come to know when he worked for Zions Bank, but he kept putting me off. Then Day 8 arrived, and I was in panic mode. I called Rich's house repeatedly, and his 11-year-old daughter answered the phone each time. I continued to call Rich's house over and over until no one would answer the phone, not even the daughter. Rich finally answered at 11:00 that night and explained that he had been unable to find the phone—his daughter had placed it in the refrigerator so she wouldn't have to hear my calls anymore. I told Rich I needed an answer, but he didn't have one. I told him I knew that FMA/Moore's loan committee was meeting with shareholders at the Marriott Hotel the next morning. I also knew they were going to have breakfast together before the meeting, at 7:00 A.M. I told Rich I was going to crash the breakfast. The next morning—it was now Day 9—I walked into the room where the group was having breakfast. It was embarrassing, but I had to do it; I was out of options. There were a dozen men in the room sitting at breakfast, some of whom recognized me.

"Look, I'm sorry to crash your breakfast," I told them, "but I need a decision from you, and I need it now. I know this is presumptuous of me, but I'm out of options."

One of the bank officials stood up and asked me to come with him, leading me out of the room. "We'll find a way to help you," he said. "We're trying to figure out how to do it. This is one of the things we're going to talk about this morning. Don't go away."

That meant I had collected $6 million, but it was Day 9 and I had only a few hours to get the rest. By now the media was onto the story. Radio and TV stations were reporting that Zions, First Security, and FMA/Moore had agreed to help, but that American Savings had turned me down. I received a call that morning from John Woods of American Savings asking me if I had planted that report with the media. I denied it. "We've been embarrassed by this," he said. "We'll give you $1 million."

I was relieved by this news, but of course that meant I was still

$1 million short. I walked back to Zions and First Security to ask for another million, but they wouldn't budge.

At 3:00 P.M., I received a phone call from Checketts. "Are you going to get the money or not?" he asked. I told him I didn't know. "We've got a problem," he explained. "Tonight we play Portland at home in the Salt Palace. We're having a reception and dinner for 300 people, and we need you to make an announcement that you're buying half of the team. The media will be there. We've got to know." Checketts continued to call me throughout the afternoon to check my progress. I couldn't give him an answer, and 5:00 was looming closer and closer.

It was 3:30. I got on the phone again and urged all four lenders to meet together for the first time to explore ways to come up with the last million dollars. They met on the tenth floor in the First Security building behind glass doors that allowed me to see but not hear them. I was in the lobby pacing back and forth, watching nervously through the window. They were making notes and talking. I was still getting phone calls from Checketts and glancing at my watch. By now, it was 4:40. We had 20 minutes to figure this thing out. I couldn't take it anymore. I walked into the meeting and said, "Fellas, I don't want to run your meeting, but I'm going to tell you something. I've been paying my own bills since I was 12 years old, and I've never missed a payment on anything in my life. If you can find a delinquent payment, turn me down. If you can't, make this loan. I've got to make an announcement at the Salt Palace in 18 minutes and make a commitment to Sam Battistone."

At 4:53 P.M.—seven minutes before the deadline—they told me, "We'll work out the details. You go to your meeting." I raced down the sidewalk toward the Salt Palace in a suit and tie, weaving through other pedestrians like John Stockton on a fast break, and entered the back door of Salon E sweating profusely. The media was already there, as were the 300 invited guests. Layden, Checketts, and Battistone were on the dais, and they immediately looked at me for an answer. I had been given a nine-day deadline to buy the Jazz, and on the ninth day, at about 4:58 P.M., I gave them the thumbs-up sign.

Battistone stepped to the microphone and announced that I was buying half of the Utah Jazz.

Even as he spoke, the bankers were still trying to figure out how to accomplish this. In the end, First Security, through its leasing company, came up with $700,000, and Zions, through its leasing company, produced the remaining $300,000. That made six lenders, counting the leasing companies.

When I woke up on Day 9, I had only half the money. Somehow, it had all come together at the last minute.

The next day I flew to New York to meet with the NBA Board of Governors to get their approval as Sam's partner. I arrived early, and as I sat there Red Auerbach walked into the room, as did Ted Turner and Jerry Buss. This was heady company. David Stern, the NBA commissioner, introduced himself to me.

Sam had been paving the way with the other NBA team owners for my approval. These were some high rollers. They had serious fortunes. They were worth 20, 50, even 100 times more than I was. I wasn't even in their league. That made it more difficult for Sam to convince them of my viability as a part owner, but he needed to recapitalize the team and make the team's debt go away, and the other owners knew it.

After dinner, the advisory finance committee gathered. It is composed of eight owners, usually based on seniority and hand-picked by Commissioner Stern. We sat around one table for the purpose of approving my ownership. Angelo Drossos, who owned the San Antonio Spurs at the time, sat next to me. I laid out my financial statements showing earnings and equity and the debt structures of my business. Angelo, for some reason, took the lead in the meeting and asked me a question. Midway through my answer, he interrupted and asked me another question. Midway through my next answer, he interrupted me again with another question. He did this five times. He had made up his mind that he didn't want me there and wouldn't listen to my answers. After the fifth interruption, Buss, whom I had never met, interrupted Angelo.

"Angelo, why don't you shut up and let him answer a question!"

Then Jerry started asking questions, and that led to a discussion of my numbers. The group knew I was on a firmer financial foundation than Sam, so if they cast their lots with the existing owner they needed me. Within a half hour, Jerry said, "I'm satisfied. Let's go with him." Jerry saved me that day. I won approval from the owners.

On May 10, 1985, some three months after receiving the Jazz's letter, I officially became part owner of an NBA franchise.

The Land Cruiser that Larry bought, restored, and sold to pay off all of their debt.

Larry and Gail with Greg in front of their apartment in 1968.

Larry and Greg. Larry tended Greg while Gail worked at the telephone company.

Larry and Greg "worked" on the 1932 Ford coupe that Larry bought in 1965 with his partners, Howard Schaelling, John Copier, and Dave Grant. In its prime the car ran about 11.50 seconds and approximately 120 miles per hour in the quarter mile.

Larry and his youngest son, Bryan, at the ballpark, summer 1978.

The family had to "kidnap" Larry to get this portrait taken.
Clockwise from left: Bryan (on Larry's lap), Steve, Greg, Roger, Karen.

Karen was too young to play baseball so she spent her time at the ballpark "protecting" her "little" brothers. Left to right, Steve, Karen, Roger, and Greg ready for the day's games.

Larry and Gail share a rare moment away—on a vacation in Monte Carlo.

Larry was chosen to be on the All Star team his first year in Little League.

When Larry stopped playing ball, all that was left was to own the team.
He bought the Triple A baseball team from Joe Busas in 2005.

Larry was inducted into the Softball Hall of Fame for his accomplishments as a softball player.

Larry tries his skill at "taming the bull" and he and Gail enjoy a variety
of other activities on a Toyota-sponsored trip to Mexico in 1973.

Larry kept this picture of Gail on his desk at the office during the 1980s.

Larry started his career in the automobile business at American Auto Parts in 1964 as a result of spending so much time there replacing parts that got broken on the Falcon when he drag raced it.

Larry became Toyota's first "Million Dollar Parts Man" at Stevinson Toyota in Lakewood, Colorado.

Because of his hard work in the parts department, Larry was promoted to General Manager of Stevinson Toyota. His parts associates had his notepad chromed and inscribed with the words "Is this your first day?" because that was what he said to them when they didn't get an order right. He kept it on his desk until his retirement in 2008.

The first Toyota dealership Larry and Gail bought. It launched his adventure as an owner in the business world in 1979.

In 1983 Larry opened the first building he built himself to replace the original dealership. Mr. Makino (in front, looking up) and other Toyota dignitaries attended the grand opening.

The proud moment of selling the first car (it was actually a truck) in the first dealership.

On September 29, 2007, the one-millionth car was sold at one of Larry's dealerships in Arizona.

Larry at the grand opening of his new Chevrolet dealership in Murray, Utah.

Chairman and Mrs. Toyoda (second and third from the left) traveled from Japan
to attend the grand opening of Larry's first Lexus dealership.

Larry got a much-appreciated second chance to be a father to his grandson Zane, who lived with Gail and Larry from birth.

Zane was homeschooled during his high school years and was very excited to graduate and get on with the big adventure of life, following in Larry's footsteps.

Larry with granddaughters Carisa
and Courtney after a fun ride in
the Falcon convertible.

Gail and Larry on the occasion of their first
granddaughter, Carisa's, blessing.

Larry was just as enchanted with his youngest granddaughter, Elizabeth, as he was with the first.

Sons Steve and Greg enjoying an outing with Larry at the family cabin in Idaho.

Larry loved being "grandpa" at the cabin.

Three generations of Miller boys sharing a fishing trip to the cabin.

Granddaughter Sabrina helps Grandpa
grill hamburgers for lunch.

Four-wheeling was a favorite family vacation
when the kids were young.

Even after the children started to leave home, the family would gather for
extended family vacations. Mount Rushmore was an especially fun trip.

CHAPTER 14

THE JAZZ II

My pen was hovering over the document. All I had to do was sign the agreement, and the sale of the Jazz would be complete—the Jazz would go to Minnesota and I would more than double my personal net worth at the time. With my signature, I would receive $14 million for my half of the team, which, after paying off my debt, would leave me a slick $6 million profit after owning the Jazz for just 14 months—not a bad return on my investment. Sam Battistone, who owned the other half of the Jazz, had placed the contract on my desk.

"Sign these papers and I'll give you a check for $5 million in earnest money today," he said, and he stood there waiting for me to sign.

The room was quiet. I bent over the desk to sign, but then I froze. Thoughts were racing through my mind. What would I do with that much money? What would it mean to me? What would

Salt Lake City be without the Jazz? What kind of hole would that leave in the community? And how could I face the fans who would be upset by this?

The reality and enormity of the decision hit me. I actually started to get dizzy and used the desk to steady myself. Part of it was the surprise. I had been caught off guard. Sam had showed up at my office without warning, and yet he wanted a decision right now.

Nobody wanted to believe this at the time, but I never bought the Jazz to make money, either on the operations side or as an investment. Almost as soon as I bought half the team, people were wondering when I was going to sell it—and perhaps, given the team's myriad owners and staggering losses, this was understandable. But Gail and I always viewed the Jazz as the grand gift we could give the city and state. There were always offers to buy the Jazz and move them to another city. All I wanted to do was ensure that that would never happen.

We were the smallest market in the NBA, and it was very clear to me that if the Jazz ever left there would never be another major league team here—at least, not in our lifetime. I saw the team as a rallying point for the state.

Money is replaceable; the Jazz are not. For me, it wasn't even difficult to pass up the money, especially when it was merely on paper. One time, while we lived in Colorado, I cashed a $20,000 bonus check and took the money home and laid it out on our king-sized bed—100s, 50s, and 20s. The money covered the entire bed. I stared at it, and it was intoxicating. But when I see money only on paper, I can put emotion aside. It was not tempting in the case of the Jazz, especially after I had worked so hard to keep them here. I wanted the Jazz to be here so much more than I wanted the money.

There was only one thing that could cause me to pick up the pen and sign a document that would take the Jazz from Utah: the Texas Option.

The Texas Option, which had been written into the original

contract with Sam, is a provision that is used frequently in business ventures. The Texas Option states that if either partner wants to buy out his partner or sell his share, for whatever reason, he can make an offer to his partner to that effect. But it also starts something he can't stop. If, say, Partner 1 declares that he wants to buy out Partner 2, now Partner 2 can turn the tables and say he wants to buy out Partner 1 for the same price he offered, and Partner 1 must agree to it. That means Partner 1 must have a good idea of where the other partner stands before declaring his intentions to buy or sell.

When I bought half of the team in April 1985, the franchise was valued at $16 million. Even though I wasn't in this to make money, it was difficult not to notice the remarkable timing I had had in buying half the team. Almost immediately, the value of an NBA franchise increased a million dollars every month! My purchase of the Jazz did nothing to stem the rush of investors who wanted to buy the team and move it elsewhere. One of those was a partnership from Minnesota, Marv Wolfenson and Harvey Rattner. They had tried to buy the Jazz a year earlier when I had beaten them to it, and now they were back again. They had been keeping in touch with Battistone, and they knew about the Texas Option clause.

Gail and I traveled with the Jazz that winter for a road game in Phoenix, and the morning of the game Sam called me in my hotel room and asked to meet with me over breakfast. He began our conversation by asking me how much of a return on my $8 million investment it would take for me to walk away from it.

"I don't know," I said. "Why?"

"I can get you a million dollars right now and probably another half-million."

"I don't know," I said. "That's not why I did it."

Sam explained that Wolfenson and Rattner, the two Minnesota investors, were still pursuing the Jazz and were prepared to offer $18 million, and maybe even $19 million, for the franchise.

I continued to remind Battistone that I didn't buy the Jazz to turn around and sell them, just as I had been telling the media for the past few months. But Sam continued to talk about the offer. It was almost as if he were saying, "What's wrong with you, Larry?" We ended our meeting with the assumption that Wolfenson and Rattner would pay $19 million, which would mean a $1.5 million net profit for me.

In fairness to Battistone, he was not the bad guy in this situation. He held his Jazz ownership in a publicly traded corporation called StratAmerica, of which he had majority ownership (65 percent). As such, he had fiduciary responsibility to StratAmerica shareholders; even if he didn't like it, he had to do what was best for the corporation, and in this case that meant selling the Jazz.

In the coming weeks, the offer climbed to $20 million. Battistone showed me the agreement, and I told him that from a tax standpoint it was a bad deal, and that if we were going to sell, this was a bad way to do it. I realized later that this was the wrong thing to say because now it sounded as if I *would* sell if the agreement were changed. I realized my mistake when Battistone set up a meeting with the Minnesota buyers at the Denver airport to discuss the tax ramifications. As it turned out, my slip of the tongue had been a great bargaining tool. They thought I was there to raise the price, and they did—to $22 million. Again, I said I didn't want to sell, but Wolfenson and Rattner persisted. They kept coming back to Battistone with bigger offers.

In May of 1986—one year after I bought half of the team— Battistone came to my office at the Toyota store and said, "You've done a great job of doing two things: moving these guys' price up and ticking them off. Now they're offering $25 million!"

None of these guys—Battistone, Wolfenson, Rattner—got it. They thought I was saying no because I was holding out for more money. They thought it was a bargaining ploy. Finally, Battistone acknowledged the elephant in the middle of the room: the Texas Option.

"Larry, this is getting embarrassing," he said. "I would sell for $25 million, and that would enable them to buy my half and exercise the Texas Option."

I could see what was going to happen, of course. They would come to me and say they owned half the team and wanted to buy me out for $12.5 million, and I would either have to sell to them or match their offer. They would know I didn't have the money to do that. I would have to sell to them.

A couple of weeks later, on Friday, June 13, Sam returned to my office with four copies of the contract, each of them three-eighths of an inch thick. Each was turned to a signature page, where I could see that Battistone, Wolfenson, and Rattner had already signed a deal to sell the team for $28 million! Sam put the agreement on my desk. With some resignation, I picked up a pen to sign the documents. I was beaten. I couldn't overpower this anymore because of the Texas Option.

This was one of the moments of truth in my life, a time to find out what I was about. It was a real test. As Sam made a point of saying, he could actually deliver a check for $5 million in earnest money that very day. As far as he was concerned, it was a no-brainer, a done deal.

My pen was hovering over the blank space and remained there frozen for 10 to 15 seconds while I wrestled with my thoughts. Finally, I threw the pen down and backed away from the desk.

"Sam, I can't sign this," I said.

"This is a tough time to decide that," Battistone said, unable to hide his irritation. "This is a good deal."

Now I took the leap. "What will it take to keep the Jazz here?" I asked.

"You know what they're paying; if you want to pay StratAmerica $14 million, you can keep them here."

Was I crazy? Instead of owing $8 million, I could turn a $6 million profit on a 14-month investment. Now I was not only going to pass up the fat profit, I was going to take on more debt—$14 million more, or a total of $22 million.

"Give me overnight to develop a plan that I will present to you tomorrow, and we'll see if there is a way to do this," I said.

I went home, and for the next couple of hours I simply tried to clear my head and think about this situation. Finally, I began to make notes on a yellow legal pad, searching for ways to structure a deal; then I would crumple the pages up and throw them away and start again. I did this over and over. How could I do this? Thirteen months earlier I had thought $8 million was over my head to buy half the team, and now I was looking at $22 million. I was already making monthly payments of $180,000 to service the original debt. How could I assume more debt? I stayed up until 3:00 A.M. The next morning, I was too weary to deliver the terms of the deal to Sam myself. Gail delivered my handwritten proposal to Sam's house and asked him to meet me at my office later that afternoon.

The proposal I made to Sam was this: I would forgive a $3.5 million loan that I had made to him a year earlier and assume payments on a loan he was paying off with that money; I would assume a $1 million loan that Khashoggi and Sam had defaulted on; and I would pay $2 million in cash. I also needed StratAmerica—remember, Sam was majority owner of the company—to loan me $5.5 million, with the stipulation that I would provide demo cars annually for both him and his wife. Nan would get a Chrysler New Yorker and Sam would get a Chevrolet Caprice, along with ten Jazz tickets (four in the front row) each season until I paid off the loan from StratAmerica (which I did in one year). I thought the cars and the tickets were relatively trivial, but I knew Sam's hot buttons, so I used them to sweeten the deal. Well, at our meeting later that afternoon, Sam read the proposal line by line while I sat there, and he worked his way through the financial numbers with little comment—until he came to the deal sweeteners.

"Everything works for me," he said, "except two things. I need two more front-row tickets and ten more tickets elsewhere." After I agreed to this, he resumed. "I don't like Caprices. It's an old man's car. I'd like a Corvette."

"Okay," I said. "Do we have a deal?"

"Yes."

Three days later, on June 16, 1986, we held a press conference to announce the deal. I have been part of dozens of press conferences over the years, but this is the only one in which no one—not even the media or Jazz employees—knew what it was about. They were shocked. Later I learned that Jazz employees were both angry and relieved—they were ticked off that they came so close to losing their jobs or being forced to move to Minnesota, and they were relieved the team was going to remain in Utah. One of the first questions I was asked was whether this transaction meant the Jazz were here to stay. I turned to Sam and asked him, "Do you have any more halves?" He said no, so I turned to the media and said, "The Jazz are here to stay."

A few months later, I was asked to speak to a group of students at Weber State University, specifically about the way I had financed the purchase of the Jazz. After hearing that I was paying $333,000 in debt service each month for the Jazz, one of the students asked me, "Doesn't it make you nervous having to pay that much money each month?"

"No," I said. "I just think of it as $10,000 a day."

From my perspective, my car dealerships were for-profit ventures, but the purchase of the Jazz was a community gift. As I explained to the media that day, it will remain just that as long as we don't lose so much money that it endangers the rest of our businesses and our employees.

Deedee Corradini, who was mayor of Salt Lake City at the time, told me that during Game 6 of the 1997 NBA Finals, when the Jazz were playing the Chicago Bulls in Salt Lake City, the police did not receive a single call regarding a crime. The Jazz have crossed all lines—age, gender, religion, and school loyalties—in a way that is rare for a professional sports team. They have captured everyone's interest, even non–sports fans. There is nothing else like this in our state that has such a broad appeal. It is exactly what I wanted for the state and city I love so much.

I think back often on the conversation I had with President Hinckley about keeping the Jazz in Utah. We felt at the time that someday in the future it would be clearer why it was important for the Jazz to stay here.

That has proven to be true. As just one example, I attend all of the Jazz's home games, and I'm quite visible because I always sit in the same seat down on the floor, but I don't go to the games on Sunday for religious reasons, and everyone has seen that as well. My absence is noticeable. This has opened so many doors to questions about the Church from reporters and fans and players and other observers.

During the Jazz's great playoff run of 1997, when they went all the way to the NBA Finals, ultimately losing to Michael Jordan and the Chicago Bulls in six games, I found myself answering questions in a press conference in Chicago. And one question I was asked was why I did not attend games on Sunday. On worldwide TV, I explained our church's beliefs about keeping the Sabbath day holy.

Later that year I was invited to BYU for a celebration of the Church's 150th anniversary. It was held in the football stadium, and I was invited to sit with some of the leaders of the Church. At some point, one of them said to me, "I saw your press conference in Chicago when they asked you about not attending games on Sunday. I was in London when I saw it. You did great. Do you know how many people were watching you? It was 225 million."

But our impact has gone well beyond religious considerations.

I've had this said to me hundreds of times: "My mom is the Jazz's biggest fan." Many women who are older and widowed start to think of the Jazz players as their kids. They can't come to the arena, but they watch on TV and know the players' names and stats, and it fills a void in their lives. There are thousands of those women out there.

The purchase of the Jazz really helped launch my entrepreneurial career and changed my life in so many ways. People have been very good to me because of the Jazz, but when that happens I always think of something Franco Harris—the former Pittsburgh Steelers running back—said when he returned to Pittsburgh for his jersey retirement ceremony at halftime. As he waited in the tunnel to be introduced, he heard the roar of the crowd while the current Steeler team ran onto the field, and right then Harris had a moment of clarity: "All those years, I thought the cheers were for me, when, in reality, they were for the team."

POSTSCRIPT

How much did Larry love the Jazz? After he was diagnosed with calciphylaxis, a doctor was explaining the options: He could either continue care, which would prolong his life a few months, or discontinue care, leaving him only days. Larry interrupted and asked, "How did the Jazz do last night?"

CHAPTER 15

THE ARENA

I n the fall of 1988, I was sitting in a Board of Governors' meeting in New York when David Stern, the NBA commissioner, delivered the next hurdle in my long struggle to keep the Jazz in Utah. The owners had been briefed on the phone about negotiations for a new collective bargaining agreement (CBA) with the players association. We came to the meeting expecting to hear an updated report on the status of the negotiations. Instead, Stern stood up and presented a CBA that the players had already accepted; all the owners had to do was sign it.

As Stern explained the terms of the agreement—in which costs would skyrocket during the first two to three years—alarms went off in my head. The thought crossed my mind that what I was listening to was the death warrant of the Utah Jazz. Costs would escalate so fast that there was no way to generate revenue streams to cover them. I did some quick calculations in my head as Stern continued to talk, and I determined that if we were going to cover the first year of the proposed increases simply by raising ticket prices, those ticket prices would have to be increased 250 percent in the entire arena, and we'd have to sell out the arena every night. A $50 ticket would increase to $125.

In my three years as sole owner of the Jazz, the franchise had been profitable, but just barely. We made $113,000 the first year and about $100,000 the next year. Collecting pop cans would have been more lucrative, but at least the franchise was profitable for the first time in its history.

Now I was sitting here listening to Stern chart our demise. There was no way we would survive under the terms of the new CBA. I felt sick to my stomach all through the remainder of the meetings that night and the next day. It was a long, worrisome flight back to Salt Lake City.

Three years after I had bought into NBA ownership, the playing field had changed. Our total payroll during the 1985–86 season was $2.3 million; by 1988 it was $5 to $6 million. Under the terms of the new CBA, the salary cap would leap to $9.8 million in 1989, then $11.9 million in 1990, then $12.5 million in 1991, and it would continue to climb. (In 2008, the salary cap was nearly $59 million.)

How would we survive? After a few days of mulling this over I began to believe there was only one remedy: We needed a new arena to produce new revenue streams. The Salt Palace was too small, which meant we couldn't make enough money to cover salary increases through ticket sales. We also had no benefit from any of the revenue streams from the catering, parking, suites, and concessions that could make this work. The county owned the Salt Palace and those revenue streams.

I was faced with the biggest financial decision of my life, and that's saying something. I had already risked everything and leveraged myself to the eyeballs to buy several car dealerships, one half of the Jazz, and then the second half of the Jazz, all in a seven-year period. Now I was faced with the prospect of building an NBA arena. I decided that if I could find a way to do it, I would do it. I was confident I could pull it off, and I didn't think much about not doing it; if I had dwelled on the risks, I might have lost my nerve. I believed we could cover our maintenance, operations, and debt service with a new arena.

It was another lonely time, trying to figure this thing out. I didn't have many confidants, aside from Gail. One day in the middle of all this, Jon Huntsman Sr., the billionaire industrialist and philanthropist, called me. He knew what I was going through. He invited me to lunch, and we chatted about the arena and the need for it, as well as the risks and costs. As I got ready to leave, Jon offered me a final word of advice. "In case I haven't made my position clear, as a friend I would try to dissuade you from building this arena. You have no obligation to the community to risk your livelihood again, a third time." He said this twice, as if to emphasize the point.

"I appreciate your input," I said. "Maybe you're right."

I got up to leave, and just as I reached the door, he said, "Larry, I know you, and I know what you're going to do, so I'll give you the first $100,000. And if you get in trouble, come see me again."

"I won't take the money right now," I replied, "but the moral support is worth more than that to me." And that was the truth. I never did take his money. Jon and I have an interesting relationship. We don't see each other often, but we can call on each other in circumstances that most people wouldn't understand and talk to each other in a way we couldn't talk to others.

I decided I needed to talk to people who could help me with this project, namely government agencies, Mayor Ted Wilson, the Salt Lake City Council, the county commission, the redevelopment agency, and the legislature. I met with the Republicans first. They said they didn't think any money was available to help build an arena but suggested there might be other ways. They were going to get back to me. Then I went to the Democrats. They said, "Whatever you want, we'll give it to you." I explained what I wanted. "Well, we can't give you that," they said. The city, county, and state people all told me the same thing.

One day I received a surprise call from Mike Chitwood, who managed the city's redevelopment agency. He turned out to be one of my heroes. "I have an idea that will get you what you need to get this thing going," he said. "I'm pretty sure we can sell a bond that you would have to repay in 15 years. I can get you $20 million, and the bond costs would be added onto that." He explained how it worked—you had to declare a certain area as "blighted," which could then justify the use of RDA money to build something new there that would increase the value of the property and reap increased property taxes for the city in return.

In my appeal for the bond, I told the city council, "I turned down enormous amounts of money for this deal [by not selling the Jazz]. I am committing $45 million for the arena. Yet the question continues to be asked: What is to stop Larry Miller from selling the Jazz to another city if we give him a $20 million bond? I have to tell you that I do get offended when people keep raising that question—because I've shown my colors. I can move John Stockton and Karl Malone; I can't move an arena. . . . We have before us an opportunity to do something very special that will affect our community and state in a positive way."

The bond was eventually issued, but it wasn't that simple. (Nothing was.) To make it work for us, we needed to change the law governing RDA agencies in Utah, and then we needed to convince various public entities—sewer district, mosquito abatement district, school district, and more—to defer their share of property taxes from our property until we had constructed the arena. Of course, everyone familiar with the machinations of government was skeptical. *You'll never get them to agree to it,* they all said; *it will never happen because each entity will protect its turf.* So I called the various districts and invited them to a meeting. I was told no one would show up, but they did. I explained what I needed from them and why, and I explained that in the end it would increase property tax revenues. They all agreed to do it; they all wanted to help. The amendments to the state statute passed 73–1 in the house and 29–0 in the Senate. The city did benefit as planned—annual property tax revenues increased from less than $100,000 to roughly $750,000 on the arena lot once construction was complete, not to mention the increased valuations of adjacent properties.

Ultimately, the bond gave us three things: ten acres that the city leased back to me; infrastructure on the exterior of the entire block—everything from the sidewalk out, including the curb, gutter, sidewalk, utilities, and so forth; and parking. Mike Chitwood was right—now I had an anchor. I could go to lenders and tell them I had all of these things. Now all I had to do was raise $66 million for construction of the arena (a figure that would grow to $71 million).

When you're talking about this amount of money, you go to a whole new level of lenders. Nobody wants to take on the whole loan. I discovered that it normally costs a fortune just to find lenders. I was receiving calls now from brokers around the country wanting to broker the loan—in other words, they would find the money. They wanted $500,000 up front and then a percent of what the loan turned out to be—a fee of close to $1.5 million. I thought this process must have been difficult if those brokers were able to command such fees. But I applied one of the fundamental tenets I follow in all aspects of my life—the only stupid question is an unasked question. I decided that before I spent that much money just to find a lender, I would make calls myself and ask questions to build a storehouse of knowledge about loans for projects like the arena. I wanted to find out what was involved in getting those loans and why it was so difficult.

I instructed my two CFOs, Clark Whitworth and Bob Hyde, to call various experts in this field to discuss our pro forma statement—what the projected costs would be for the operation, interest, construction, and so forth. We made presentations to 40 prospective lenders and each presentation lasted three to four hours, if not all day. It was exhausting. The three of us became very knowledgeable about the pro forma and how to present it. We learned what information bankers wanted to hear. The bottom line was that we brokered the deal ourselves.

During this process, in February of 1989, we received a call from Ninoos Benjamin, who worked for Toyko-based Sumitomo Bank and Trust out of their Los Angeles office. I don't even know how he found out about what we were doing, but he had attended the University of Utah and he was a bright, demanding, high-strung guy. He said he needed to know the parameters of what we were doing—costs, what we could afford in interest and repayment, collateral, and pro forma. We gave him our presentation.

I went home and wrote in my Day-Timer, "Ninoos Benjamin came here. I believe this is the lender we're going to do this deal with."

And that was exactly what happened, but not for another year.

We were making all these presentations, but no one was calling us back, or if they did, it was only because they wanted more information. Nobody was offering money, and we were very frustrated. I told Bob and Clark that we needed to narrow the field to two to four lenders and really work those. We narrowed it down to one: First Interstate Bank. They sent representatives from Amsterdam, Buenos Aires, and Los Angeles. When they do something like that, you're pretty sure they're going to do a deal. They threw me one curve—they said they would finance the project if we had a local lender that would finance 10 percent of it. They wanted someone locally who believed in the project that much. I called First Security, and they agreed to do it.

The representatives from First Interstate met with us at First Security for six and a half hours to complete the loan agreement. All of First Security's top officers were there. We had a letter of credit from First Security for $10 million, which represented 15 percent, instead of 10 percent. We finished the agreement by 4:00 P.M. The representatives from First Interstate had to go to the airport for an appointment in Houston, so they said they would take the agreement with them that we had just completed. The next day they sent us a fax of their understanding of our deal, and if you had been at the meeting you'd have thought it was totally different. They changed everything—the pricing, the collateral, everything. What they were saying was that they got cold feet. Nothing they changed was favorable for us.

We were now about 18 months into this process with nothing to show for it. It had been a year since we had secured the $20 million bond from the city, and we still didn't have financing for the arena. I was depressed. We had built up to this crescendo and done a lot of good work, and they cut the heart out of it. The problem was that in narrowing our prospective lenders to one, we had been stuck on them for two months, so there was a big enough gap from where had we left off with everyone else that the thought of starting over was more than I could handle. I was emotionally drained.

Three or four days later I received a call from Ninoos Benjamin. It had been a year since I had talked to him. "Do you remember me?" he began. "My boss just asked me why we're not funding your new arena."

I reviewed what we needed, and he said what they were willing to do. We flew to California and met with them that night, and although they moved almost every term of the deal we had discussed on the phone, we agreed to their terms. And just like that, after more than a year and a half of work to secure financing, we had a loan agreement. We came home with a deal in May 1990. I had financed the Delta Center—as it would be called when the airline bought the naming rights—for $86 million, including the $20 million bond.

Now for the difficult part: construction.

Time was not on our side.

Every year we remained in the Salt Palace I would lose lots of money because of escalating salaries—$2 million in losses the first year, $4 million the second year, $6 million the third year, and so forth. There was no way around it. I could handle the losses the first couple of years, even though I didn't like it, but I was not in a position to lose $6 or $8 million. I had to get the arena done before the start of the 1991–92 season or I would take those kinds of losses.

It was now May 1990. We had 16 months to get this thing done—which, I learned, is nearly impossible for the contruction of a 20,000-seat arena. I had assumed that once we gave the go-ahead to FFKR Architects—the firm we employed for the job—to begin designing the arena, the plans would be finished in six to eight weeks and we could start building. But it quickly became clear to me that such expectations were unrealistic, so I asked Jeff Fischer, my FFKR liaison, "If I locked you and the other architects in a room and said, 'Don't come out until the plans are done,' when would I see you?" And he said 14 to 15 months!

"We've got to build while we're designing, then," I said.

This is known as fast-tracking—in other words, the owner's conception of the building, the architect's design, the engineer's design and calculations, and the construction of the building all occur at the same time. You build while you plan, with the planning and design staying just one step ahead of construction. For instance, while you pour the first-level floor in one corner of the building, the other corner is being excavated. An hour before the concrete is poured, changes are being made.

Much of the work was done off-site to speed things up. By precasting the bleachers—which, if placed end to end, would have covered eight miles—at an off-site location, we shaved one year off construction time.

The crews worked around the clock during much of the project, using portable lights. They would build forms at night so they could pour concrete during the day. It got so cold that winter that we were unable to pour concrete and had to shut down for two weeks, but other than that it was full speed ahead. We poured 90,000 cubic yards of concrete—enough to make a sidewalk from Salt Lake City to Las Vegas.

Even the trusses we used for the roof enabled us to save construction time. Each of the 12 trusses was 342 feet long, weighed 120 tons, and spanned the entire length of the building. They were dubbed "super wings." It's Japanese technology. It was the first time they had been used in America. They were built off-site, assembled with bolts and cables, and lifted up with super cranes. The advantage is that you can continue construction on the rest of the building while the rafters are being put up; usually you would stop the rest of the project. We expected it would take 12 weeks to do the roof system; we did it in 29 days.

The Delta Center was completed on October 4, 1991. We built the arena in 15 months and 24 days—by far the fastest construction of a major arena in the United States—and that included the two-week shutdown for cold weather. It took longer to finance the building than to build it.

I was now fully committed to the Jazz. I had risked everything I had and more to keep the team in town. When you add it all up, I spent about $95 million on the Jazz, counting the purchase of the team and the construction of the arena. As of 2009, I owe about $20 million, which will be paid off with four more annual payments. Each year I am approached by prospective buyers, some offering as much as $400 million for both the franchise and the arena. I have never seriously considered selling the team.

I marvel at the chain of events that changed my life so

dramatically. I was a career car parts manager and general manager. I was steeped in the car business and thought that was where I would spend the rest of my professional life. Yet within six years almost to the day after I bought my first car dealership, I owned half of an NBA franchise, and a year later I owned all of it. Even when I wasn't certain how I was going to accomplish something—such as pay off all that debt—I had developed enough confidence in my abilities to know that I would find a way.

When David Stern came to town for the arena topping-off party, he asked me, "How long are you going to keep playing for table stakes? You put more than your net worth on the line when you bought the first half, then you put way more than your net worth on the line for the second half, and now you're building an arena by yourself and putting it all on the line again."

I've never had to do it again.

POSTSCRIPT

"You've got the Mormon Tabernacle Choir, you've got the lake, and you've got the Utah Jazz," says Frank Layden. "That's what people know. I travel all around the world, and everywhere I go that's what people talk about when they learn you're from Utah. The Utah Jazz. John Stockton. Karl Malone. The Jazz have been critical to this city. If you don't have that arena and the Jazz, we don't get the Olympics. And we don't get the NBA All-Star Game and the NBA Finals.

"I'll tell you this: Larry's name should be on that arena somewhere. On the floor or on the building, whatever. When he got into something, he took it seriously. You'd see him down on the ground with a hard hat on when they were building that thing. When he built the Delta Center it was the best arena in basketball. It's first class."

CHAPTER 16

LIFE AS AN NBA OWNER

W hen John Stockton sank his famous last-second shot in Houston to beat the Rockets in 1997, sending the Jazz to the NBA Finals for the first time, I was in a parking lot. I missed the greatest play in the history of the franchise because I was too busy to go to Houston to see it live and too nervous to watch it on TV.

Actually, I did watch most of the game on TV, until the Jazz fell so far behind that I couldn't take it anymore. With a few minutes left, Zane, Gail, and I went for a drive and listened to the rest of the game on the radio. We didn't get far. The Jazz rallied, and the game became so close and intense that I parked at the Cowboy Grub restaurant and listened to the end of the game sitting there in the car. When Stockton hit that shot, we shouted like little kids. I mean, we hollered and screamed. I was surprised by my emotions. I guess it was all those years of suppressing my feelings and working hard to keep the Jazz here and create a championship-caliber team. Zane must have thought I was crazy. Suddenly, everything was released with that single shot. In that moment I realized that if there had ever been any question about whether it had all been worth it, this was the answer.

I bought the Jazz to keep them in the community, but later of course I became swept up with the team like everyone else. If you can't enjoy it, you shouldn't be doing it; there are easier and better ways to make money.

I changed the culture of the team from one in which the owner maintained a distant, traditional business relationship to one that was considerably more hands-on and personal, which of course is the way I operate in all of my business endeavors.

In the early days of my involvement with the Jazz, I went to the Salt Palace on game days, put on sweats and a T-shirt, and participated in the shootaround with the players, shooting baskets or shagging balls and chatting it up with the guys. I wanted to be a part of it, and that's where the relationships with the players began. It enabled me to understand the way they thought and the way everything worked. It enabled me to see things from their perspective. I got my own locker in the locker room, with my name on it. Once we had a retro night and I came out in a Jazz uniform with a headband on. That caused quite a sensation, especially since the retro look consisted of short shorts. Often, as part of my game routine, I would sit by my locker during Jerry's pregame talk with the team, then again at halftime and after the game. Before the game I'd go on the floor and shake hands with the players. Every now and then I would scold the team for a poor effort. I can't tolerate anything less than a full effort. That's what I built my career on.

Unlike most owners, instead of sitting in a suite during the game, I sit in a floor seat to be more involved in the game—Section 17, Row A, Seat 20—directly across from the visiting team's bench. A suite would be too removed for me. I don't go there to wine and dine clients during the game. I like to take guests to dinner in the upper level of the arena before games, but once the game begins I'm pretty focused on what's happening on the court, and I'm not very sociable, or so I've been told.

I developed a personal relationship with many of the players. I took Mark Eaton and Karl Malone fishing at my cabin in Idaho, and I took John and Karl for rides in my Cobras. After the Stockton-Malone-Hornacek era ended, I decided maybe I shouldn't become so involved with the next generation of players, and yet I find myself getting drawn in with these guys now and developing relationships with them, although not to the same degree yet. I've just concluded that's who I am. Relationships get built. It has worked for this franchise. We wouldn't have had Karl and John as long as we did without the relationships I had with them. Kent Benson—a former Jazz center—once told someone, "Can you believe the owner of the team picked us up at the airport personally?" That's just how I do things. It seems natural to me.

I get to know players from other organizations, as well. In the late 1980s, I tried to woo Julius Irving from the 76ers. We arranged to meet near Morgan, Utah (Julius had been vacationing in Jackson Hole), and we drove back to my home together. He came over to our house to share a barbecue with our family, Dave Checketts, and Frank Layden. Afterward, we chatted in the family room about the possibility of having him spend a year or two in a Jazz uniform. Eventually, he wound up in the driveway playing basketball with Greg and the other boys. Greg says that even now he thinks of that day when he drives by that house. Julius was a tremendous gentleman and remarkably personable and down to earth for a man who was so famous and successful. It made an impression on our family, especially on Greg. Years later, Greg reintroduced himself to Julius at the NBA All-Star Game, and as soon as he made the connection, Julius treated him as a friend.

I'm on friendly, sociable terms with players from other teams. I was sitting courtside in my wheelchair this season (2008–2009) when Shaquille O'Neal and Steve Nash stopped to talk to me. It was a nice gesture.

We have been fortunate that the vast majority of our players have been good guys. This wasn't an accident. As an organization, we have made a point out of trying to sign players of good character because this pays off in many ways. We are mostly successful on this front. We've had very few players get into trouble. I've received many compliments from owners over the years about the type of players we have, especially during the era of John Stockton, Karl Malone, and Jeff Hornacek. Some of the owners envy us for that and lament that they have some knuckleheads on their rosters. I insist that we bring in players of high character, and with a few exceptions we pull it off. We aren't going to bring an idiot in here just because he can play ball.

We also aren't going to let the inmates run the asylum. One of the best things we have done was hire Jerry Sloan as coach. At the time, he said, "I am only going to ask you for one thing—if I get fired, let me get fired for my own decisions." I've always honored that. Too often management makes decisions that affect the team and the coach, and the coach takes the fall for it.

From the start, we gave Jerry complete charge of the team. In this era of multimillion-dollar player salaries, the players are often given more power than the coach in this league. Owners and management bow to the demands of their star players because they have invested so much money in them. We let Jerry run the team the way he sees fit. He runs a tight ship, even in the way he insists that his players dress. The Jazz way is old school. It is about little things. It is wearing your socks the same length (four inches above the ankle), it is wearing shoes the same color as your teammates' shoes, it is tucking in your shirt and keeping it there, it is having your shoes tied at all times, it is sitting in a certain order during time-outs. Karl Malone once announced that he was going to wear black shoes in our next game. Jerry told him, "You're not going to be on my team if you wear black shoes." He would've been the only player in black shoes, and Jerry wants them to look like a team. Karl wore white shoes.

Jerry tolerates little nonsense, although once in a while he lets things slide. Once, in the locker room at halftime, Jerry was talking to the team and said something that Greg Ostertag didn't like. Ostertag threw a bag of ice at Jerry's head. Jerry simply moved his head to one side to dodge the ice and then kept talking as if nothing had happened.

The other thing we do is to strive for stability on the court and in the front office. As any sports fan knows, most sports franchises are quick to fire coaches and administrators and equally quick to trade players. We try to pick good people and then let them do their jobs, and we stick with them and maintain our faith in them even through trying times. Sloan has coached for a single team longer than anyone in NBA history (the 2008–09 season was his 21st season), and he is the fourth-winningest coach ever. His assistant, Phil Johnson, has been with the Jazz for 24 years. We've had only three trainers in 36 years. Stockton and Malone were here almost 40 years combined, which is almost unheard of in this day. Our head scout, Dave Fredman, has been with the Jazz for 28 years. Our director of basketball operations, Richard Smith, has been with the team since 1984. The voice of the Jazz, Hot Rod Hundley, was here 35 years before retiring. Our vice president of game operations, Grant Harrison, has been with the Jazz since they came to Utah in 1979. Team president Randy Rigby and CFO Bob Hyde have both been here 25 years. We've pretty much had only two men serve as general manager in all those years—Scott Layden and Kevin O'Connor. When Frank Layden decided he had had enough of coaching, we made him team president and essentially turned him into our ambassador. He traveled, watched games, did interviews, made commercials, and filled speaking engagements—and got paid to do it.

We were grateful to Frank and appreciated all he had done for the team and repaid him with a very generous retirement package.

Our stability has certainly been a big part in our success. Think about it: The Jazz have been a model of consistency and stability for a quarter of a century. They own NBA records for the most consecutive seasons of finishing with a .500 record or better, with 21. That's more than the great Auerbach Celtics (19), more than Magic Johnson's Lakers (16), more than the Celtics of the Larry Bird era (14). The Jazz also own the NBA record for most consecutive winning seasons, with 19. They rank third in NBA history in most consecutive playoff appearances, with 20, trailing only Wilt Chamberlain's 76ers (22) and the Portland Trail Blazers (21).

Think about it: In 26 years, Jazz fans have seen one losing season. Along the way their team ascended to the NBA Finals twice and the conference finals six times while winning eight division titles.

We have been a harmonious operation, one in which all the members are supportive of one another, from top to bottom. Of course, when you're dealing with some of the egos we deal with, sometimes your patience is tried. During Karl Malone's last contract negotiations, after we had pretty well established what his salary would be, his agent concluded things by dropping another request in our laps. "Oh, by the way," he began, "Karl doesn't like to be on the same floor as the rest of the team in a hotel, and he wants a room away from the elevator and in a corner. Also, when he arrives at the hotel, Karl has nutrition needs. He needs a fruit basket in his room when we're on the road."

He wasn't finished. A short time later, he told Jazz president Denny Haslam, "Could we have the chef at the arena fix wings for Karl after each game?"

It was a little irritating. We had just agreed to pay Karl $14 million for his final season with the team, so what's a bucket of wings?

I guess the clincher came about six months later when the agent called Denny again and said, "I need to talk to you about something that's pretty important to Karl. Lately, the fruit baskets have been getting smaller." Denny swallowed real hard and said, "What do you want—more apples or bananas?" The answer, "More of everything."

My passion and temper—and my involvement with the team—occasionally got me into trouble. During the 1994 season, I lost my temper a couple of times. The first time was when Elden Campbell, the big Laker forward, threw an elbow or fist at John Stockton, and I came out of my courtside seat and yelled at Campbell. I told him to pick on someone his own size, which led to a brief war of words. The league office called and wanted to hear my side of things, but nothing much happened beyond that. Anyway, the worst was yet to come.

About a month later I made national headlines during an embarrassing incident that occurred at halftime of a 1994 playoff game between the Jazz and the Denver Nuggets in Salt Lake City. It was an eventful night for me, to say the least. During the first half, I became increasingly irritated because I felt a couple of our players weren't playing hard, which is the one thing I can't tolerate. One of the players was Malone. I was tempted to shout my feelings across the court, but I decided I didn't want to say anything stupid, so I restrained myself. Just before halftime, I got up, intending to leave the court, but as I neared the bench on my way to the tunnel I could no longer resist speaking my mind. "We got some guys who didn't show up tonight!" I shouted to Jerry. He didn't hear me, so I repeated it. "They should be on the bench!" I added.

I headed for the halftime locker room once the players were in there, but John Stockton stopped me and told me to go cool off. I took his advice and went to get something for my headache in the training room. I returned to the locker room and listened to Jerry's speech, and then as I returned to the arena I noticed several Denver fans in an area near my children's seats. I guess they had left their seats, which were behind the basket, and wandered to the courtside seats to watch the Nuggets warm up for the second half. I asked them to move. One of them said something like, "Is this your seat?" And I said, "They're all my seats!" Anyway, things got ugly. We yelled some bad things at each other. There was some pushing and chest bumping and name-calling. I lost it. Greg and one of our security people restrained me. It was silly and stupid for me to get caught up in all that. It became a national story—the owner of an NBA team gets in a fight with a fan.

I was chagrined by the episode. The league and I agreed that I would not attend the next two games, and I elected not to attend the third game, which was Game 7 at home. Three days later, I ended my silence on the incident and apologized at a press conference. It was broadcast on live TV in Denver and Salt Lake in the middle of the afternoon! Nothing else resulted from the confrontation, but it was an incident I would just as soon forget.

NBA owners are all successful, competitive men, and, as I learned, sometimes our meetings could get heated. Mark Cuban made billions at a young age in cable and computer businesses, which allowed him to buy the Dallas Mavericks. He quickly developed a much-deserved reputation for being outspoken and brash.

Soon after buying the Mavericks, Cuban showed up for a meeting of the NBA's Board of Governors. During the meeting, he got on his soapbox about something and started talking and went on and on like this for some time. I guess you would say he was full of himself. Bill Davidson, the 80-year-old owner of the Detroit Pistons, listened to this rant patiently, and finally, when Cuban stopped, he said, "As far as I'm concerned, you're a snot-nosed little punk who got lucky." There was some colorful language in there somewhere, but anyway, he put him in his place. Cuban shut up for the rest of the day.

The 1999 negotiations for the collective bargaining agreement became so contentious that they resulted in the loss of 32 regular-season games. The negotiations polarized the public, but the players really did themselves a disservice with nonsensical comments like the one Patrick Ewing made: "We [players] make a lot of money, but we spend a lot, too." Kenny Anderson tried to garner sympathy by announcing that he might have to sell one of his eight luxury cars because things were getting tight. That didn't work. Even though he was retiring, Michael Jordan wound up leading the players' cause. I was on the league's negotiating committee, and during one of our CBA meetings I challenged something Jordan said, and we got into a debate about it that continued in one-on-one meetings. Michael said they didn't need the owners, that they could play anywhere. I told him, "You've got that wrong. The owners have the arenas that bring in the fans and provide a place for the players to play. How much money are you going to make if you play on the playground?" I have reflected on that discussion a few times. I don't think players appreciate the capital outlay and the risks that owners undertake; owners don't get in this business to make money. There are a lot better ways to do that. You can make money with an NBA team as an appreciating asset, but in terms of annual profit, it basically just pays for itself. Greg pointed this out: If the Jazz were a Toyota car dealership, they would have been only our fourth-largest Toyota store in terms of annual revenue in 2008.

But of course the profit margin was never the reason I bought the Jazz. Sometimes, when I am sitting at a game, I'll find myself looking around the arena and watching the fans have a good time. They're smiling and cheering and talking with their neighbors or their kids or spouses. That's very rewarding. That's another thing that tells me this has all been worth it.

POSTSCRIPT

A photo appeared in the newspaper the day after the Nuggets game that showed Greg restraining his raging father. Greg recalls the incident: "Normally, I got Coke and popcorn and hung out in a back room during halftime, but for some reason that night I came out early.

I had a Coke in each hand, and I was talking to Tom LaPoint and his wife next to the court, and I could see Tom was looking at something over my shoulder. Tom said, 'Uh-oh, that's not good.' I turned and saw Dad getting into a verbal altercation with a Denver fan. I handed the Cokes to Tom and ran over there. By the time I got there, Dad was fully engaged with the fan. It was getting physical. I got Dad in a headlock. 'There are cameras everywhere,' I told him. 'You don't want to do this.' That's what got him to relax. Later, one of the TV guys told me, 'We got all that on audio. That was wise counsel you gave your dad.'"

As was typical with Larry after he had had a confrontation with someone, he went to great lengths to reach out and smooth things over. He could not abide bad feelings to linger. Rich Babich, one of the Denver fans who was in the middle of the confrontation, recalls, "Right after the game, when we were doing paperwork for the police, Larry came up and apologized to me. He did not go public about that. He wanted me to know he felt bad about it. He gave me his business card with his private number on it and told me I could be his guest at a game anytime. He was a gentleman throughout the whole process. There was quite a media frenzy for several days. Neither of us knew it at the time, but a TV station hooked us up for live interviews at the same time, and Larry apologized to me again on the air. Other than those ten minutes, he was always a gentleman."

When Larry and Gail attended a Jazz game in Denver a year later, Babich left his seat and walked over to sit by them before the opening tipoff. "It was very cordial," recalls Gail. "He said, 'Do you remember me?' and they talked." Babich recalls, "When I walked over there I could see the security people were getting nervous. Anyway, Larry again invited Al Leiberman (another of the Denver fans in the confrontation) and me to be his guests at a Jazz home game. Later that year we took him up on it. We sat with him in his courtside seats and visited with him at halftime in one of the club rooms."

A few days after Miller had exploded at both the Jazz bench and the Denver fans, he told newspapers it was a strangely emotional night for him, and that he didn't know why he let the situation get to him the way he did. There was media speculation that Miller's controversial selling of his minor league hockey team and the shouting match with Elden Campbell—which had both occurred a month earlier—had gotten to him. "If you look at the time proximity, there's certainly an argument for it," he told newspapers. "I am not aware of any outside forces at work, but it sure came on me strong."

The truth is, there were outside forces at work. Gail says there were some personal family issues that were deeply bothering Larry that night that they wish to keep private. Those family pressures (which were eventually resolved), combined with the Jazz's poor play, seemed to cause Larry to snap that night, first at his team and then at the Denver fans. The Jazz lost that night, but they ultimately won the series.

"He was just an overexcited fan who was irritated by how his team was playing," says Babich. "If he had not been the owner, it would have been a non-incident and no one ever would have known about it."

Miller was contrite during his press conference. He said, "I'm not planning on being as involved with the basketball team as I've been. . . . If I get to a point . . . and I don't have the good judgment to stay out of there and [not] cause this kind of problem for all of us, then I need to figure out a better way to do it. Whether that means not watching games, I don't know."

But Gail notes, "After the incident with the fan, Larry said he needed to pull back and not get so emotionally involved—for everyone's sake. It didn't really last too long, though, before he was right back out there with the team before the games."

As evidenced by the incident, Larry was very intense about the Jazz, as he was about everything in which he was involved. "If the Jazz lost," says Gail, "you couldn't talk to him at home. He had to learn that he couldn't let things like that affect his whole life. I had to learn *that it wasn't me he was mad at. It really affected our relationship for a long time. It was hard for him when the team played poorly because he felt that the fans weren't getting their money's worth, and he felt responsible to make that happen. There were many times we'd be at a Jazz game and he would say, 'I am so embarrassed that people paid money to see this product tonight.' I'd say, 'But look at them; they're having a great time.' He could not handle it if players were not giving their best effort all the time. He told the players, 'I'll never ask you to win, but I will ask you to put your best effort on the floor every night.'"*

Gail continues, *"I was always worried that Larry would say too much and get fined [by the NBA], but I came to accept that his passion was what it was, and for what he put up to make the Jazz happen and stay in Utah, I was not going to try to restrain him. He generally seemed to keep things in check. His bark was much worse than his bite. The fans either loved the way he showed his emotions or thought he should set a better example. Larry didn't worry about that—he just did what came naturally, and it was usually okay. He had a good relationship with just about all the players in the league. He would go out of his way to be friendly to them and treat them with respect on and off the court."*

Like he did with everything else, Larry took the time to learn the business when he became an NBA owner. He studied the subject the same way he studied auto parts behind the counter in his youth. He visited with the players to learn the game and picked the brains of veteran front-office personnel and coaches, as well. "Pro sports is unique," says Frank Layden. "There's nothing like it. In how many businesses do the employees make more than the bosses? Larry was very good about listening. He didn't jump on it like a fan or someone who knew everything. He listened and developed a philosophy. In the early days we would sit down and put our feet up and chat—Larry, Checketts, and I—and talk about the league. He was learning. After a game he would ask, 'Why do you do this, and why do you do that?'

We'd come back from a road trip and he'd want to know what was going on. He was interested in the draft. The one thing about Larry is, he didn't want to sound like a fool. He was going to be questioned about the Jazz, and he wanted solid information. We were all united in purpose. If we drafted a guy, we'd stick together on it. Nobody was going to take a fall for a bad pick. We're still trying to decide who got John Stockton.

"Larry's relaxation was the game and being a part of that and going into the locker room. It was like he was a player or a coach. I remember at the All-Star Game in Salt Lake in 1993 he asked, 'Can I sit on the bench and help coach?' I told him, 'Yeah, sure. Listen, you paid a big price; you can do what you want. If this isn't fun, get out.'"

Layden continues: "This sums up Larry Miller. If you wanted to do something—whether it was buy equipment or stay in camp longer or whatever—he didn't necessarily want to spend money, but he would always ask: 'Will it help us win?' If we said yes, he'd say, 'Then go ahead.' Never once did I hear him say, 'No, you can't do that.' I used to take the team to New York two days ahead of the game to give us a chance to recover from jet lag. I told him why and he said, 'Okay.' You can't have a better owner than that."

CHAPTER 17

STOCKTON

One of the questions I am frequently asked is, "What is John Stockton really like?" I tell people this: He's exactly the kind of person you hope he is.

During my years as an NBA owner, I have had the chance to meet many great athletes and coaches and other people involved with the game. And Stockton was one of a kind, the type of guy who made it a pleasure to be involved with the game.

He saw me as a father figure and told me that. We still visit on the phone, and he's been retired from basketball for six years. He is a straight arrow and came from a good family. In his house, the kids respected the parents. John teaches his kids the same way. And he treated me that way. Shortly after I was released from the hospital after my heart attack, he showed up at the house with his five kids all dressed up. He said they were in town and they were worried about me. They sat in my living room, and we talked for two hours.

After I got sick, he came to the house and to the hospital a few times to see me. He was very thoughtful and considerate.

John was a bit of an enigma to those who didn't know him. They failed to understand that he was not motivated the same way as most players—or most other people, for that matter. He didn't hunger for attention or awards or recognition; all he wanted was victory for the team. Everything else was extraneous. When he set records for assists and steals, he did not want us to stop the game for a ceremony in his honor, but we convinced him that it was necessary.

He would not even look at a stat sheet. I've seen other excellent players who wanted to see the stat sheet at halftime and after the game. John didn't care about that; all he cared about was the success of the team. He would ice his feet for 20 minutes after games, and I'd talk to him while he did that, and I noticed that even then he wouldn't peek at the stats. He had no personal agenda or ego invested in such things. He couldn't have fun; he was just waiting for the games.

John drew his teammates in. If they couldn't score or wouldn't score, he would do it. He would do whatever it took to win games: If it meant passing the ball, he did that, or if it meant scoring, he did that.

For some reason we became friends. It's probably his single-mindedness—he's like me in that way. I've never seen anyone else like that. I remember standing at center court to present him the game ball the night he got his 10,000th career assist. I said, "Now we have to think about 15,000." He said, "Never happen." He didn't think he would play that long. But he got a good chiropractor and kept playing at a high level. And in the blink of an eye we were out there again for number 15,000.

John understood the game. From my seat on the floor, I'd be at such an angle that I could see him throw the ball on a bounce pass to someone at the other end of the court; it was like a rifle shot and just as accurate. He changed the plays ten times a night. He'd move defenders where he wanted them and then take advantage of it. He was a clutch player, as we all know. I busted his chops once about missing technical free throws in a regular-season game. He said, "When you need me, I'll be there." And he was. Of course, it was John's three-point shot in Houston that sent us to the NBA Finals for the first time. It has become an iconic play for our franchise.

One of the extraordinary things about John was how well he could keep Karl in line. They chided each other. They knew where the hot buttons were. They were strong supporters on the court, but didn't socialize off the court.

John was a strong personality and was respected by everyone. He was the calm, steadying presence on and off the court. As I mentioned earlier, during the first half of a 1994 playoff game in our arena, I became very upset about the effort of our team. At one point I shouted at Sloan to bench Karl. At halftime I entered the locker room with steam coming out of my ears ready to unload on the team, but I was intercepted at the doorway by Stockton, who told me, "If you're too mad to be here, don't." I turned around and headed for the training room instead and cooled down. His words of wisdom allowed me to get a grip on things, at least momentarily.

A lot of people didn't understand John or were put off by his aloofness. He prized privacy and family time. He wanted to create a sense of normalcy for himself and his family and didn't want his career to intrude on that. He managed to do it, but at a price. No one got to see the real John, who's a very bright, witty, and warm man in private. He could be brusque with fans and autograph seekers who were trying to reach out to him. He had a contract with a card company stipulating that he would sign a certain number of basketball cards, and that was all he would sign. But for me, he would make some exceptions. I'd ask for an autograph for a sick kid, and he'd say, "You know where I am on this," but usually he'd sign anyway. I didn't push him hard, but one time we were hosting the Russians and I heard that the head of the Russian delegation had a board on which he had mounted all 12 of the Dream Team players' cards. All of them were autographed except John's. I told John about this. He said, "You know my deal on cards." I told him, "This is going to be on a wall in Russia, and it will have everyone's autograph except yours." He said, "If you make me sign it, I will." I told him, "I'm not going to make you." He said, "Come to me when I'm retired."

Some of this seems a little cold, but let me tell you a story that might explain John's attitude toward autograph seekers. The team was in Chicago for a game early in John's career, and as the players walked from the plane to the bus, a lady was waiting there with a yellow legal pad asking John for an autograph. He signed one. Then she flipped the page and said, "Sign this, too." He wouldn't do it. The players have a saying: "One autograph is for you, two is to sell." What happens is that some people collect numerous signatures from the same player so they can sell them. This is a lot different from a mere fan or some kid asking for an autograph for himself. It's a business enterprise, and you can imagine what would happen if a player signed a dozen autographs for every professional collector. Anyway, John and the other players got on the bus and were driven to the hotel. When they walked into the hotel lobby, the lady from the airport was there, and she began screaming at John. She called him all kinds of names. Everyone stopped to listen. She was screaming, "You should sign every page of my book!" The players were embarrassed. That experience, along with many others—such as people asking for autographs at funerals—was so hard for John that he said to heck with autographs.

Let me tell you one final story that illustrates John Stockton. There was a teenage girl in Farr West who had cancer who was brought to my attention. She was a big John Stockton fan, so I called John and asked him if he would go visit her. One of the first things he asked was if the media was going to be there. When I told him no, he said he would go and asked if I would go with him.

I asked John to let me go into the house first, so I knocked on the door and the girl's mother answered and I entered the house. The mother told the girl, "You have someone here to see you." I walked in and met the girl. She had a John Stockton poster on the wall. I told her, "I've brought somebody here to see you." Then John came in. Her face lit up like a Christmas tree. I watched John with her. He was so kind and considerate and very gentle. That's how John is. More important, he did things for the right reasons. He wasn't doing it for attention—in fact, he wouldn't have done it if the media were there. He was doing it for the girl. He didn't want anyone to know.

POSTSCRIPT

During the last few years, everyone who knew Larry noticed his decline. "Larry doesn't look too good," acquaintances were saying. When Stockton, who had returned to his native Washington after retiring, learned of this from Greg Miller, he plotted with Greg to "kidnap" his former boss and force him to seek treatment and rest.

Stockton called Larry and told him he was in town and that it was urgent that he meet with him that day. Larry politely declined, explaining that he had a family meeting to attend that day at the arena. Stockton persisted, saying that it would take only a few minutes and that he would meet him in his car in the parking lot behind the arena. As agreed upon, Larry climbed into Stockton's car—and then Stockton took off. By the time they reached I-15, Larry was angry. Stockton, a devotee of chiropractic and naturopathic medicine, didn't stop until he reached Pocatello, Idaho, and the office of Dr. Henry West, one of Stockton's chiropractors. John stayed with Larry and the doctor through the evening before heading home, leaving Larry behind for further treatment. Larry was stuck—he had no transportation, not to mention no change of clothes and no toiletries. His family arrived the next day to show their support and concern while Dr. West conducted tests and gave him various treatments. They headed home together that evening. Larry continued to visit Dr. West regularly for treatments, commuting from Salt Lake City, for about six months. Following West's directions, Miller took packs of pills for his heart and kidneys. Later, when Miller grew too sick to travel, he discontinued the visits to Pocatello. But this revealed a great deal about how Stockton regarded Miller and to what lengths he would go to help him.

One of Larry's favorite Stockton stories was the visit to the Farr West teenager. He liked to tell the story because he thought it said something about Stockton, but, when asked about this, Stockton recalled the story largely because of what it revealed about Larry. As Stockton tells it now, "He called me and said, 'I need you to do something for me.' He asked me to do things from time to time, and if I didn't feel comfortable or didn't want to do it, he wouldn't pursue it. He could have put his foot down, but he was good about it. If he thought I was wrong, we might discuss it. But he let me decide. Anyway, he asked me to visit someone who was sick. I said, 'I'll go if you go with me.' Now, Larry was a busy guy. I realize it more now than I did during my playing days. He had all those businesses and the Jazz and thousands of people asking him for things. I figured there was no way he could go, and I was going to go anyway. But he agreed to go with me. He picked me up and we had a great talk driving up there and back. The girl's mother was there when we arrived. I remember it was a humble abode. They didn't have a lot. They welcomed us into their house, and we visited with them and signed a few things. But one of the things I remember about the visit is that Larry would do something like that. How does a guy that busy get a phone call asking for something like that, and how does he pick it out as real and unique and take the step to do it? He must've gotten thousands of calls like that, but he made time and told someone he would do it and he did it."

CHAPTER 18

MALONE

In the summer of 2007, Karl Malone called and asked to meet with me. We had stayed in touch, even though he had moved back to Louisiana since retiring from basketball in 2004. He said he was in town and there was something he wanted to talk to me about.

As anyone knows who has followed our team, Karl and I had our ups and downs during his long career with the Jazz. One week he was my adopted son; the next week he was complaining in the media about how the Jazz and I had mistreated him. Over the years, I tore up many of his contracts and gave him new ones to make him feel appreciated. I even set him up with his own car dealership. But nearly every season he lashed out at me in the media with some complaint or imagined slight. Sometimes I had no idea where he was coming from, which was hurtful because we were close. Like John, he considered me a father figure. He was a visitor to my home—he lived just minutes away. We drove to my cabin in Idaho and fished together. I took him for rides in my Cobra. We enjoyed each other's company and had a lot of good talks about life in general.

As arranged on the phone, Karl drove to Jordan Commons to meet me. He said he was going to come up to my office, but I told him I would meet him in the parking lot. I climbed into his car and, after we exchanged greetings, he did something that was very meaningful and moving to me: He apologized. For everything—for the many public diatribes against me over the years, for the way he had lashed out at me. It wasn't just the words he said; it was an aura about him, a maturity and self-confidence. He explained that during his career he always felt that he played best when he was angry at someone or something, and so he turned that anger on me. He said I hadn't deserved that. It meant a lot to me. I was very moved by his gesture, which I could tell was very sincere.

POSTSCRIPT

I called Karl Malone one morning in Louisiana just as he was launching his boat. "The bluegill are out," he said. "I've got to get out there. Can we talk later when I can really sit down and spend some time talking about this? I want to give you all the time you need." Malone continued: "I'm glad you called because I want to be part of this book. It's funny. Larry once asked me if I was going to write a book. I said, 'No, are you?' He said he had thought about it a couple of times, and I said, 'Maybe if you write one, I'll have a page in there.' Then Gail called and said you were writing his book. I'd be honored to be in it."

So I called again the next morning, and Karl couldn't have been more gracious or eager to talk about Miller and their relationship. He recalled that visit with Miller in 2007, a year before his former Jazz boss had his heart attack.

It had been weighing on Malone's mind for years—he didn't feel good about the way he had treated Miller. "I wanted to talk to Larry and tell him how I felt, and I wanted to do it before too much time passed," Malone said. "In life, we always wait until it's too late to apologize or tell someone how we feel. It was on my mind for a year or two, and one day I thought, What if something happened to Larry and I showed up at his bedside and told him all these mushy feelings? He'd appreciate it, but he's going to think I'm just saying it to cheer him up. What if something happened to Larry, and I hadn't said what I needed to say?

"So I didn't wait. We sat in my car in the parking lot, and I said, 'There are a lot of things I said and did that I regret. I should have said those things in private. I apologize for what I said and how I handled it. I handled it more like a kid, not like a man.' Larry looked at me and said, 'Big Guy'—that's what he called me—'you don't need to say that.'

"I said, 'Yes, I do. I have to swallow that pride and say I'm sorry. I should have handled it a different way.'

"I said what I needed to say. Do you know how much I replayed that day in my mind when he got sick? I was so glad I had said those things when I did. I'm not too proud to tell everyone who reads this book that I should have handled it a different way. I'm 46 now, and I guess as we get older we mature."

The following summer, when Larry had his heart attack and was hospitalized for weeks, Malone flew to Utah again and spent four days in the hospital with him. During the first three days of that visit, Malone tried to convince Larry to move from University Hospital to the Huntsman Cancer Institute. He had been impressed with the way Huntsman had cared for his mother-in-law when she was ill with cancer; also, his brother-in-law was a chef there. Miller finally relented on the third day. Malone immediately jumped out of his seat, saying, "Okay, I'm going to make the arrangements." After Karl was gone, Gail asked Larry, "Are you doing this for you, or for Karl?" Larry said, "For Karl." Karl made the arrangements by calling Jon Huntsman himself, and Larry was moved to the Huntsman hospital.

During those four days, Malone sat by Miller's bedside from morning till night. "I punched in like I was going to work," says Malone. "I'd get there at 7 or 8 and leave at about 8 or when he got too tired, and I'd spend the night in a hotel and show up the next day." Malone became another nurse for Miller. He fetched cold towels and glasses of water; he massaged Larry's arm and wiped his mouth and helped him in and out of his wheelchair and bed.

"It was an awesome experience," says Malone. "Larry has done so much for so many people, and the times we had together were often interrupted. I had an opportunity to do things for him, and we spent a lot of time talking without interruption. You know that conversation every young man wants to have with his dad in which he tells him how he feels? I had that with him. He was like a father to me. We told each other how we felt. It was funny. We were both trying to say the same things and beating each other to the punch in saying them. It was gratitude and tears for both of us. Of all the neat things I have done in my life, that has to be the best—those four days. I would come there some days, and he'd ask, 'Do you feel like talking about business?' And we'd talk about it, and two hours later he'd fall asleep. He'd wake up and say, 'How long have I been asleep?' When I told him two hours, he said, 'What did you do for two hours?'

"'I went to the bathroom, got something to eat, read the newspaper.'

"'What else?'

"'I sat right here in this chair, watching you sleep. It's very entertaining watching you sleep.'"

During one playful moment, Miller looked up at Malone and said, "Big Guy?"

"Yes, Mister Miller."

"When's the last time somebody kicked your butt?"

"Well, my track record is clean, and you're not going to break it.'"

Malone laughs at the memory. "He said it in front of the

nurses—he did it for them—and they didn't know what to think," says Malone.

A security guard was posted at the door to Larry's room. He had a list of those who were allowed to visit. Malone confessed that once, while Larry was sleeping and the guard had momentarily left his station, he sneaked a peek at the list. "I couldn't resist; I had to see if I was on the list," says Karl.

Larry and Karl reminisced during their daily visits. They recalled the time Miller took Malone for a ride in one of his Cobras. Miller placed a $100 bill on the dashboard and told Malone it was his if he could pick it up. Every time Malone reached for the money, Miller accelerated, slamming Malone back into his seat. "Never did get that money," says Malone. "He knew what he was doing. Everytime he accelerated, I was hanging onto that grab bar he had in there. I had white knuckles. We were going 100 miles per hour on a one-lane road. The more he saw me cringe, the faster he drove. He loved it. He had this smile on his face. He always wanted to one-up me. It was as if he were saying, 'Now you know I'm better than you at driving.' He loved those Cobras."

Malone recalls the first time he met Miller shortly after being drafted. Malone got word that Miller wanted to meet him at his office, which was then at a car dealership. "I was looking for someone in a double-breasted suit and tie, and out walked this guy in a polo shirt, jeans, and sneakers," says Malone. "He said, 'Let's go get something to eat,' and we went to Wendy's. I thought, I'm going to like this guy."

Malone, a marvelously talented athlete, would become the second highest scorer in NBA history and a two-time Olympic gold medalist, but, quite incongruously, he was still an insecure kid from rural Louisiana whose father had died when he was three. Miller seemed to fill a need for Malone, odd as it might seem for a white middle-aged Mormon from Utah and a young black man from the Deep South.

As Malone recalls, "I told Larry thanks one day in the hospital, and he said, 'For what?' And I told him, 'For being that father figure for me.' I used to go over to his house all the time. He talked to me about everything—religion, race, basketball, marriage, family, business, you name it."

The relationship survived Malone's nearly annual public ventings against Miller and the Jazz, as well as Miller's occasional outbursts directed at Malone. "Sometimes, to get my attention, you've got to come with it," says Malone. "If you came at me soft, I didn't listen to you. I appreciated it. I needed that edge."

Malone thinks about how rare it is for an owner to be so close to his players the way Miller was with him and Stockton and a few others. "I don't think it will happen again," says Malone. "A lot of other owners who were concerned about our relationship told Larry they didn't think he should be that close to a player. They'd say to him, 'You do know this is a business, don't you? You need to be careful when you mix business and friendship.' And Larry would just say, 'I'll keep that in mind.' But he told me, 'Big Guy, I never wore a suit and a tie and never fit in with them, so why should I fit in now?'"

Malone's visit finally wound to a close on the fourth day when his wife, Kay, arrived at the hospital and announced to Karl that she was going shopping.

"Why don't you go with her?" Larry said.

"Come on, Karl," Kay said, "you've overstayed your welcome."

It was the last time Karl saw Larry alive.

PART IV

OTHER VENTURES

CHAPTER 19

JOSEPH SMITH PAPERS

There have been many times in my life when I have felt guided or led to some new venture, and the Joseph Smith Papers was one of those ventures.

It began in 2000 when David Brown, who had served as my bishop during my Colorado years, my reactivation period, was called by the LDS Church to serve as the director of the visitors' center in Kirtland, Ohio, site of much early Church history. He called Ron Barney of the Church Historical Department and asked him for a crash course in Church history to prepare him for his new assignment. Ron set up a display for him that chronicled Church history and invited him to come to see it in his department at the Church Office Building.

We had stayed in touch with David and his wife, MelRae, over the years, so when he was in town he invited Gail and me to go with them to see this display. We were dazzled by the exhibit, which included original manuscripts of the Book of Mormon, Joseph Smith's diaries, the Book of Commandments, and Eliza R. Snow's hymnbook. We were blown away to be right there next to them. While we were there, I met and visited with Ron, who we learned was working on the Joseph Smith Papers.

Later, after we had returned home, I told Gail, "There is something I need to be doing here. I need to call Ron Barney." I called him and asked if I could meet with him. We met at the appointed time, and at some point I told Ron, "I don't know why I'm here; do you?"

"I don't have a clue," he said.

"Well, I think it has something to do with something you're working on that you need help with."

The meeting ended after we had discussed a variety of projects without reaching any conclusions. Both of us were perplexed.

A few days later, I called Ron and told him, "We need to meet again."

"I know why I am here," I said when we met.

"So do I," Ron replied.

"Why?"

"You go first," Ron said.

"It's the Joseph Smith Papers."

"You're exactly right."

At the time, Ron and other Church historians were working on a Joseph Smith history and had limited funds to operate with. They needed more researchers and funding. They were trying to produce a set of books that would publish everything Joseph Smith wrote or was involved with in his life—personal diaries, the Book of Revelations from the president's vault that had never been published, letters, and so forth. We set out to produce 30 volumes.

What we did was provide funding for the project and hire a great team of scholars, archivists, manuscript experts, and so forth to examine Church history documents. We gave BYU a donation of

$10 million worth of bonds. The interest mostly supports the Joseph Smith Papers project. We make up the difference that the interest doesn't cover each year.

In the case of most scholarly historical books, you're successful if you sell 1,500 over a lifetime. Our first volume sold more than 60,000 at a cost of $50 per book. The next volume, which was bigger and pricier, at $100, received more than 2,900 orders before it even came off the press. The books themselves are beautiful and the contents are mind-boggling. The researchers have found some fantastic stuff. They have discovered some things no one knew. The project has also included a companion TV series that airs on Sunday evenings. We have completed 40 of the 100 episodes we plan to produce.

Only a few days before I learned of the Joseph Smith Papers, I had been assigned to speak in a Sunday sacrament meeting and spent some time preparing my remarks. But en route to the chapel, I decided I wasn't going to use the talk I had prepared; I decided I was going to talk about Joseph Smith, and I did. Afterward, I was approached by a woman who had sat in the congregation. She said, "I don't live in this ward, but I felt I needed to go to a new ward today for some reason and wound up here. Your talk was for me." I felt like I had been prepared for this project. I was in my office one time studying various things about Joseph Smith, and I felt he was there with me.

POSTSCRIPT

Larry's involvement in the Joseph Smith Papers project consisted of more than providing funding. He advised on what researchers were needed to keep the project on course, as well as how to invest and spend the money he provided to them. He received nearly weekly updates from the JSP team and visited Church leaders often about the project. He organized a trip for the JSP team and their spouses to visit Church history sites to enable them to see the scope of the project and meet other researchers on the team (which is where the material for the Joseph Smith Papers TV program came from). He hosted annual dinners for the group so everyone could receive firsthand reports about what other groups had discovered in their research. Larry was passionate about this project right to the end of his life. As his obituary noted, "Of his many philanthropic endeavors, the Joseph Smith Papers project was one of the dearest to his heart." Referencing a well-known Mormon hymn, Church historian Marlin K. Jensen said this of Miller: "He had as one of his objectives in life to make sure that billions 'will know Brother Joseph again,' the words he uses when he talks about this."

CHAPTER 20

FOR THE LOVE OF CARS

There's this smell you get when you race cars. It's a combination of super-heated brakes and oil and high-octane fuel. That smell is intoxicating to me. I breathe it in the way others take in perfume. It might sound strange to those who don't have 10W30 oil coursing through their veins, the way I do, but I love smelling that smell and hearing the sounds that come with it out there on the racetrack. The sound of an engine when it revs up is music to my ears. It's like the purring of a cat.

When I'm driving one of my sports cars, I love the explosion of power under me. I like to take a car to the racetrack or one of the canyons near Salt Lake City and ask the car to do something special. I know what's going to happen—I've done it before—and still what happens is a huge thrill. I almost always say to myself, "Wow. I didn't remember it being quite like this." You can't quite remember the full force and effect of it and the thrill that comes from it.

Much of my personal and professional life has involved cars. I have repaired cars. I have managed auto parts departments and dealerships. I have raced cars on the street and on the track. I own car dealerships and collect vintage sports cars, and I built a motor speedway and a race car museum and assembled a racing team.

I like to get in a car and go for a drive after work or on Sunday after church as a way to unwind. One of my favorite things to do is take Gail or one of my kids or grandkids for a drive in one of my Cobras with "Hey, Little Cobra" playing full blast on the radio. It is a good way to visit with loved ones and to see the scenery while also feeding my passion for automobiles. I like to drive up one of the canyons early on a Saturday morning and drive fast—sometimes 100 miles per hour through the mountains. Gail worries; she'll say, "You're going to get hurt." Usually I don't even push the car hard. I just love to listen to that engine and know what's there. It becomes part of me.

My favorite car—as anyone who knows me will tell you—is the Shelby Cobra, the small, two-seat roadster built in the '60s. I look at them and melt. Even the sound of the engine affects me. It revs up so well, and you're going to 7,500 RPMs, and it doesn't fight back; it just goes, as if it's saying, "Let me run, let me run."

I have a deserved reputation as a frugal man, but Gail laughs at that because she knows how my frugality falters when it comes to Cobras. I own 15 of them, which is the largest private collection in the world. Only 1,011 of them were ever made. I paid as much as $4 million for one of them and none is worth less than $250,000. I had to outbid movie maker George Lucas to buy one of my Cobras. I know the serial numbers of all 15 of them the same way parents know the names of their children. I used to keep five of them in my garage at home. I have files and history books for each of the cars. It pained me to have to put two of my Cobras—serial numbers CSX2175 and CSX3202—up for collateral when I bought the first half of the Jazz.

I also have a fondness for GT-40s and Shelby Mustangs—I gave one to each of my kids, all of them different colors.

When I am asked about my great affinity for Cobras, this is what I say: I deal so much with people and I have such high expectations of those people. I work with a lot of very good people, but they're still people and, despite all the preparation, they don't always deliver as you hoped. You still can't determine the outcome. With Cobras, you do certain things to them and you get certain results. You get out of them what you put into them, and you can count on that. I like that about my Cobras.

The Cobra was developed by Carroll Shelby, a legendary name in auto history. He was a race-car driver, but heart problems forced him to quit. He turned to designing and building race cars. He made a deal with Ford to put small-block Fords in an AC Cobra body—a 221, then a 260, then a 289. The Cobra is an aluminum roadster. They're tight and small. They have no creature comforts. Shelby liked to say there was nothing on a Cobra that wasn't there to make it faster. Shelby was way ahead of his time. The Cobras were the fastest production cars made until the '90s. They could travel from zero to 100 miles per hour and come back to a complete stop in 12 seconds. It took more than 30 years for other cars to catch up with Cobras.

Shelby was a master marketer, and in 1962 he touted the car to the media. It was in every publication. In its first race, the car proved to be exactly what Shelby said it was. It didn't win, but only because it lost a rear wheel axle bearing. The car was way out front at the time. It instantly became the car to beat. Cobras dominated Europe, the road tracks, and the drag strips. They were just neat cars. They became part of folklore in auto circles. In 1964, a pop group called the Rip Chords released a hit song titled "Hey, Little Cobra." I own the car that was on the cover of that record.

I was a high school senior when the Cobras arrived on the scene, and they instantly caught my eye. When the cars came out in

1963, they sold for $5,995. Two years later, they retailed for $7,495. That was a lot of money at the time, and much more than I could afford. I settled for racing cars with Cobra engine components in my youth. I also settled for a car that was a little short of a Cobra.

I bought my first car when I was 17. It cost $20. It was a two-tone metallic green 1952 Oldsmobile Rocket 88, with a 303 engine. I was forced to learn about cars thanks to that Rocket 88. It was a great car for a teenager, but it had one problem: When the engine was warmed up, it wouldn't start. I'd have to let it sit and cool off for 15 to 30 minutes before it would start again. I couldn't diagnose the problem, and because of this I took an auto mechanics class from Mr. Wynn at West High.

After that, I continued to dabble with the workings of a car and learned how to build engines. In 1964, shortly before we were married, Gail bought a year-old Ford Falcon convertible with 13,000 miles on it. I started making minor modifications to it and eventually converted it into a customized race car that was fast and loud. I also helped my friends work on their race cars, mostly small-block Fords. So I fussed with Gail's Falcon—I put a four-barrel carburetor on it to make it quicker, then a solid lifter and cam shaft that made it significantly different, then high-performance heads. Now we were starting to get somewhere. Then I realized the rear end was not strong enough to handle that much power, so I changed the eight-inch rear end to a nine-inch one. It gave me the capability to put in much lower gears. I added slicks to manage the power, along with exhaust headers and a 289 motor. For its time and class it was pretty quick. I was racing it all that time, but when I started I was getting beat badly, so I increased the horsepower from 132 to 331. Gail didn't like it, but she put up with it as long as it kept running. This is the car we took on our honeymoon that attracted the attention of the highway patrol in Oregon.

It wasn't just the twisting of nuts and bolts. You can't spend that much time with something and not develop an affinity for it—and that certainly describes what could be considered the beginning of my love affair with cars. What I saw was the development of my association with, and my subsequent love of, cars. For a while cars were just transportation, but if you work on a car—as you do in racing—you come to know the car and its personality. You can feel the car. If I drive a car a fair amount, I can feel when something is wrong with it—a slight vibration or a different sound. Every car is different, even if they're the same type. In a way, cars respond to people like pets do. If you do something to a car, it responds.

I learned about cars from a number of sources—in shop class and at drag-racing events and in car magazines and while working on cars. Then I got Gail's car fully built up, and I was really hooked on racing. That also led to my affection not only for cars but also for their history. Look at what the car has done since 1900—the work, the reliability and speed. It's remarkable. Cars do so much to reflect our history as a society.

This all helped me when I went into the car business. When I was behind a parts counter and heard a customer describe a problem or a list of symptoms, I could diagnose the source of the problem even from behind the counter. "Have you thought about this?" I would ask. "Have you tried this? Here's how you do it." My knowledge of cars was very helpful. The best way to learn the car business in a dealership is to work in the parts department, where you're exposed to all aspects of a car.

My love for cars, racing, and Cobras lay dormant for about eight years as I turned my obsessive nature to work, softball, and my entrepreneurial career. After moving to Colorado, I was preoccupied with supporting a family, playing softball several times a week, and working. Then, late one night in 1975, I was in my office—I had just become general manager of a Toyota store in Colorado—when for some reason I suddenly decided to check *Hemmings Motor News*, a large national magazine that caters to traders and collectors of exotic cars and car parts. I wanted to see what had happened to

Cobras. I had been told they had become just another used car, nothing special. In 1973 and '74 that might have been true, but by 1975 they were being rediscovered. In 1973, for instance, you could buy a Cobra for $1,000 to $3,000, or maybe $5,000 for a 427. Thumbing through the pages of *Hemmings*, I found a couple of Cobras in Wisconsin. I called the owners, and they wanted $9,500. I thought that was too much money, but I learned later it was a good deal. I called the people again, but the cars had been sold. This happened to me again a couple of times. Meanwhile, the price of a Cobra was escalating at a rate of about $1,000 a month.

Later, I was in the Toyota regional office and asked if anyone knew of someone who had a Cobra. The odds of that were slight, but to my surprise someone said he had a cousin in California who not only owned a Cobra but had put it up for sale for $13,500. I went to see the car. It had 12,000 miles on it and had had just one owner. Gail flew to California to meet me, and we drove it home. We parked it in a parking lot in Las Vegas overnight, and the next day we drove over Rabbit Ears Pass in a snowstorm with no top and no windshield wipers. We were bundled up in our coats trying to stay warm while we braved the snow for 30 miles in April. Gail reached over the window to wipe away the snow every few minutes. That was my first Cobra—CSX125. I hardly drove it, except to take it out for a spin occasionally.

In 1978, I learned of a badly wrecked, big-block 427 Shelby that was located in Michigan's Upper Penisula. I flew to Gladstone, Michigan, to see the car, but there wasn't much to see. It had been disassembled and now consisted of parts piled into boxes. The car had had seven owners since it had been wrecked. The current owner had bought the parts hoping to put it back together, but he couldn't do it. He had restored the frame, which is the biggest problem when a car gets hurt. The frame was what we wanted to check. We made a deal to buy it and returned to Colorado. I sent two employees to retrieve it. They bought a pickup truck in Green Bay, and then drove it to Gladstone, where they loaded up the parts and brought them to Denver. I hired the renowned Bill Murray—I will tell you more about him later—to restore the car, and it turned into a two-year job. We entered the car in shows, and it won the judges' and people's choice awards in about everything we entered. It was beautiful. During contests, one judge would lie on the floor just looking for flaws in the paint, and he couldn't find any on my car.

So now I had two Cobras—a 427 and a 289—both street cars with no racing history. They sound soooo good. You shift the big blocks at 7,200 RPMs when you race them, and the small blocks at 7,800. Those two cars sat for a long time in the garage here at the house. I'd drive them a little; I'd warm them up occasionally and drive them around the neighborhood just to keep the oil good. From the time I bought them until 1997, I drove those cars a total of just 700 miles.

The 289 led indirectly to a defining moment in my life. The car needed some work, and the guy I trusted to do the job was Murray. He didn't have time to do it immediately, so I decided to leave the car with him for the winter. I put it on a trailer and drove it to his shop in Longmont, Colorado. While I was there, he invited me to see his museum of vintage race cars. To me, that museum, which was housed in a building with a band of windows around the top to let the light in, was like holy ground. It was mind-boggling and exhilarating. There were about 30 GT-40s, Cobras, and Shelby Mustangs. I was ooohing and ahhhing. "This is so cool," I gushed to Bill. He turned and said, "Let me tell you what's cool. In the history of Cobradom, Cobras won 57 professional races. Cars that won 28 of those 57 races are in this building." Wow! For me, that was like being in a room with a dozen Super Bowl champions. He pointed out nine cars and said, "Those nine cars won 28 of those 57 races. Last Saturday, all nine of those cars raced at Steamboat; that's what they were built for, not to be museum pieces."

I didn't say anything, but in that instant I said to myself, *We're going racing.* We began acquiring Cobras that were either already fast or we made them fast. Most of my cars are extremely fast or have a significant racing history or both. My favorite car in the world is CSX2229—it's one of six Daytona coupes that were built. It is drop-dead gorgeous. That car won the world manufacturers championship in 1975 and raced all over Europe. I ended up buying it and raced it in Goodwood, England. The first person I turned to, of course, was Murray. He was my builder, driver, mechanic, and restorer. When it comes to the restoration of automobiles, Bill is an artist, a master. We got a tech crew and driver and bought a transport that can haul five cars. In 2000, I bought a racetrack in Mead, Colorado, that had once served as a practice track. It was located on 60 acres north of Denver, ten miles from Bill's shop. We'd take four to ten cars over there and go through our race preparations, breaking in engines and making sure they were okay. Sometimes I'd take a guest with us. We'd fly him over and spend the day on the track.

Soon I wanted to build a better track in what was then a 160-acre cornfield next to our existing track. I hired Alan Wilson, a famous track designer from South Africa who has more than 20 tracks to his credit (*Automobile Magazine* called him "the world's most prolific race track designer"). I paid Alan $125,000 to design a three-mile track on the 220-acre parcel, but we couldn't get the zoning changed. They believed it would be too noisy, even though a decibel check revealed we weren't as loud as the adjacent I-25, plus we would more than double city revenue with sales tax at the track. They put it on a referendum and we were routed 93 percent to 7 percent. We decided enough was enough; it wasn't worth the fight, plus it was too far away and difficult to get to.

In 2003 we began looking for another race site, preferably in the Salt Lake Valley. We made a deal to lease a plot of land on Kennecott property, and once again I paid Wilson $125,000 to design a track—and once again we never built it. After two years of jumping through hoops for federal and state agencies and battling wetland and environmental issues, we got tired of waiting for approval. We looked farther west to Tooele, where they didn't have those issues. We leased 500 acres from Tooele County for 99 years. So here we were again. Wilson and I were looking over the proposed site for another track, now in the fall of 2004. The land, consisting of fields and sage, didn't look like much. "Can you do it?" I asked him. He looked at me and said, "I have only one question: Are we going to build this one?" We broke ground on my birthday, April 26, 2005.

The original plan was to build a fun little club track where we could take our GT 40s and Cobras and drive ourselves silly and not worry about getting speeding tickets or hurting someone. Our budget was $7 million, and Alan started his design of a Le Mans–style road racing track. Well, the budget quickly went a little past $7 million—to $100 million.

I became immersed in this project just as I had during the construction of the Delta Center and the purchase of the Jazz and so many other things. I wanted to add buildings. One is a Grand Prix garage with 27 bays that empty onto the pit lane; there aren't any tracks like that in the U.S. Alan wanted a clubhouse built on a hill for a nice, upscale experience. Then we built day garages with huge sunscreens and cinderblock enclosures. That way the racers can work on a concrete surface in the shade. We put in shaded stands, restrooms, and concessions with an acre of lawn and shade trees— we call them oases—and we put these all around the track. The 4.5-mile track—which is the longest in the U.S.—consists of 24 turns. The course has three additional possible configurations: the 2.24-mile highly technical East Course, the 2.24-mile West Course suited for larger cars and motorcycles, and the 3.06-mile Perimeter Course, which is one of the fastest track layouts in the country. You can see much of the track from any place on the grounds.

Well, this became a huge project. We moved 2.5 million cubic yards of dirt. I never intended to build a track like this; I just wanted a place to drive my cars. But then the architects and I saw it and pretty soon we were saying things like, "We ought to do this, and we ought to do that, and wouldn't it be great if we did this," and it got away from us.

Alan was very good at writing what the experience would be like on each turn. He could visualize it. These are well-thought-out, engineered turns that are challenging, each for a different reason. Even the good professional drivers say the turns are tough, but they learned to handle them, and I like it that way because the real racers can do well and we haven't made it too easy for the wannabes.

I've been surprised by the comments drivers have made about the track. We've had drivers from 27 countries out there, and they often tell us it's one of the two finest tracks in the world. It was engineered that well. There are five double-apex turns and one triple-apex turn (the apex being the high point of the turn, of course).

I was thinking no one would use the track—people wouldn't know about it. Well, Gail called this shot. She said the track would be so heavily used that I wouldn't be able to get on it. I have not turned a wheel on the track because it's so busy. People go out there to race—motorcycle guys, Jag and Corvette guys, the Porsche Club, and so forth. It's constantly in use. There are practice days and racing days and national and international races out there.

The first year I went out there a few times and drove myself silly. It's good R&R for me. Part of the problem is that a lot of the cars I own have greater abilities as cars than I do as a driver, and that can get me into trouble. I can drive those cars, but I can't get all the car can give me because I don't have the skills to handle it.

About five years ago I took John Stockton out there. We drove the Cobra—I think it was CSX3032. I drove it first, and then I let John drive. I should tell you that the passenger and driver sit in basically a box with their feet up on a thin aluminum wall that separates them from the engine. That wall gets very hot. Well, John drove for quite a while, and when I removed my shoes later that day

188

I discovered that my feet were bloody. I had burned my toes on that aluminum wall—I actually melted my shoes—and hadn't realized it because one of the symptoms of diabetes is loss of feeling in the feet. My toes were so damaged that they would never heal. Eventually, the bone became infected and the first joint of three small toes had to be amputated.

I should also note that I have the dubious distinction of committing the first crash on the track, and it was a doozy, something straight out of *The Dukes of Hazzard*. I drove my Lexus out to the track one Sunday evening, accompanied by Gail and Zane. No one was there that day, but the track was still being poured and there were a few large dirt berms across the track so that trucks could cross to the infield without harming the track surface. I wanted to see if drivers would be able to feel the seams in the track, so I decided to drive the Lexus on it. After checking to make sure my passengers were wearing their seat belts, I asked Gail to watch the speedometer and tell me when I reached 110 miles per hour because my eyesight is poor. Remember those berms? Well, I didn't. I had reached 100 miles per hour when Zane shouted from the backseat, "BUMP!" We hit one of the berms and went airborne. We flew over the berm and landed 20 feet past it. Parts were flying off the car. The airbags deployed. I knew I had to keep the car steady when we landed or we would roll. At that speed we could have died instantly. Gail said later that she was thinking that this must be what it feels like to die; it happens in an instant, but it doesn't hurt. Finally, I managed to stop the car. It was still running and I didn't dare shut it off. I told Zane to get out of the car and collect all the parts that had flown off. I drove the car to the Lexus dealer the next day, but it was declared DOA—totaled.

We also built a museum out there in which we display my collection of vintage race cars—Cobras, GT-40s, and Shelby Mustangs as well as a lot of other auto-related memorabilia connected to

Carroll Shelby. We rotate the cars between my museum and the Carroll Shelby Museum in Boulder, Colorado.

But, as Bill said, those cars are meant to be raced and driven. Keeping them in a museum is like locking up wild animals in a zoo. I assembled a racing team—drivers, mechanics, crews, and all—and I pay their expenses to race around the country and beyond. We have raced in England, Germany, France, and Belgium. I actually drove one of the cars in Goodwood, England. We made two trips over there, and my family accompanied the team.

To tell you the truth, the motor speedway has been an ugly stepchild for The Miller Group. It's losing $2 million a year. It's just too far ahead of its time. Auto racing has taken the country by storm in the last few years, but not Utah. It's just difficult to get people out there for race events as spectators. The track has worldwide recognition, but few in Utah know about it.

I go out to the track at dusk occasionally when no one else is out there. The entire 26-acre paddock will be empty except maybe a security guy and a few hawks and seagulls overhead hunting mice. It's quiet and serene as the sun sets over the Oquirrhs. And just 12 hours later the place is transformed. The paddock is crammed full of vehicles six inches apart, bumper to bumper, motorcycles and cars. There is so much going on. It's a beehive, with men working on cars and loading and unloading trailers and technical inspections and practice sessions and qualifying sessions and races, and it's acres of semis and race cars and the sounds and energy that go with them and thousands of people.

The track was a realization of a dream.

POSTSCRIPT

Those who knew anything about Miller had to smile when they saw that his coffin was designed to look like one of his beloved Cobras—blue with two white racing stripes running the length of the casket and an official Cobra medallion attached to one end. It was Greg's

190

idea. *During the last week of his father's life, he told his father about the Cobra casket to see how he felt about it. "I guess that would be okay," Larry said. Greg sent the casket to one of the Miller body shops to be painted, and he asked the Cobra racing team for the emblem (the team showed up for the funeral in their blue Cobra uniforms). Among the flowers that were placed atop the casket during the viewing was a black-and-white checked ribbon. All they needed was "Hey, Little Cobra" playing in the background to complete the picture. As a final salute to their father's love of cars, Miller's sons drove Cobras, Mustangs, and his beloved 1963 Ford Falcon convertible in the procession to the cemetery.*

The man who painted the casket was an employee who felt especially indebted to his boss. Years earlier he had requested a week off of work so that he and his wife could drive to Texas to pick up a baby they were going to adopt. After waiting several days for the baby to be born, they learned that the mother had changed her mind about putting the baby up for adoption, so the heartbroken couple began the long drive back to Utah, only to learn en route that the mother had changed her mind again and would allow the adoption as planned. The man needed two more weeks off from work. He called his boss repeatedly to ask if he would still retain his job when he returned. When word of this reached Miller, he wrote a note to the employee telling him to take all the time he needed and that his job would be there when he was ready to return to work.

As for the racetrack, Greg Miller says, "It was bad timing. Sponsorships have been cut back and entertainment dollars are not being spent. But my father held it close to the vest. He wouldn't involve the sports entertainment division of The Miller Group. He did it personally." In the end, those close to Miller were philosophical about the track. "Some people build swimming pools or tennis courts in their backyards," says Greg. "He wanted a racetrack and his yard wasn't big enough."

CHAPTER 21

SOFTBALL

The routine rarely varied: Every afternoon during many of my teen years, I laced on my cleats and walked across the street to the Ashtons' backyard and pitched—first, five minutes of throwing just for control, striving to pitch so accurately that my catcher, Stan Olsen, didn't have to move his glove; then five minutes of pitching for sheer power, with no concern for control or form; then five minutes of pitching various pitches—riseballs, dropballs, changeups, sliders, fast knuckleballs, slow knuckleballs. The pace was fast—pitch, catch the throw back from the catcher, pitch, catch the throw back from the catcher, pitch, and so on, as fast as we could go, especially when it was cold, because then I just wanted to get it done and get out of there. I threw more than 100 pitches in that 15 minutes.

I practiced this routine every day for five years, year round, never mind that softball was a spring-summer sport. In the winter,

I would dig out a foothold in the ice and snow with my cleats. If the weather was too severe, or I couldn't find a catcher that day, I'd practice the same routine by throwing darts at a plywood target in my basement. I would throw so hard that it would bury the dart to the hilt. Even as an adult, when I was working long hours, I would throw darts in the basement late at night.

Those daily practices paid off. I became a pitcher in an adult league at the age of 16. I pitched in my first world tournament at 24. I played softball for nearly three decades, 18 years at the highest levels of fast-pitch, before retiring in 1985 at the age of 41. By then I had pitched in 1,081 games and collected 819 victories. In 1992, I was inducted into the International Softball Hall of Fame in Illinois. I pitched for some great teams. We finished second in the world tournament in 1982 and second in the national tournament in 1985.

Softball became my great passion. It filled a huge need in my life. I just loved it. As a kid, I looked forward to the games so much that a rainout was devastating for me. With the stresses of home life and, later, my career, there was nothing I loved more than to be on a diamond on a weekend night, under the lights, in a highly charged, competitive game. There are a bunch of lines in the movie *Field of Dreams* that describe how I feel about the game. At one point the character Doc yearns for "the chance to squint my eyes when the sky is so blue it hurts to look at it, and to feel the tingle that runs up your arms when you connect dead-on. The chance to run the bases, stretch a double to a triple, and flop face-first into third, wrapping my arm around the bag. That's my wish . . . that's my wish."

Softball became a major gathering point for our Capitol Hill neighborhood. We didn't even have Little League baseball until I was 12—I was a catcher and an unbeaten pitcher that year and made the all-star team. For some reason I didn't sign up for Little League again the following year, and that was the end of that. From then on, I played softball.

LDS Church softball was a big event in those days. The climactic event was the All-Church tournament, which was played in Salt Lake City and featured the top teams from around the world. I started playing Church softball at 13. I was a catcher, but in a late-season game Coach Glen Lloyd put me on the mound, even though I told him I had never practiced the underhand softball pitching motion. I had a reputation for throwing hard from my Little League baseball days, so even though I was lobbing underhand pitches with a six-foot arch on them, guys were jumping out of the box for a while. I struck out a couple of batters in two innings and liked the experience. After the season, the stake athletic director, Reid Ashton, told me, "With the athletes we have in this neighborhood, we could put together a good team if we have someone who can pitch." I made the decision right then to become a good softball pitcher. We succeeded as 14-year-olds because I could throw strikes and we had good position players and hitters.

By the time I was 15 I realized that if I was going to be good, I had to work at it. That was when I began my daily training routine with the peculiar single-mindedness that became my defining trait. While doing this I developed all the usual pitches, plus pitches that other pitchers didn't have. My repertoire consisted of a riseball, a dropball, an out-curve, a hard knuckleball, a change knuckleball, and a changeup. Over the years, I taught myself the pitches by asking other pitchers about them during tournaments. Some of my teammates laughed because I was asking for help from opposing pitchers, but I was driven to learn. I also grew during the next couple of years, from 115 pounds as a sophomore to 190 pounds as a senior, which helped improve my pitching.

Over the next three years we became a force on the local softball scene. We would usually win the tournaments. We were so dominant in the junior program that we were asked to play in the senior division against the men, with the proviso that it wouldn't count on the seniors' win-loss record and we would be granted an automatic berth in the post-season junior tournament. We were unbeaten against the seniors, as well. We went to the All-Church tournament and finished second after blowing a 3–0 lead against a team from Sacramento.

I began to play in recreation and open leagues about this time, against men. A year later, I played for a farm team of the Metro League, which was the equivalent of the big leagues in softball. I was the number-two pitcher and produced a 15–0 record. A year later I was the number-two pitcher on the top team in the Metro League, West Construction. The following year I was the number-one pitcher for another Metro League team, YD Motors, which had several weak players who were on the team because they were related to the team's sponsor. I pitched our first six games and we lost each of them, even though I had an ERA of under 1!

We won about half our games that year, and then in the off-season we got another sponsor—Western Floor Coverings—so we weren't obligated to play relatives anymore. We picked up some good players who had played baseball for the University of Utah. We were young and brash and wore our tricked-out uniforms—green sleeves and chokers, white shoes, white and green pinstripes—with pride. In the first tournament of the season, I was on the mound nursing a 2–1 lead in the last inning against powerhouse West Construction, with a man on second base. I turned to teammate Roger Burt and said, "It's game time, Rog," and I blew the next pitch past the batter for the win.

With a young team, we began to earn a reputation, winning tournaments around the West. When one of the dominant teams in the West, Vern Hagestead of Colorado, saw what we were doing, they recruited me. When I was 26, they lured me to Colorado with the promise that they would set up job interviews for me. One of the primary reasons I moved to Colorado was to play softball. I played fast-pitch at the national level for the entire eight years we lived there. As I noted earlier, Gail brought the kids to the ballpark on weekends just as a means to get us together. We were there most weekends and a couple of evenings during the week. The games lasted 90 minutes, plus there were warm-ups and travel time, and if it was a tournament, you might have to wait ten hours or so for your next game. We traveled seven to twelve weekends a year, to Arizona, California, Canada, Montana, Nebraska, Illinois, Iowa, Texas. Gail and the kids traveled most of the time with us. We drove to a lot of the tournaments in our Toyota station wagon. Once my family and I drove 100 miles to Pueblo on a Thursday for the opening game of a tournament, drove back to Denver that night so I could work on Friday, got home at midnight, I went to work the next morning, drove back to Pueblo after work, and played games at 6:00, 7:30, and 9:00, stayed in a hotel that night, got up on Saturday and played games at 10:00, 11:30, 1:00, 2:30, 5:30, and 7:00. I pitched nine games in less than 24 hours and won seven of them, while also batting .458, and I was named tournament MVP. My arm was a limp rag hanging at my side at the end of that last night.

Softball was a great outlet for my emotional and competitive nature. I was very aggressive. When I was on the mound, my feeling about hitters—even if I was facing a friend—was this: If a guy had the nerve to pick up a bat and walk into the batter's box and try to hit a ball off me, he was the enemy. I was going to do everything I could to throw the ball past him.

There were summer nights when I was on the mound, staring at the batter, with a soft breeze blowing in my face—ideal for making my pitches move—playing against an opponent who was so good that I couldn't afford to make any mistakes. And not long into the game—somewhere in the first inning, usually—I would actually have this thought: *This is cool. Things couldn't be any better.* There was one night when we were playing West Construction, our league's version of the Yankees, and it was 0–0 in the bottom of the last inning. I remember the moon had just come up over Mt.

Olympus, and right then I hit a triple off the fence and scored on a sacrifice fly.

These were the occasions when I was really able to enjoy the moment and, on a larger scale, fill a competitive need. When you get right down to it, the things I did on the job—the long hours, the search for better ways to work faster and more efficiently, the record sales, and so forth—were all the result of my competitiveness. I wanted to beat the other guys; I wanted to succeed. But to do something physical felt so good after a day in the office. To be part of a team and to see our team perform like a machine and to compete— this feeling was difficult to beat. I went stir-crazy in the winter when I had no place to release the energy and competitiveness.

This is how much it filled a need for me: If I was stuck on the bench as a potential relief pitcher and didn't play, I'd come home from the game and go for a run at 10:00 at night just to run off the energy. Otherwise, I'd lie awake in bed. I got so wound up. This intensity did create challenges. I had problems with my temper. I'd get mad at guys for not catching a ball that wasn't really catchable. When I was in the dugout, I would get into the occasional shouting match and one or two shoving matches. I was intense, as I was in everything I did.

The other part of softball's appeal was that I made many great friendships that have continued over the years. Some of those people have come to work for me. It also opened a lot of doors for me. Without realizing it, I was networking while I played.

When I moved back to Salt Lake City, I sponsored my own team—Larry H. Miller Toyota—which I continued to sponsor for some 20 years, even long after I retired as a player. I told the team that as long as we had a legitimate chance to win a national or world tournament, I would sponsor them. It reached a point where we were always ranked among the top ten teams in the nation and qualified for the national tournaments, but we'd wind up finishing sixth or eighth or tenth or whatever, and it wasn't satisfying to anybody. We finally called a big meeting of the players and discussed it. We had aged together. We stuck with our players, like we do with the Jazz. But now we were slowing down, and we had watched each other get grayer or balder.

We talked about all the great times we had had together. We had traveled thousands of miles and played hundreds of games and had become quite close. It was a great time, but we decided it was time to quit. If we couldn't be what we had once been, it was time to move on to other things. As much as we hated to quit playing the game, everybody arrived at the same conclusion.

Every once in a while, I just flat-out miss it, even 23 years later. I miss being on a field of competition. Other than the times I've spent with Gail, I will say that some of the happiest times of my life were when I was in uniform competing at the ballpark.

CHAPTER 22

THE MOVIE BIZ

H ere's how naïve I was about the movie business. During construction of Jordan Commons—our complex of offices, restaurants, and 16 theaters—we had actually completed the foundation, with concrete and steel above ground, when I turned to Steve Tarbet, who was overseeing our theater operations, and said, "I wonder how you get movies."

As I discovered, it's a very involved process. We had completed the design and were getting ready to construct the above-ground building. We'd already spent $25 million, and I hadn't thought this part through. I mean, we didn't want to rent our movies from Blockbuster.

Like the racetrack and other projects I have undertaken, Jordan Commons grew into much more than we had originally set out to do. Once again, it demanded all of my entrepreneurial skills. The original driving force for the project was that the people in our company were scattered around the valley. We wanted to put everyone—IT, automotive, leasing, sports and entertainment, and so forth—under one roof in an office tower. We thought that would be more efficient. I told my guys that we were going to do some fun stuff there. I was thinking of a restaurant and a park and theaters.

As with the Delta Center, we did a lot of the work ourselves after researching things and learning about the business. There are design consultants for theaters and people who buy movies for you and people who tell you what kind of equipment to buy. You're supposed to hire these people to do all this for you. We didn't hire any of them. We wanted to throw away the book on theater design. We were going to create the type of theater experience that we would want if we took our families to see a movie. We had a list. We wanted stadium seating in the theater that was so good that Mark Eaton could sit in front of you wearing a cowboy hat without blocking your view. We wanted zero bad seats. Also, in most theaters there are too many seats that are too close to the screen. Wheelchair patrons get the worst seats because they're in the front row. So we moved our front row 15 to 25 feet farther away from the screen than in conventional theaters. We gave up extra seats that we could have sold in exchange for having no bad seats. We also dug down deeper into the ground to set our foundation so that people could enter the theater from the middle of the theater instead of the bottom. People in the industry told us that wouldn't work; they'd never seen it done. Since then, it's become a standard in the industry. Now wheelchair patrons can sit on the middle deck and have the best seats in the house. We've gotten so much goodwill from that. It was revolutionary, and we have a high utilization rate.

It was only later that we hired an expert to critique us. We also hired a design expert to make sure there were no major flaws. Our design included four pods with four theaters in each, and we wanted one grand 600-seat theater in each quadrant. We paid this consultant $30,000 to tell us what we did wrong and what we did right. The first thing he said was, "Man, you can't have these 600-seat theaters. They're passé. Nobody uses them anymore. They're too big. It's a theater of a bygone era. You can't sell that many seats, and you can't get enough big movies to do that." So we modified the floor. We cut it back to two 600-seat theaters. Later, when it was completed, the consultant returned, and when he saw the 600-seat theaters, he said, "Wow, this is cool; you should have built all four of them."

We wanted some other unique things in our theaters. We wanted wide aisles. We wanted no sticky floors I hate sticky floors. I've hated them since I was a kid. We do something that is financially insane: We go into every theater after every movie and clean the floor. We vacuum the popcorn, mop the floors, and pick up items for the lost and found, so when people arrive for the next movie, the theater is completely clean. We also put a 70mm screen in the complex, which was the only one in Utah at the time. We have since created a reserved seating system, which has been a big hit with our patrons.

We had a lot of fun with this project. We built the center food court area to look like Salt Lake City circa 1877. We went to the Utah Historical Society to look at photos of what Salt Lake looked like in that era. We studied all the details, right down to the hand railings and the tables and the facades on the fronts of the stores. The expense went off the charts—a $7 to $10 million difference. We did it just 'cuz. We didn't have the restraints that traditional theaters have.

We put a video game room in the theater complex and offered a lot of food that isn't available at traditional theaters—pizza, fish and chips, a deli, an ice cream parlor, a hamburger stand. And we designed it so people can take the food into the theaters on a tray that fits into the cup holders. Most theaters won't risk the mess and potential damage to the seats. In the area around the theater, we built four restaurants as well.

Anyway, all we had to figure out was the minor detail of procuring movies. We started calling around and got educated, and everything fell into place. Jeff Goldstein, the head of Warner Brothers, said it was the finest movie complex in America. That was a huge accolade.

CHAPTER 23

PETER, NATASHA, AND THE AMERICAN DREAM

P eter and Natasha Serdiukov were both teachers in Russia during the Cold War—he was a professor of languages, she of physics. As Russia began to break up, the country became more interested in a market economy. Utah Valley State College, as it was called then, was putting on a seminar in "managing a market economy," and the Russians came to town to learn. One of the guest speakers canceled at the last minute, and I was asked to fill in. Later the Russians came to my Chevrolet store to learn about how a dealership was run, and they brought a translator with them—Peter.

He was 5-foot-6, 120 pounds, with a spirit as big as all outdoors. We had a good session about how to start and grow an American business. They had taken a group of 42 of these Russian visitors to a Footlocker store a day earlier as part of their training, and after a half hour none of them had made a purchase. Finally, they were asked why they hadn't bought anything. They asked, "How do you

203

choose?" They had never been in a situation like that. In Russia, commodities like shoes were so rare that you just bought the size that was the closest fit. All those choices blew their minds. When I heard about it, I gave them each $100 and took them to a Fanzz store to buy what they wanted.

We also took them to a grocery store. I went in ahead of them because I had an idea of what was going to happen. They barely got inside the store when they stopped dead in their tracks. They couldn't believe what they were seeing. They were in shock and talking in rapid-fire Russian. That night four of them left the hotel and walked down to the same grocery store to make sure no one had fixed it up just for them.

I tell the story of Peter and Natasha for many reasons, but primarily because it illustrates the greatness of America and what it can offer people in so many different ways—the advantages of the free enterprise system; religious freedom; the superiority of our education system and our health care. These Russians discovered all these things in this country, things they could not have found anywhere else.

Peter and I developed a friendship. He had been sent to the United States—BYU, actually—as part of an exchange program for the government. One day I took him for a ride, and as we headed toward Emigration Canyon, Peter asked me to turn into the park at This Is the Place Monument. We walked around the park, and I pointed out the image of my great-great-great-grandfather Jesse C. Little, whose likeness was reproduced in bas relief on the monument. He was one of the early Mormon pioneers.

Peter turned north and looked out at the grassy fields waving in the wind and began to talk. "From the time I was a little boy I have had a recurring dream. I was seeing a place, but I didn't know where it was. I came here one day and saw the green trees and shrubs— we don't have greens like that in Russia—and I heard the song of a bird. I found out it was a meadowlark, which we don't have in

Russia—and I knew when I turned west I would see the lake, and I turned west and there it was. In my dream I had always wondered what was the scar on the mountain, and I knew if I looked south I would see it [the Kennecott mine]."

Peter eventually joined the Church, and I was his escort as he went through the LDS temple and was happy to be part of that. (Natasha, his wife, is a true Christian, but she didn't join the Church.)

Quite suddenly, Peter decided to return to Russia and told me so one day. I was shocked. He explained that his country needed him—inflation was 3,000 percent. He was willing to return because he knew America had something better, and he wanted his people to have it. He had been gone for a year and a half when I received a call from him one day.

"I need to talk to you about Natasha," he began. "She has breast cancer. We went to the hospital and they said she could have surgery, but we would have to bring our own equipment and medical supplies because they have none. Natasha couldn't get the equipment, so I turned to herbal medicine. It's not working, she's getting sicker. She's in late Stage 1 or early Stage 2." (There are four stages in cancer, the fourth stage being the worst.)

I believe Natasha was a victim of the Chernobyl disaster in 1986, the worst nuclear power plant disaster in history, one that resulted in the release of radioactivity. Natasha had lived just 50 kilometers downwind from the plant when it exploded, producing 400 times more radioactive fallout than the atomic bomb that was dropped on Hiroshima in World War II.

"What can I do?" I asked.

"I don't know," he said, but clearly he was reaching out to me for an answer. "We can't get her out of Russia because of visa problems."

I thought about it for two days. I knew nothing about cancer. I got in one of my modes, and I thought, *This is nonsense, she's coming.* I called Peter and said, "You've got to come now."

"I have no money and no visa," he said.

"Are you willing to come if I get it handled?"

"Yes."

I called Senator Orrin Hatch and told him I needed a visa, and then I went to Dr. Russ Shields and asked him, "Who's the best oncologist you know?"

"There's a guy at the university, but he's taking patients two to three years out. And he's really arrogant."

I called that doctor's secretary and explained the situation. He did call me back that same day, and I told him the story. The first words out of his mouth were, "How quickly can you get her here?"

"Maybe within a couple of days."

Well, Senator Hatch came through like a champ. Natasha got her visa and was on the plane within 48 hours. I went with them to the doctor's office, and three and a half hours later her evaluation was finished. The doctor informed her that she was in Stage 4, which basically means "go home and die." The doctor assembled a team of four top doctors that he supervised. They did a mastectomy and reconstructive surgery, followed by outpatient treatment for four months. I put her up in one of my condos, and people from my ward took turns taking her to the doctor.

That was a dozen years ago, and Natasha is still alive. One night Gail and I went to dinner with her and Peter. When dinner was finished, Natasha reached across the table and took Gail's hand and then took my hand and said, "Thank you for life." I don't know if I've ever had anything as profound said to me as that simple sentence. She's alive and doing well.

POSTSCRIPT

I included this story in the book because it illustrates many things about Larry—his ability and willingness to "build bridges" or make *things happen; his penchant for "developing relationships," as he always called it; and, finally, the advantages and privileges of life in the United States, which was the reason Larry often related the story. Larry paid Natasha's medical bills, which totaled more than $300,000. The Serdiukovs eventually settled in California and have stayed in touch with the Millers over the years. The day before Larry died, they flew to Salt Lake City to say good-bye to their friend. This is an excerpt of one of their letters to the Millers, written shortly after they had returned to Ukraine, leaving their son Vova in America to attend the University of Utah:*

"Dear Larry and Gail:

"We arrived safely in Kiev and immediately got to work in our universities. The situation in education has deteriorated further—now we have to increase the teachers' workload (without additional pay and payment of long overdue salaries) and at the same time laying off a great number of highly qualified faculty. . . . We certainly miss Vova. . . . We are happy for him to be in Salt Lake City, nevertheless. It is better for him, particularly in view of the current situation in Ukraine. As Vova left, we were able to move from our dining room where we had to sleep almost all of our married life on a folding sofa, to his room, which became our bedroom in the 29th year of our betrothal. We even bought our first double bed and enjoy the liberty of not unfolding the sofa and bed clothing and moving some furniture each night and doing the reverse every morning. And again, as everything else in our life now, it became possible thanks to you, our dear friends. We talk of you and pray for you every blessed day. . . . God bless you and all your family and all of America."

CHAPTER 24

PASSING ALONG AMERICA'S HERITAGE

I could not have accomplished what I have if not for the free-doms and the free-enterprise system that exist in America. Where else could a man from working-class roots have a chance to do the things I've been able to do through my own hard work and effort? I have had the freedom to live the American Dream.

In the entrepreneurial class I taught with Keith Hunt at BYU, one of our recurring themes was the connection between freedom and free enterprise, a principle that is under assault these days.

We must preserve these freedoms. Freedom to live your life the way you want to. Freedom to earn as much as you want. Freedom to do whatever you want with your earnings. Freedom to benefit the lives of others by providing employment, goods, and services. Freedom to live according to the values and beliefs you cherish as true.

Ronald Reagan once said: "It has been said that history is the patter of silken slippers descending the stairs and the thunder of hobnail boots coming up. Back through the years we have seen people fleeing the thunder of those boots to seek refuge in this land. Now too many of them have seen the signs, signs that were ignored in their homeland before the end came, appearing here. They wonder if they will have to flee again. But they know there is no place to run to. Will we, before it is too late, use the vitality and the magic of the marketplace to save this way of life, or will we one day face our children, and our children's children, when they ask us where we were and what we were doing on the day that freedom was lost?" (from an address given November 10, 1977, at Hillsdale College; see http://www.hillsdale.edu/news/imprimis/archive/issue.asp?year=1978&month=01).

It is important that we educate people about our heritage and our freedoms, and I have striven to do this, whether teaching at BYU, teaching my employees, or providing an educational program for high school teachers.

In our entrepreneurial class, Keith and I urged businessmen to protect free enterprise and to understand the system and why it was set up the way it was. It's more involved than running a business. You have to be involved in the health of the country and community and the things the government does that affect you as a businessman. You have to protect the freedoms you have. You can't assume they're always going to be there. You have to be aware of what it takes to live in a free country and preserve it.

Today people believe *profit* is a dirty word, that it means you are taking advantage of people. Well, you can't run a business without a profit. It's important to understand what's involved in the business world and capitalism. Everyone does not have equal material possessions—nowhere is that guaranteed—but they do have equal opportunity, which *is* guaranteed. Otherwise, you have socialism, and that will be the downfall of the small businessman. Everyone has a

209

right to earn a living and earn as much as he or she can with hard work and initiative.

I am profoundly grateful for and indebted to America for nurturing this wonderful life I have and for the opportunities we all have. I am grateful for the Founding Fathers and for our pioneer heritage in Utah. My ancestors came across the plains and settled here.

For years Gail urged me to take some time off from work to attend Education Week at BYU with her. I finally agreed, and we attended a class about the American Constitution. The class rekindled my deep feelings about America and free enterprise and freedom in general. The speaker referred to a book called *Miracle at Philadelphia* by Catherine Drinker Bowen. It became one of my favorite books. I refer to it frequently while speaking to my employees and in the many speeches I give each year. My renewed interest in our country led me to read other books on America's origins, including *1776* and *John Adams*, both by David McCullough, the Pulitzer prize-winning historian. He made John Adams and history come alive for me. John Adams is one of my heroes. His story is my story.

Twice each year we have a managers' meeting in our company in which I discuss the business and my feelings about business in general, the state of the economy, and our duties as businessmen to protect the free-enterprise system. I like to do something extra for my general managers' meeting in the fall. We hold a retreat somewhere special for them and their spouses. A couple of years ago we went to Boston, the seat of the Revolution, to get a firsthand look at American history as well as discuss the business. I gave all of our managers a copy of McCullough's *1776* and told them to read it before we went to Boston. As a special surprise, I made a few phone calls and managed to track down McCullough himself. I invited him to be our keynote speaker, at a cost of $40,000, which should tell you how much I respect McCullough and how important I think it is that we understand our history and our freedoms. David spoke for an hour about patriotism and history and signed everybody's books. Afterward, he took Gail and me to lunch and to an art museum and finally to dinner. We talked nonstop the entire time about patriotism and free enterprise and helping people to learn history. From this, a friendship grew. We really hit it off. He was another kindred spirit. We had a lot in common. We felt the same way about many things. He is a very inquisitive man, which I suppose is natural for a historian. He peppers you with questions—he just wants to know everything.

We wrote letters back and forth—like me, he is a letter writer. David told me that the reason he was able to do the research for his books was because John and Abigail wrote letters to each other, and he was able to study them. Who writes letters today, and where is our history going to be preserved? It's all e-mail now. Like me, David doesn't use a computer. He writes his books on an old Remington typewriter.

Recently, David came to Utah to speak to a group of students at Ogden High School. He was our houseguest for two nights while he was in town, which was way cool. While he was here, I took him on a tour of Temple Square, the Conference Center, and the Tabernacle. I also arranged for him to meet with President Gordon B. Hinckley, the President of The Church of Jesus Christ of Latter-day Saints at the time, but I didn't tell David about it until we arrived at President Hinckley's office. During the ride over to Temple Square, we discussed education. David was saddened that many students were no longer choosing a liberal arts education and that history was no longer required for graduation from many universities and colleges. Well, as fate would have it, President Hinckley and David began talking about their educations. President Hinckley had earned a degree from the University of Utah and David had studied at Yale. David asked his host what he had studied, and when President Hinckley replied that he had studied liberal arts, David stretched his hand across the table and said, "Put 'er there, pal!" President Hinckley eventually presented David with a leather-bound copy of the Book of Mormon, and he also brought out his copy of *1776*. They each signed the other's book—signatures only, with no salutations, because true collectors know a book is worth more with only a signature and nothing more.

David and I both believe it is important to educate people about our heritage. Otherwise, many of the freedoms we have had in America are going to be lost to future generations, and they won't even know what they've lost. In some places, American history isn't even a required class anymore—that's a tragedy. With all this in mind, David told me about a program in his home state of Maine that took teachers to historical sites—the idea being that if you can get the teachers to experience history firsthand, they will become more knowledgeable and more passionate about the subject, and this will trickle down to the students. I took this idea with me back to Utah and grew it bigger. We call it our "Teach the Teacher" program, or the Education Project.

We started the program in the summer of 2007, and it has been growing since then. In the summer of 2008, we sent out three groups: one focused on Utah and Indian history in southern Utah, one on westward migration, and one on colonial America and the Civil War in the Washington, D.C., area—Monticello, the White House, the Capitol, Philadelphia, Gettysburg, Yorktown, and so on. We sponsor 30 teachers in each group, and we had more than 300 teachers apply. Each tour lasts a week. We pay per diem and travel and lodging expenses. It's a rigorous program. They're up at 6:00, on the bus by 7:30, and don't return to the hotel until evening, and then they meet in a conference room and discuss what they learned and how they're going to teach it. They take photos and create lesson plans. It seems to have had an impact. We have a book of letters from grateful teachers. Many of them say they have always taught history out of a book; now they've seen it firsthand and they are much more passionate about teaching.

POSTSCRIPT

Although he wouldn't live to see the event, Larry also spent $50,000 to have McCullough speak to the University of Utah's commencement exercises in the spring of 2009. "Larry did it because the U does not (or cannot) pay commencement speakers," says Gail, "and he felt it was worth paying for it if David would do some other speaking for him, as well." While he was in Salt Lake City, McCullough went to the new Church History Library and spoke to the historians who were working on the Joseph Smith Papers, and addressed an LHM employees' luncheon at the arena. On Saturday afternoon, he spoke to a large group of teachers as part of Larry's Teach the Teacher program—the event was held in the Tabernacle to accommodate the large gathering. On Sunday morning, McCullough returned to the Tabernacle to listen to the Mormon Tabernacle Choir's weekly radio broadcast of Music and the Spoken Word. *After the choir finished the broadcast and signed off the air, they sang "The Battle Hymn of the Republic" especially for David.*

"He said it was the most moving performance he had ever heard," says Gail.

Gail notes that Larry had strong feelings about freedom and free enterprise. "He would be horrified by what's happening today in government," she says. "He frequently warned in his management meetings about the need to protect freedom. He loved the Founding Fathers, those who built the foundation of this country. He learned a lot about leadership from the Founding Fathers and the process they went through to author our country's foundational documents—the basic principles that guided them. He saw a lot of himself in John Adams—his attitude, his way of life, his thought processes, the things he was passionate about, his hard work and sacrifices."

PART V

LESSONS LEARNED ALONG THE WAY

CHAPTER 25

FATHERHOOD AND REGRETS

S purred by the epiphany I had as a young man, I worked nearly every waking hour. Initially, it was fear that drove me to work those 90 hours a week for 20 years—this overwhelming feeling of being responsible for the needs of my wife and children and not having a college degree to fall back on. My solution was my ability to out-work everyone else. I worked when other people were home watching TV or sleeping or eating breakfast. I was getting the next day's work done a day early. I was sleeping about six hours a night.

It made me successful.

It made me a failure, too.

I missed most of my children's youth. I missed ball games and science fairs and back-to-school nights. I missed the first day of kindergarten and playing catch in the yard. I missed dinner at home with my wife and kids. Gail had to do everything. She was basically a single parent with our five children—Greg, Roger, Karen, Stephen, and Bryan.

I didn't take any time off. I worked all the time. I worked six days a week, and on the seventh day—Sunday—I played softball. As Gail likes to say, I didn't go to my kids' ball games; they came to mine.

Even when I was at home, I wasn't really there. Greg, our oldest child, says he learned that when the door to my home office was shut, you didn't open it, and if it was ajar you entered at your own peril. Gail says that if there was a family problem I would get really angry and make it worse, so she just didn't tell me about it unless it got so bad that she had no choice. By the time a problem reached me, it had already spiraled out of control, and I would step in and overreact. I was the bad cop to Gail's good cop.

The kids were in bed when I got home from work. The only time I saw them was at church on Sunday or at my softball games. Gail says we raised our children at the ballpark. It was part of her effort to put the kids and me together. When they were young, Gail would bring them to the dealership in the evening and we'd go to dinner, and then afterward they'd drop me off at work again. When the kids were about 12, I started to give them jobs at the dealership, which was another way for them to at least be around me. But as they got older, they resisted the trips to work and softball and became angry.

Gail had to create ways for me and her to be together, as well. She would find something to do at the office, for instance, such as posting parts in the evening. When we dated, we were inseparable; once we married, we hardly saw each other. When I came home at night, I would soak in the tub to unwind, and she would sit on the floor in the bathroom and listen to me talk and talk and talk. Or we'd go on a late-night walk, which was another way for me to unwind and be with Gail. I would have Gail walk with me to the car in the morning to see me off to work. These were our dates.

The great irony of my life is that I originally began working those long hours to benefit my wife and kids, but wound up hurting them. The children suffered without a father figure in the home. Most of them were strong-willed and angry; some caused trouble and did poorly in school. Four of our five children did not graduate in the traditional way. Greg was kicked out of one high school late in his senior year and had to graduate from another. Roger married in February of his senior year and graduated from Alta High School's adult program. He divorced twice. Bryan wound up at Valley High, which is for nontraditional students, and eventually graduated from Granite High with college credits from Salt Lake Community College doing concurrent enrollment. Karen didn't graduate—she got a GED. She had a baby at age 15, and she was in and out of the house. I remember Greg standing at the bottom of the stairs once shouting at me, "I hate the car business! I'll do anything but the car business." The kids all said things like that, but all four boys are now in the car business, and Karen worked for the company in various capacities for a while before deciding to be a stay-at-home mom with her twins.

It's remarkable that Gail was able and willing to handle all this. She didn't like it, and it did create serious stress in our marriage. She needed more parenting partnership. I look at it now and wonder, *What was I thinking?* After one of these belated realizations, I asked Gail, "Why didn't you tell me?" She said, "I did; you weren't listening." She tried many times to get me to slow down, to be home more, but after a while she decided two things: It made no difference, and it was actually easier not to have me home. I was so wound up all the time that I was difficult to be around. Gail says that when I *was* home it was like I was running another business (with the family). One day she scolded me, "I'm not one of your employees."

The only thing I can conclude—and I have given this much thought—is that I didn't know how to be a father. As I achieved success in my career, I felt safe and confident in that environment. I knew what I was doing. As a husband and father, I viewed myself much more as a breadwinner than as an emotional leader. As long as I provided for my family financially, I fulfilled my role, or so I thought. I didn't realize, until my late 40s, that not only did my kids and wife have an emotional need for a father and husband, but it was my responsibility. I had grown up in a family in which we didn't talk about emotions or feelings; we talked about work and achievement. I didn't have much interaction with my father. He was a breadwinner and that was pretty much it. For me, things got worse as I got older. It was a case of moving to higher planes (as the world sees it), and of those worldly things demanding more time, and of me allowing myself to cater to those demands. I was repeating my father's life, the life that had left me emotionally wanting.

Part of the problem was that I was not a good delegator in my professional life. Even when I was overseeing 80 businesses and employing 7,000 people, I tended to get wrapped up in the details that should have been delegated to employees. Earlier I mentioned how involved I was in determining the type of trees that would be planted in front of the Delta Center. That was 100 hours' worth of work. I look back at that now and think, boy, that was dumb! I was employing people who were paid to do that kind of thing—I was employing horticulturists!—and I wasn't even using them. If you ask someone who works for me to tell you how involved I was in details, they'll roll their eyes.

It got to be too much as we grew. I tried to hire someone to run the day-to-day operations in 1993, but he was the wrong guy for the job. In 1997, I tried again. I hired Richard Nelson to run the automotive side and Denny Haslam to run the sports and entertainment side, and that relieved me of a lot of the detail work.

So I am often asked these questions: Would I do it differently if I had it to do all over again? And, if so, would I have been as successful if I had worked fewer hours and spent more time with my family?

If there is one thing I'd do differently—only one—it's this: I would have been there for the Little League games and the scraped knees and the back-to-school nights. Would we have accomplished as much? There's no way to know. Fifteen years ago I would have said no. Today I think I would say I probably could still do it. Instead of working 90-hour weeks and missing all that stuff, I'd work a more balanced schedule, 55 or 60 hours, and the important things would still get done. Perhaps I wouldn't have accomplished as much back then with fewer hours, but today I could because I know how to delegate.

If I had to choose between working long hours and being closer to family, I would choose the latter. That has come to mean more to me now, but, unfortunately, I didn't see it until after my kids were grown and gone. I am able to sit back and enjoy my grandkids more than I did my own kids.

Gail tells me I am too hard on myself. I don't think so, but I will say that everything is a tradeoff. It could be argued that many people benefited from the sacrifices I made to work those long hours. By building up a business, I was able to provide quality jobs for thousands of people and their families. Job security and a good wage produce better, healthier families, which in turn raise better people. We try to provide a wage that allows one parent to stay home with the children, which I believe is better for the family.

Our success also enabled us to create a family foundation that has helped a lot of people through private and public philanthropy and through our company scholarship program for our employees' children. We could not have done these things if we hadn't grown into a billion-dollar business empire, and that might not have happened if I hadn't worked all those hours.

Despite my shortcomings as a father, I have been fortunate in my family life. I have good relationships with all five children. There could have been permanent damage, but the kids are doing well. Things are better than ever. We work hard on this. The kids feel like they can speak up and express their feelings now. They probably were angry along the way, but we've worked hard on communicating, so I don't think it's something constantly gnawing at them. My children and my 23 grandchildren and my one great-grandchild are doing well. They live in the area, so we can and do see them often. We meet one Sunday a month to hold a family home evening and to celebrate birthdays for that month. The entire extended family takes vacations together each year. Every Friday Gail and I meet with our sons—Greg, Bryan, Roger, and Steve, all of whom have management positions in the company—in our home to discuss the business and pass along my business methods and philosophy. This has been a gratifying experience for me. Greg will tell you that he learned a lot from me—he learned what he should do and what he shouldn't do. He's a very good, attentive father who makes time for his family.

The weekly meetings with my boys have been an opportunity to make up for the lost time in an intensive, compressed way. I was hard on my children, I suppose. I never coached my kids' Little League teams. Gail will tell you that maybe part of this was that I didn't want to give my kids preferential treatment. I was always sensitive to that. This was the case even when it came to our business. I had people coming to me in our company telling me, "Your sons are ready for this position or that position; you are holding them back." I just didn't want people to think the boys were getting something they hadn't earned. In the end, I got to teach and interact with them in a very focused way.

Greg, of course, is CEO of The Miller Group. Steve is the company's used car manager, and he has made a major difference in the organization—a $5-million-a-year difference. Roger is our IT guy. He's trying to get automotive and sports and entertainment on the same page as much as we can, but automotive has a lot of different accounting needs. Bryan works at the track in promotional sales. The plan is to get him ready to be general manager of the track someday. He thinks and talks a lot about being a teacher or artist. He likes teaching, and for a while he worked as a volunteer writing tutor at Salt Lake Community College. He's the one most likely to go off in another direction. He has the artist's mentality of being all over the place like me. Karen is 35 now and raises horses, chickens, dogs, and cats on 22 acres. My children are all doing well, which is a source of comfort to me.

A great irony occurred in my life. I was granted a second chance at parenthood, in a way. When I was in my mid-40s, our daughter had a baby and was unable to care for him at the time. Zane came to live with us. We considered it temporary. We thought that when our daughter matured, she would reclaim her baby. After Karen gave birth to the baby she lived with us for three years, and then when she left home we kept Zane and cared for him. Gail home-schooled Zane for all four years of high school. I confess that at first I resented the intrusion on our middle-age years when we should have been freed of child-care responsibilities (perhaps this was karma, given my absence during my own children's formative years).

Then something happened: He started to grow on me. By the time Zane was four, I was sure we'd passed the point for his mother to reclaim and raise him, which was good because I didn't want him to leave. Besides those feelings, I realized that here was a second chance life doesn't always give you. Raising Zane, I saw what I had missed with our own children. For me, it was almost like having a first child. When Zane was a baby, I'd run to Gail and say, "Did you see what the baby just did? How come our kids didn't do that?" She would calmly reply, "They did; you missed it." I have really enjoyed Zane. We raised him as our son—he calls Gail and me "Mom" and "Dad."

I try to pass these painful lessons to others who might be tempted by the allure of professional success. Mine is a cautionary tale. For years I taught a weekly three-hour entrepreneurial class for MBA students at BYU. Near the end of each semester Gail was invited to speak with me to the students and their spouses about the trappings of the business world. I tell the students that success, as the world defines it, is very intoxicating. I tell them they should understand that it's important to be home with their families and be more than breadwinners.

When we agreed to do this class, Gail and I decided there would be no value in it if we didn't tell them the truth, and so Gail was brutally honest. I mean brutal. She talked about how much I was gone and how hard it was. Gail says these lectures became therapy for her and for our marriage, and I agree. She says she found a safe place in front of the class to let it all out, and I had to listen. Then we would talk about it on the way home. I began to take notes in class when she spoke. Gail says the first time she did it, she was really angry afterward, because she was reliving the emotions and because she had just laid her soul bare in front of a roomful of strangers. Each time, Gail got a little braver in what she told the class. It seems every time she talked she remembered something else she hadn't thought of previously. She never used notes; she just talked from the heart.

It really helped our marriage, and her message left its mark on the students. In the class evaluations at the end of each semester, she always received the highest marks of all our guest lecturers. The students wrote about how much she helped them with her presentation and made them aware of things they hadn't considered. I still get comments about it from people who were in the class years ago.

So I missed all those years with my family, and I can't have them back. In some ways, it's so simple. All you've got to do is be there. You have to listen and you have to understand what's going on at home.

Frank Layden (coach of the Utah Jazz), Larry, President Gordon B. Hinckley, Wendell Ashton, Sam Battistone (former owner, Utah Jazz), and Dave Checketts (general manager, Utah Jazz) shortly after Larry purchased the team.

Larry waves to an appreciative crowd at the game the night it is announced he is the new owner of the Utah Jazz, April 11, 1985.

The bankers who made it all possible observe as papers are signed by Gail, Larry, and Sam Battistone to make the sale of the team official. Dave Checketts also looks on.

Co-owners of the Utah Jazz in 1985: Sam and Nan Battistone with Gail and Larry Miller.

Salt Lake Mayor Deedee Corradini, Larry, Gail, and NBA Commissioner David Stern enjoy a few moments together before the All-Star game in Salt Lake City, Utah.

Commissioner Stern talks basketball with Larry and Gail at the Delta Center in Salt Lake.

Karl Malone and Larry enjoyed a "father-son" relationship.

Legendary Utah Jazz point guard John Stockton had a very special relationship with Larry.

Larry assesses the situation at a game, with grandson Zane following in his footsteps.

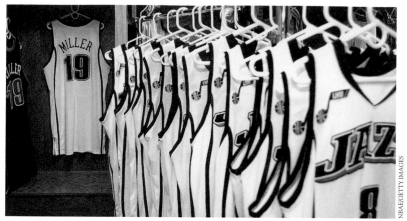

Larry was an unusual owner in that he had his own uniform and locker and was a regular both in the locker room and on the floor with the team during warm-ups before each game.

Larry had a very good relationship with many of the referees . . .

And with the team members.

Frank Layden, Utah Jazz center
Mark Eaton, and Larry Miller.

Larry and Darrell Griffith during the
retirement of Darrell's number.

Sharing a bit of fun with Kyle Korver
and assistant coach Tyrone Corbin.

The Utah Jazz coaching staff.

Larry respected the talent of the great players. Michael Jordan shares a moment with Larry on the court before the game at the Delta Center.

Larry shows off his moves to Stockton and Malone during the shooting of a commercial.

Retro night at the Jazz game. Larry poses with Denny Haslam, COO of the Sports and Entertainment division of the Larry H. Miller Companies.

Ninoos Benjamin (standing, right) and other representatives from the bank look on as Larry and Gail sign the papers to finance the building of the new arena.

Dignitaries join in the groundbreaking ceremony for the arena.

Larry visits the arena construction site in the beloved Falcon convertible.

The arena was a massive undertaking—built on time, on budget, in less than 16 months, in time for the opening game in the fall of 1991.

Sam Battistone, Larry Miller, and NBA Commissioner David Stern inspect the progress on the arena.

On the way to the arena, the truck carrying the new floor had a mishap and the floor was destroyed, so the arena had to open with a temporary floor while a new one was being built.

Aerial view of the nearly completed arena.

Larry outside the finished arena. Larry planted daffodils
and roses for Gail because they are her favorite flowers.

VIP seating for the arena dedication, the culmination of an enormous effort.

Larry and Fred Rollins from Delta Airlines exchanging gifts of appreciation at the naming ceremony of the Delta Center.

Gail and Larry cut the ribbon for the grand opening of the arena.

"If you build it, they will come." Larry welcomes the crowds on opening day.

Steve Creamer of Energy Solutions and Larry announce the renaming of the Delta Center to Energy Solutions Arena on November 20, 2006.

Senator Orrin Hatch is a big Jazz fan. He and Larry share a few moments together during a Jazz game.

Larry always stood with the team during the National Anthem
and enjoyed the "pure" renditions the most.

Larry and Gail attended almost all the games and enjoyed taking
friends with them to share the experience.

POSTSCRIPT

A few weeks after Larry passed away, I met with Gail in her home. Once we were seated, I asked her how she was doing. With trademark Miller candor and tears, she said, "I don't want to sound cold. I've been waiting for him my whole life. It's not that different now." She began to cry as she added, "The only time we were really together was when he got sick and could no longer go to work. The relationship that never failed was the business connection. He always shared what happened to him in business. So we had time together, but it was one-sided. I listened. I was his sounding board.

"In reality, we didn't have many common interests. I don't like race cars, and I hated to go to business things where people put on airs—all those people who thought they were something and thought we were something. I began to resent going to Jazz games—that's 41 games a year. If I talked to one of our guests, Larry would ask why I wasn't watching the game. I wanted to stay home sometimes, but Larry felt that people would wonder what was wrong between us. So I always went to the games. It was another way to be together. We had dinner upstairs in the arena before the game, and that turned out to be a great thing. We'd always invite guests. It was the only real socializing we did; the rest was obligatory."

CHAPTER 26

WYOMING GAS

I t was Labor Day 1966, and Gail and I and our four-month-old baby, Greg, were driving across the high plains of southern Wyoming late at night. We had gone for the weekend to Colorado Springs to watch a regional softball tournament—I was just emerging as an open-class softball pitcher and wanted to learn what level of expertise I had to attain to compete at that level. Now we were returning to Salt Lake City so I could report for work the next morning. I could see the glow of Rock Springs on the horizon of the night sky when suddenly the car began to falter. My stomach dropped. I was out of gas. It was 3:00 A.M.

I thought I would be able to push the car up the slight incline that lay in front of us and then coast down the other side to Rock Springs, but as I began to push the car, the "slight" incline proved to be longer and more formidable than I had believed. My legs and lungs burning, I quickly realized that I would be unable to push the car any farther.

I didn't want to leave Gail and our baby alone on the dark freeway while I went to get gas, so I decided to flag down the next car for help. A feeling of dread came over me as I contemplated the vulnerability of my little family out there in the middle of the night. I was greatly relieved when a car soon approached and pulled off the road in front of us, backing up until he was 20 feet from my car. A man climbed out of his white El Camino, and we walked toward one another, meeting about halfway between our cars. We chatted briefly. I learned that he was a repairman on the oil-drilling rigs of southern Wyoming. The back of his car was filled with tools—and a pair of 30-gallon gas tanks, complete with a hand pump. He pumped several gallons of gas into the fuel tank of my Ford Falcon and then added a teaspoon of fuel to prime the carburetor. He looked on while I tried the ignition and the car started immediately.

I was overwhelmed with a feeling of relief and gratitude to this stranger for his kindness. I offered to pay for the gas. He said he was happy to help and refused payment. We shook hands as I repeated my thanks. He opened the door of his car and was nearly seated when he seemed to remember something. He got back out of his car and approached me again. He said he had changed his mind; he wanted payment for the gas, but not in the way I would expect. The next time I saw someone stranded on the side of the road, he said, he wanted me to stop and assist them. I readily and eagerly agreed to his request. I would "pay it forward," as we say now.

I have remembered his words many times over the years. It has been more than 40 years since that night on the side of the road, and I can still see the man's face and hear his request. I have come to realize that each of us during our lives "runs out of gas," either figuratively or literally. Each of us has the opportunity to be the giver and receiver of help in some way. I have tried to remember that stranger's example throughout my life and to keep my promise to him.

POSTSCRIPT

The Millers didn't have much in 1966. During the trip to Wyoming, unable to afford a hotel, the three of them slept in their car for two nights, once at a rest stop and once in the parking lot of the softball complex. But in the fall of '66, just a few months after they were helped by the stranger on the Wyoming freeway, Larry received a phone call one night from an acquaintance. After Larry hung up the phone, he told Gail that the caller had asked if he could borrow $300. "That was all we had in our savings account," recalls Gail. Larry asked her to deliver a check for that amount to the man that night.

On another occasion, Larry and Gail were walking in downtown Salt Lake when they were stopped by a man on the sidewalk. He said he knew Larry, although Larry didn't remember him, and that he needed to borrow $250. Larry pulled the money out of his wallet and gave the cash to the man.

Somehow word reached Miller that one of his new employees—who worked in one of his parts departments—had recently married and couldn't afford a refrigerator. Miller summoned the man to his office and told him, "Come with me to Costco." Once inside the store he told the employee, "Pick out a refrigerator."

There was a hamburger restaurant in downtown Salt Lake City, Snappy Service Lunch, where Larry liked to eat. One day he learned that it was going out of business—the lease was up and the property had been sold—and Morris Daras, the restaurant's owner and proprietor, had no job prospects. He had started working there as a fry cook in 1957 and then bought the place in 1969. Larry visited Morris, whom he had known since he was a teenager. "I have a plan for you," he told Morris. That plan was to move Morrie's business to Jordan Commons, Miller's theater/restaurant complex in Sandy,

Utah. "We'll set you up near the theater, and you'll never be out of work again," he said. And that's what happened.

"He did stuff like that all the time," says Gail. "He was looking for things to do."

Near the end of his life, while he was still in the hospital, Miller heard of a patient who was about to lose a job and needed to travel to California for personal reasons. Larry told Gail, "Write a check for $7,000."

A hospital aide who was fighting her own battle with cancer was especially patient and kind to Larry. When he learned that she needed a car, he told her to go pick out a car from his lot, and he would help her with the price.

"I could tell you all kinds of those stories," says Gail.

Years ago he paid doctor bills and a car debt for a retired high school teacher who was having health and financial difficulties.

He paid off mortgages and car debts and medical bills for too many people to count.

Part of his largesse sprang from his lifelong empathy for the underdog. "He was always that way, even as a boy," says Gail. "He was always for the underdog. When he was in third grade, there was a kid in his class who wasn't popular or athletic, and the other kids picked on him. One day, after a heavy snowstorm, this kid found himself surrounded by a dozen kids who were throwing snowballs at him. He was defenseless. Larry ran up to the scene and began pummeling the bullies with snowballs until they stopped."

Larry simply found pleasure in helping people. "It's just satisfying to help," he liked to say. During winter storms, he and Zane liked to climb into their Land Cruiser and drive the roads looking for people to pull out of the snow. They'd hook up their tow rope and pull a vehicle out of a ditch or snowbank and then search for someone else, sometimes helping a dozen in a night.

Sometimes all Larry gave someone was his time. Someone would ask for advice about his business and they would spend hours talking about it. He made public speeches 265 times in one year—an average of five per week—after which he says he decided, "I can't give people that much of my life."

Larry and Gail spoke at the prison occasionally, and sometimes inmates asked Larry if he would hire them after they got out of prison. Yes, he would say, and then hand them his card. Several of them eventually called him and were hired.

Larry did little things that touched hearts. Gail grew up in a poor family of nine children. To help the family, Gail's mother hosted cooking parties representing a certain company because the hostess was promised a gift by that company. One of those gifts was a waterless cooking pot. She did much of her cooking in that pot, and it became known in the family as "the potato pot." When Gail's mother died, the only thing her children wanted from her estate was that pot—it had priceless sentimental value—but there was only one pot and nine children. Larry secretly took the pot to a specialist, who analyzed the composition of the metal and reproduced the pot with specially made molds.

"He didn't tell me anything about it," says Gail. "At Christmas, he said, 'Come out in the garage with me.' He had a box full of those pots. He gave one to each of my siblings for Christmas. They were absolutely delighted. I got calls from each of them the minute they opened the gift."

He provided financial assistance to numerous people who wanted to start businesses, ranging from motorcycle shops to fishing stores to finance institutions to car dealerships.

When two men in his LDS ward lost their jobs, Larry found jobs for them in his own company. A young, newly married man in Larry's neighborhood couldn't pay his mortgage. Larry told him he'd help him, but only if the man would help himself. Larry advanced him money and gave him a job, and when he still couldn't keep up with his mortgage payments Larry continued to advance him money.

When a man was unable to continue working on the Joseph Smith Papers because of financial problems, Larry paid his salary.

At Thanksgiving time, Larry bought thousands of turkeys for the food bank.

He gave substantial sums to an array of artists—sculptor Steve Neal, painter Al Rounds, and singer Michael Ballam, among others—because he believed in them.

He served on the governor's policy partnership board, which advised the governor on matters that needed his attention and on ways to streamline government, besides serving as a sounding board for his initiatives.

One of Miller's favorite stories—and everyone close to him will tell you this because they heard him talk about it—is the famous "starfish story." A woman sees a girl dancing along the beach tossing starfish into the ocean. The woman asks her why she is doing this. The girl explains that she is trying to save the starfish. The woman scoffs. "There are thousands of starfish washed up on the beach. How can you possibly make a difference?" The girl picks up another starfish and tosses it into the ocean, then tells the woman, "It made a difference to that one."

That was Larry, those close to him say. "Larry loved to save people," says Clark Whitworth. "We called them 'FOLs'—friends of Larry's. People knew that if they came to Larry he would fix things. People in our company looked askance. Some of these people who came to Larry for help were wolves in sheep's clothes. Larry was the good Samaritan. He had to fix it. He couldn't leave a problem alone. They'd say, 'Larry, I need your advice,' but what they really wanted was his money, and he knew it, but he wanted to fix things and solve problems. It's the 'starfish' story in action—you could tell him he wasn't going to save everyone, and he'd tell you, 'Yeah, but I'm going to save this one.' He didn't just recite this story; he believed it and lived it to his core. And if he made one starfish better, that was satisfying to him. But there were so many. He tried to teach them correct principles so they could be self-sufficient—he was teaching them how to fish. Larry knew how to fish so well and assumed others could learn too. He helped people whose finances were a disaster, and he could always see a way to help make things work. Through his eyes, he could always see how it could work, but the people he was helping weren't Larry Miller and couldn't do those things without help."

CHAPTER 27

MONEY

When Greg was five months old, Gail took him to the doctor because he was vomiting repeatedly. After a quick check, the doctor asked if Greg had fallen recently. She told him, yes, he had fallen off the bed. The doctor immediately placed Greg in the hospital for tests, suspecting a subdural hematoma. Greg wound up undergoing two operations, one on each side of his head, to remove blood clots. He recovered well, and thankfully there were no side effects except this one: We were left with a large debt. I had no medical insurance, but Gail did; however, we were stuck with $3,000 worth of medical bills, which was a huge sum for us in those days.

Our financial situation was already tight. I had been changing jobs frequently, either because I was looking for something better or because my employer reneged on our compensation agreement. When we moved to Colorado to take yet another job, we took our $3,000 debt with us and then added a mortage to our obligations with the purchase of a new house for $24,800. Gail, pregnant with our third child, quit her job at the telephone company in Utah, and we decided it was time for her to become a stay-at-home mother. This made our financial situation all the more tenuous.

We devised a plan to pay off the $3,000 in medical bills. We listed all of our bills on a sheet of paper, starting with the biggest debt and working down to the smallest, and each month we paid a certain amount toward each of them. As the smallest debts were paid off, that money would be applied to the next smallest debt the following month. It was slow progress.

I finally figured out a way to pay the balance of our debts. Someone brought an old Land Cruiser to the dealership, and I bought it for $800. In my spare time, I fixed up the vehicle and paid others to do some of the work as well. Eventually, I sold it for $2,500, which I used to pay off the balance of our debts. We were debt free. After that, Gail and I vowed never to go into personal debt again. We wanted to be in control of our own destiny. We didn't like being at someone's mercy. We didn't take out loans or use credit cards. If we didn't have the money for something we wanted to buy, we just didn't buy it. It was as simple as that.

To obtain financial independence, I decided that whenever I was given a raise in my salary, instead of increasing my standard of living, I saved it. The mistake many people make is that when they get pay increases they buy boats, fancy cars, bigger houses, designer clothes, or exotic vacations, so they never get ahead. They're earning more money, but they're increasing their expenses, so they merely maintain the same level of debt relative to their income. We didn't do that. When I was promoted from parts manager to general manager, for instance, I received a significant raise. We saved that money. When we had saved enough money, we invested it and opened savings accounts for our children, making monthly deposits for their education.

It wasn't because we didn't want things, but we wanted to build security more. Gail and I were uncomfortable with debt. We had always lived within our means. It's important that husbands and wives share the same philosophy about money because it can be such a source of contention. We were fortunate because we shared the same upbringing and outlook on money. As Gail says, if one of us had been different—if one of us had coveted worldly things or if Gail had been a wife who put pressure on me to have the latest things—we couldn't have done what we did. Our work ethic, our beliefs, and the way we viewed money were the same. We never bought anything on credit, and our priority was to pay off bills. We had both been self-sufficient as teenagers, even while we were dating. We felt capable of orchestrating our lives without help from our parents, so we never went to them for money. Gail babysat and cleaned houses. I had a paper route and worked other odd jobs as a teenager. I saved up money and bought a Schwinn three-speed bike, and we used that as our transportation for dates—we'd ride double. We had been working since we were 12 years old. Gail says we grew up together; she didn't get to travel and see the world and didn't need it. Those things were all to come, as it turned out.

When we got married, we continued to live frugally. On our honeymoon, we stayed in cheap hotels and bought our food at the grocery store and fixed sandwiches while we drove. We just didn't spend money. We didn't have a power mower for years. We owned one of those old-fashioned hand mowers with the twirling blades that was powered by sweat. We stayed in the same house—1,700-square feet, three bedrooms—for four and a half years, remaining there even after we had our fourth child. We didn't landscape for years because we couldn't afford it. We had no lawn. Our yard was dirt and weeds so tall that you couldn't see the kids when they were playing out there. We finally laid 10,000 square feet of sod, doing the work ourselves. A friend of mine who was a banker saw our small home and large family and took us to see houses. He showed us a $35,000 home; we considered that way over our heads. In reality, we could have afforded it, but it just didn't feel right to take on that kind of debt when we were so frugal. That would have been splurging for us. It didn't feel comfortable. Just because the bank says you qualify for a certain mortgage doesn't mean you should do it. We finally bought a bigger house when our fifth child was born.

Our one luxury was an annual family vacation, but even those were spartan events. We'd go four-wheeling and stay in Motel 6, all of us in one room, and eat fast food.

I advise people not to change their standard of living as their income increases. Protect the base. It's tattooed on my brain. I still won't spend $60 at a restaurant. We eat at restaurants that have good food but are cheap—$15 or so for a meal. Gail still shops at Costco and buys things on sale. It's just ingrained in her. If she buys something nice, it's the exception. I drive what most would consider a normal car. That's intentional—I don't want to convey ostentatiousness or attract attention. (Besides, I am a high risk for death threats, so I'm careful for that reason, too.)

It was never a temptation to change my standard of living. I don't need anything better than what I have. I don't buy fancy clothes, as everyone who has seen me can attest. I could afford Armani, but that wouldn't be me, and I wouldn't be comfortable. My "uniform" is a golf shirt, sneakers, and jeans or khakis. There's a story behind this. When I was managing five dealerships in Colorado, some of the guys asked me if they could dress casually because of the hot weather. I asked my boss if that would be all right, and he looked me right in the eye and said, "A white shirt and tie is as casual as we're going to get." I thought, *If I ever get on my own, I'm not going to impose that on myself.* You work better if you're comfortable. Well, my casual dress became my trademark with the media. If I ever wore a suit or a tie, people were wondering, *What's up with Larry?* Some of my employees have to dress up because they're out making business contacts, but I can get away with the casual look because of my persona.

My conservative nature has proven to be advantageous and has put me in a position to do some of the things I've done. One of my investments was a joint purchase of 48.8 acres of land near Littleton, Colorado. It was in the middle of nowhere at the time. But we could see that Denver was going to expand southward, and we figured land there would appreciate. Eventually, a dam was built out there, and then things started to develop, and we sold the land to a developer. When we returned to Utah, I had saved $88,000—which I used to buy my first car dealership. By saving that money, I was able to start my own business, and everything in my professional and entrepreneurial career began with that purchase.

Through the years, as my wealth grew beyond any of my wildest expectations and I could afford to buy things, I still spent money sparingly, with two notable exceptions—my Cobras and our current home. I have always been determined not to let money change me, and I hope I have achieved that. I have not wanted the accumulation of money to change my lifestyle or the way I treat others, or to cause me to lose perspective. For me, money was the means to an end, and that end is to help others.

Postscript

Larry Miller never did change, even though his bank account did. As Lee Benson wrote in the Deseret News, he was the kind of man you hoped you'd be if you had money. Miller was arguably the most famous and beloved man in Utah, but he never acted as if he knew it. Benson recalled a quote from Kipling when he wrote of Miller: "If you can talk with crowds and keep your virtue, Or walk with kings, nor lose the common touch."

That was Miller's nature, but he also went to some pains to ensure that money didn't change him. As I sat in the Miller house with Gail, she placed her late husband's wristwatch, wedding ring, and wallet on the table in front of me. "Notice anything about them?" she asked. The ring is a plain gold band—which he liked to tell people cost

$22—and the watch is a nondescript $100 Seiko with a worn leather wristband. He wore the same watch for years, changing only the band when it began to crack. He didn't buy a new wallet until the stitching fell out of the old one. "He wanted to keep grounded and remember where he came from and not put on airs," says Gail. "He made a conscious effort to remain the same."

Larry wrote this in his notes: "The worry I have with having nice things is getting dependent on them and not having the toughness to survive without them."

He was naturally frugal anyway. Greg has a story he delights in telling. He and his father had just left a meeting in which they had discussed plans for building the $80 million arena and were driving to a downtown deli for lunch. As they approached their destination, Miller slowed the car near an open parking space directly in front of the deli, but then sped up and drove past it.

"Change your mind?" asked Greg.

"No," said Larry. "There wasn't any time left on that meter."

Recalls Greg, "We drove a half block up the street so he could save 25 cents!"

During family business meetings, Larry and Gail passed documents around the table for each family member to sign. Each document had a colored tab on it showing where to sign. As they worked at the table, Larry noticed that Gail was peeling off one of the tabs to throw it away. "Gail!" he said. "We reuse those!"

On several occasions Larry would castigate Gail for buying expensive apples until one day she snapped, "I think we can afford the apples!"

Even the sneakers Larry wore were discounts. Rather than buy his own, he wore the ones that were sent free to Jazz players.

He could have afforded to fly first class; he flew coach instead.

So, with all that wealth, what did he buy? "Nothing," Gail says. "He never bought anything."

Actually, he bought a softball mitt for $64, which for years was the most extravagant thing he purchased for himself.

Gail continues, "His idea of splurging was buying a Water Pic. I bought all his clothes. He just didn't care about them. I bought him Dockers. He had 250 shirts in his closet, most of them polo shirts with Jazz emblems on them. He could have worn a different shirt every day for a year, but he usually wore only a few favorites. He'd say, 'Where is that shirt?' When he lost weight, I told him he had to buy new clothes. He was on the stake high council and needed suits. So we bought two suits, six pairs of pants, and several dress shirts. Then he wore the same black suit every Sunday. He didn't want anything fancy. He just didn't want to change how he looked at himself. He was afraid if he changed into a person who wanted worldly things he'd lose sight of the reason he had money, which was to help people. He got more enjoyment out of that. He had fun building an empire, but it was a means to an end."

Larry wasn't perfect—he had a temper that he had to conquer, and he was demanding and impatient at times—but he was deeply empathetic and utterly without pretense. He insisted that his players call him by his first name. "If you call me Mister Miller, I'll call you Mister Williams," he would say to Jazz guard Deron Williams. Center Jarron Collins never could bring himself to call Miller by his first name, and Karl Malone compromised by calling him "Mister Larry" out of affection and respect (and, on rare occasions, "Mister Miller"), but the other players managed. "He didn't like formality," says Gail.

Larry was always nonplussed when people made a fuss over him in public. "He could never understand why he was such an attraction," Gail says. "Little kids and grown-up men and women would approach him. The ladies always wanted to touch him—they'd hold his arm or pat him on the shoulder or put an arm around him. He was the common man." All of this—the lack of pretense, his open emotions and honesty in public, the way he dressed and treated others—made him approachable to everyone, and everyone, even strangers, called him "Larry."

The name of his businesses—Larry H. Miller—seemed too formal for him, but there was a reason for it. Only weeks after buying his first dealership, Miller faced a legal challenge over the use of his name on the new business. The challenge came from Mark Miller (no relation), who represented a long-established car dealership in Salt Lake Valley known as Laury Miller, named after Mark's father. Those names—Laury and Larry—were remarkably similar. Over the years Larry delighted in telling the story of how the Laury Miller company accused him of trying to ride its coattails. Legally, Larry probably would not have had to change the name of his dealership—the secretary of state had already accepted the name Larry Miller Toyota in Utah—but to avoid legal wrangling, Larry volunteered to add the "H" to his company's name. But, ever the competitor, as Larry was leaving the meeting, he told his business rival, "We'll see who's riding whose coattails."

The one incongruity in Miller's life was the mansion on the hill. The Millers raised their family in an upscale private neighborhood in Sandy, but they always hoped to return to Capitol Hill, where they had grown up. In 1997, they completed construction of an 18,000-square-foot home on a large empty lot near Capitol Hill that overlooked the entire valley. Several years ago, before I visited Miller for the first time at his new home, he was almost apologetic for the grandeur of the home and tried to prepare me for it.

"When we were dating in high school, we would drive around and see homes we wanted," he said. "Our dream houses. We'd see houses and we'd say, 'That's an obscene display of wealth.' Well, when we built this house, I told Gail, 'You know people will say that's an obscene display of wealth.' When you come down the street, you can't miss it; it is pretty lavish.

"We had always bought existing homes. Gail had always wanted to build her dream home. I told her that we had waited a long time to do it, so let's just do it. We really splurged."

Let's put it this way: When the architect showed up the first day, he plunked down a book in front of Gail and said, "See if there's anything in there you like." The title of the book: The Palaces of Marseille.

It's a granite and glass structure with a pool and a playground and a home movie theater. Bronze statues greet visitors as they approach the front door. Inside, there are marble and wood floors and 24-foot ceilings and an elevator and large paintings on the walls and another large sculpture in the entryway. The house took three years to build.

"We drew a rectangle, and then started putting rooms in," says Gail. "We worked for a year on the plans, and the architect built a model of it. The architect also designed the Delta Center and the Jerusalem Center—which is where the design for our house came from. We wanted a lot of windows and big rooms."

The house required a red iron frame and big steel beams—the type used for office buildings—and two inches of concrete on each floor.

As Gail recalls, "The first time we drove up here after they built the frame, we looked at it and thought, Omigosh, what have we done? The size of it. What are people going to think of us? We didn't want to stand out and make a statement like that. We spent $250,000 to cut the hill down so you can't see all of it from the road. However, I had a lot of fun decorating it and choosing colors and floor materials and designs. Larry said, 'You've waited a long time to do this; do what you want.' And I did. He never said anything about how much it cost. He would often say, 'You have done a wonderful job. I see you everywhere.' It was like a gift—for the waiting. I really enjoyed it. It was a growing experience for me. I had always been reticent and stood back in decisions. It was a confidence builder. I had to make thousands of decisions. Larry referred to it as a time when I put my confidence and creativity and ability all together."

CHAPTER 28

WHAT MANNER OF MAN . . .

N o fair keeping it all, because you don't need it.

In the mid-1990s, I arrived at a crossroads in my career. I had worked so hard for so long to achieve success, and now that I had done that I found myself asking the big questions: *Now what? Why am I doing this? What was it all for?*

I was really struggling with all of this. There were other things that were happening, as well. My company had grown significantly and, as a result, my role had changed. In the beginning I was involved in a hands-on way in everything the company did; I knew every employee in every department and their families and the names of their children. These relationships were important to me, and I enjoyed them. But as we grew, I had to hire people to help me run the business—there was just too much for one person to oversee—and I became more removed from things. I missed being a part of it. There was more bureaucracy. There is no other way to run a company this big. The business became much more traditional, and I am not a traditional businessman.

In some ways I was a victim of my own success. I missed the challenge and fun of structuring deals and financing in those early days. Our success and reputation enabled us to get financing easily through traditional ways. I grew disinterested in running the company on a day-to-day basis. I knew that when Greg took over for me someday, he would run the company in a more traditional manner. I was going through a transition. My real interest was in building things and bringing new businesses to life—being an entrepreneur.

All of this caused me some introspection about what it all meant—the money, the business, the purpose of it all, my role and my responsibility. After work I would talk to Gail about it. This led to a lot of conversations about where we were going. We had more than enough money. We had a nice house. Our family was taken care of. Now what? What am I going to be remembered for? Was it just about money and success in the business world? In the Book of Mormon, Christ asks his disciples in the New World, "What manner of men ought ye to be?" That's what I was asking myself.

This was a turning point in my life. I had all these resources, and I wanted to use them to bless the lives of others. Money is not an end, but a tool to build with. I decided that I needed to engage in philanthropic efforts in a more significant way. I had always been involved in philanthropy, usually on a personal basis, but now it became a big part of what we did as an institution.

It is the principle of stewardship—using what we have to do good things. I really have no choice in the matter. It is a responsibility to use our means to do good. Where much is given, much is required in return.

Each month, I began to set aside significant amounts of money for charity work rather than put it back in the business, and we began to take on big philanthropic projects. That has led to some of the most gratifying experiences of my life.

One of our biggest projects was building a campus at the south end of the valley for Salt Lake Community College. For 15 years, representatives of SLCC had asked me to help them build a building or some physical facility. I told them I wanted to help, but I just couldn't handle it at that time. I had too many other things going that required my attention.

I owned some property that was adjacent to Jordan Commons. The county wanted the property on which they could build the Expo Center. I sold it to them for what I paid for it, plus my costs for improving the property. In essence, it was a donation. Then I told them I had something they could do for me. The county owned some property at about 9600 South on the west-side frontage road that could serve as a site for the SLCC campus. The county had wanted to put a waste transfer station on that property, but there was such a public outcry about it that they couldn't get support for it. The property sat there unused for years. They agreed to sell it to me. They came out way ahead on the arrangement because the Expo property had doubled in value while the waste transfer property was just languishing. There were a lot of problems with it.

The college wanted a building, but I envisioned more than that for the 20½ acres we had purchased. We funded and built buildings that totaled 325,000 square feet. We built a library, offices, and a conference center. The school had a police academy, so we built two buildings for the Department of Public Safety—one was a 160-bed dorm to house the cadets and one contained classrooms, a gym, and a high-tech firing range. We built an entrepreneurship center where students can learn how to start and grow a real business and run it from there until they are ready to move out and establish their own offices. It is an incubator for businesses. We built an automotive building where students learn how to run a dealership. And we built a culinary arts building.

It was a very satisfying experience for me because the buildings and the campus are very busy—they're getting used for what they were intended for.

The reason I had postponed my commitment to help SLCC was because when I undertake these philanthropic efforts I usually do more than provide the funding; I am very involved and hands-on. I want to ensure things are done right. We approach these projects in an unusual way—we usually build the buildings ourselves, privately, with our own people, and then donate them. This was cheaper, faster, and less bureaucractic than if we had simply donated the money and had the government construct the campus.

In the case of the SLCC campus, I was involved in everything design and location of the buildings, landscaping, even location of the flagpole. I lobbied the state legislature to obtain computers and equipment for the buildings. Gail and I frequently drove out there on weekends—which is when I had a little free time—to check the progress of construction and determine what needed to be done.

This was one of my first major undertakings in philanthropy, and there have been many more since then. They have become a big part of my life these last 15 years. I believe entrepreneurs have the responsibility to be involved in the community and invest their time and talents in things that will help many people. We have to understand the big picture and our role and obligation.

For the 25th anniversary celebration of our company, I wrote the following mission statement titled "What We're About":

"My wife and I have been blessed with many opportunities to be 'bridge builders.' We also recognize there have been many who have gone before us to build the bridges we have crossed. As our businesses have matured and our financial capabilities have expanded, our desire has been to build bridges for others that may need help in moving forward. In contemplating the legacy we might leave to our posterity and our society, we have defined three primary elements:

"1. To create quality jobs.

"2. To help as many people as possible gain an education, thus becoming self-sufficient and, in turn, able to help others.

"3. To assist individuals or institutions that have found themselves at the edge of a chasm needing and wanting to cross, but who need help with either means or know-how to bridge the gap."

POSTSCRIPT

There was an endless array of projects that drew Miller's interest, time, and money, including the estimated $50 million he donated to SLCC to construct the south valley campus that bears his name, the $10 million he gave to the Huntsman Cancer Institute, and the $10 million endowment he gave to the Joseph Smith Papers.

Much of what Miller did in charity related to education, the arts, and businesses.

He provided financial assistance and extensive tutelage to numerous people who wanted to start or fix a business. "There are hundreds of small businesses operating in Utah today whose owners were taught and received encouragement and guidance from Miller," said A. Sterling Francom, former director of SLCC's Center for Entrepreneurship Training.

Miller funded movies such as God's Army II *and* Brigham City, *some of Lee Groberg's Church-related documentaries that aired on public television, and* The Work and the Glory—*projects he considered to be enlightening for many.*

The Work and the Glory *was based on the series of LDS historical novels by Gerald Lund, whom Miller considered a friend. Miller stayed in close contact with producer Scott Swofford throughout the production of the movies. (Miller is actually listed in the credits as one of the producers.) He read the script as it was being developed and made suggestions for it. Swofford and others involved in the making of the movie came to Miller's house with some of the rough cuts of the film, and they watched them in his home theater and solicited his opinion. Miller also was involved in the distribution process and the*

DVD release. Gail flew out to Tennessee a couple of times to visit the set so she could report to Larry about the movie's progress (and also to accompany their grandson Zane, who appears in two of the movies).

The story goes that during a company meeting Larry was informed that he had lost $18 million on the Work and the Glory movies. During that same meeting, a letter was read aloud from a woman who thanked Larry for the movies. She explained that she had been inactive in the Church, but the movies had caused her to return to full activity. "Now we know what the worth of a soul is," Larry quipped. Those close to Miller love to tell this story.

Miller, the Hall of Fame fast-pitch softball pitcher, funded construction of BYU's softball and baseball complex; Gail Miller Field (softball) and Larry H. Miller Field (baseball) sit back-to-back. Miller helped design the fields and the clubhouse, as well as advised school officials about how to maximize the benefits of the money he donated to them.

Larry had a special weakness for the arts. After Gail coaxed him to attend Education Week at BYU with her, he was so moved by the performance of operatic tenor Michael Ballam that he called him and said, "I need to meet you." A friendship blossomed, and Miller became involved in building up Ballam's pet project—the Utah Festival Opera Company in Logan. Ballam told Miller about a building the festival wanted to purchase. As he was wont to do, Miller didn't just hand him a check; he wanted more information. He told Ballam to send him a list of his needs. That summer Larry attended his first opera, and he was so moved by the performance that afterward he told Ballam, "Every child in the state needs to see excellence at this level. How can I help you?" Ballam needed several things to make the opera work—housing for visiting artists, a production facility, and an endowment fund that would guarantee future income.

Miller decided to do the project, but he didn't tell Ballam. Instead, he asked Ballam if he would give a special performance for him, Gail, and about 90 friends and employees. After the performance, Miller told Ballam and other Festival Opera staff that he wanted them to meet his employees because they were the ones who made his businesses profitable, which in turn facilitated his charity work. Continuing, he explained that he wanted his employees to enjoy the fruits of their labor on this night. At the end of the evening, he announced he had bought an apartment building for Ballam that would serve two purposes: It provided revenue for the Opera because it was already being rented by college students during the school year, and, since it was empty in the summer, it could be used to house the performers of the opera.

Miller also eventually purchased the Dansante Building for UFO and renovated it. Miller's architects turned the building's 20,000 square feet into 45,000, which enabled it to be used to build and store props and costumes, and provided rehearsal space and children's classrooms.

Miller didn't want public recognition for his support of UFO, but years later, when Miller purchased the Utah Theater for the opera, Ballam asked him, "Would it be okay if we let people know that you and Gail bought this building?" Miller replied, "If having our names associated with the Festival would be helpful, then you're welcome to use them."

Miller's philanthropy frequently targeted education. As mentioned earlier, he started a Teach the Teacher program in Utah. He provides in-state tuition scholarships to the children of all employees who have worked for his company for at least two consecutive years, and all they need to do to earn one is maintain a C average. It adds up to about 300 students per semester. Miller also provides 10 full scholarships per year—tuition, books, a monthly stipend, 20 meals a week, a job, housing, and an on-campus mentor—to several University of Utah students falling in any of the seven federally recognized minorities. At last count, 43 minority men and women were utilizing these scholarships, and, again, they only have to maintain a C average to retain them, but the students tend to do much better. (Overall, they maintain about a 3.0 GPA or better.) Each year the Millers host a dinner to welcome a new group of scholarshipped students. Miller knows most of these kids' names and something about them, and he has personally stepped in to aid students who needed help and had nowhere else to go. When Miller built the racetrack in Tooele, he wanted to do something for the students in that community, so he set up three scholarships in Tooele County.

When the LDS Church decided to discontinue its annual Christmas sing-along event in the Tabernacle, Miller revived it. He funded the event and moved it to his basketball arena. The last public event he attended, shortly after being released from the hospital, was the 2008 Christmas sing-along. The event featured soldiers participating from Iraq via closed-circuit TV.

Miller served as chairman of the board for Clark Planetarium and devised a plan that pulled it out of debt and made it profitable, using his own money to jump-start it.

He started Larry H. Miller Charities, a nonprofit organization, to operate the charitable division of his business and provide a way for his employees to participate in the satisfaction of helping others. The foundation is funded by donations from employees, Miller's companies, and the general public through fund-raisers such as "Leapin' Leaners and Low Tops."

"Larry viewed money as a stewardship rather than ownership," says Gail. "He treated money as if it were God's money and he had to find ways to do good with it."

That stewardship will continue even after Miller's death. In the last years of his life, he set up the Larry H. and Gail Miller Family Foundation. Eventually, after the last of the Miller grandchildren passes away, the Millers' entire fortune will be placed in the foundation, including his professional basketball franchise, the Utah Jazz.

"It was one of those things that we worked on as a family," says Gail, who is overseeing the trust. "He didn't want everything he built in his life to dissolve after he was gone; he wanted the business to continue and the money to do good things. If it's managed right, the foundation will go on forever."

Miller viewed his businesses as a way to help others. He often thanked and recognized his employees for helping his companies to earn the money that funded his philanthropy. At the time of his death, the foundation was already funding the Joseph Smith Papers project, the Clark Planetarium, and the Teach the Teachers program.

In the years ahead, the foundation "will provide assistance to women and children, health issues, things that primarily make life better for lots of people, not just individuals," says Gail.

Miller worked on setting up his foundation for many years. Says Gail, "It was very important to him. He was very thoughtful and deliberate about setting it up right. After working on it for years, he came to a structure he felt good about."

CHAPTER 29

BROKEBACK MOUNTAIN

I woke up in the middle of the night thinking about it. I kept replaying the situation in my mind, and sleep was impossible. The *Brokeback Mountain* controversy—the one that made me the butt of jokes for the late-night talk show hosts, including Jay Leno, not to mention the target of boycotts and hate mail and the center of a national debate—had become a weight on my shoulders. I went downstairs and wandered to our living room and looked out the large windows that overlook Salt Lake Valley, with its rows of lights winking in the black night. The piano was nearby, and for some reason I reached for the Church hymnbook that lay there and opened it to the hymn "How Firm a Foundation." I began to read the entire seven verses, but the third verse was the one that really reverberated for me: "Fear not, I am with thee; oh, be not dismayed, / For I am thy God and will still give thee aid. / I'll strengthen thee, help thee, and cause thee to stand, / Upheld by my righteous, omnipotent hand" (*Hymns*, no. 85). After finishing the song, I was comforted. I returned to bed and slept the rest of the night.

The spring of 2006 was a difficult time in my life. The only reason I am revisiting the *Brokeback Mountain* controversy is not to restate my position or to defend myself or to apologize or waffle on my original position, although I would do things differently now. I revisit this mostly because I want to discuss what happened afterward, and to do that I must return briefly to the genesis of the controversy.

I own several movie theaters. I hire people to oversee these theaters, and we have a long-established protocol for procuring movies. That protocol includes a gatekeeper in the distribution business who knows the kind of movies I consider acceptable and who knows my values. He procures the movies and, if he sees something he knows I would find objectionable, he simply does not procure that movie. Well, along comes *Brokeback Mountain*, a movie about gay love between cowboys. By the time I heard about the movie, it had already been booked by our theaters and advertised as an upcoming attraction. Our movie procurer had recently died, but we have an internal guy who is supposed to be a gatekeeper as well. He should have caught it and simply declined to procure the movie, and then it never would have been an issue. We pass up hundreds of movies and no one says anything.

When I learned about the subject of the movie, I pulled it. In my world and with my beliefs, I figured enough is enough. I'm taking a stand. It's as simple as that. Well, that started a nationwide controversy. There were calls from gay and lesbian groups to boycott my businesses. It ignited long debates on talk radio and in newspaper forums. It got ugly.

But something good grew out of all this. About this same time, I was asked by the University of Utah—via Jim Wall, the *Deseret News* publisher and chairman of the U's President's Club committee—to speak at the university for their U Days Celebration. It was part of an ongoing effort by the university to become more integrated with the community. After *Brokeback* turned into a heated controversy, the university began to catch flak from gay and lesbian groups for inviting me to speak. They started an Internet boycott campaign against my speaking engagement. They circulated petitions demanding that the U withdraw its invitation in protest. Gail read the petition online and was surprised at some of the people who had signed it. She didn't tell me all the names because she believed it would be too hurtful to me. Some were people I had donated money to. Well, seeing all the trouble this was causing for the U, I called Michael Young, the university president, and told him, "I don't want to cause problems; you can uninvite me." But President Young dug in his heels. He said no one would dictate who spoke at the U. I finally told President Young, "Let me meet with them."

A meeting was arranged. The U invited representatives of various gay and lesbian student groups and faculty members, and I met with them on campus. Greg and Gail came with me as a symbolic gesture—the traditional family, family solidarity, and so forth. Gail said, "I'm not going to let you go in there alone." To start the dialogue, I simply said, "I want to hear what you're feeling. What have I done to hurt you?" I wanted to listen to and learn from what they had to say. To their credit, they were willing to discuss the issues openly. It was refreshing to them that I was willing to come onto their turf and just listen to them.

What I learned is that while taking a stand for what I believed in, I had hurt many sincere people, and I deeply regretted that. It was never my intention. I had always been a guy who stood up for the underdog—I was the kid who fended off the snowball attack of my underdog classmate in grade school—and here I had hurt a whole group of underdogs. As I listened to the abuse they had endured and how they believed my actions had contributed to it, I was surprised and moved. I felt great empathy for them, and I learned a lot.

It was a remarkable two-hour meeting. It turned into a mutual admiration club. Instead of protesting my speech the next day, they showed up and listened. They had previously threatened to wear cowboy hats in protest as a nod to the *Brokeback Mountain* cowboys. Only a few came with their hats, and, instead of wearing them, they held them in their hands in what I interpreted as a sign of respect, which I very much appreciated. I was able to give my speech about the rewards of investing in higher education, something I think we had demonstrated in the previous day's meeting.

Yes, I would do it differently. I would either not procure the movie and not discuss it, or, if we had booked it, go ahead and run it because we were showing worse movies than that—*Hostel*, for instance. People assume I am retracting my position; I'm not. But I wouldn't intentionally hurt someone unnecessarily. Even my own secretary was upset. I regret that I caused people pain or made life more difficult for them.

POSTSCRIPT

The Brokeback Mountain controversy polarized the community. While a segment of the population was organizing boycotts of Miller's businesses, another segment was quietly happy that Miller had taken a stand for traditional families and marriage. More than 50 people called Miller in the first three days after the controversy began to say they had bought cars from Miller that day to demonstrate their support.

In the end, Miller defused the situation masterfully and with great sincerity. He did it simply by taking time to listen to the other side. People who witnessed the meeting between Miller and members of the gay community have called it one of the most remarkable, heartwarming meetings they have witnessed.

"He didn't go in there to make statements or defend himself," says Jim Wall, who witnessed the meeting. "It was obvious he was there

to listen. He wanted to find out what he had done to offend them; he wanted to understand them. One of the things he learned is that these people suffer a lot of ridicule and prejudice. People throw popcorn at them in theaters or snicker at them. They feel persecuted. They said that when Larry pulled the movie, it was as if he endorsed that bad behavior. Larry said, 'I had no idea you were being persecuted, and I had no intention to endorse bad behavior. I'm sorry that happened to you. I do have my beliefs, and they're pretty well founded in marriage between a man and a woman to propagate the human race. I disagree with your lifestyle, but I don't tell you you can't live it.' He didn't talk as much as he just listenened. He was emotional—he got teary-eyed as he spoke to them and listened to their stories. A genuine discovery occurred; a lot of bad feelings melted away. He never compromised his values, but he was empathetic and listened.

"It was one of the perfect examples of diverse, opposite points of view coming together in a dialogue in which both sides were hurt and neither side moved, but both sides understood each other better and really could have differences of opinion without being confrontational. Many expressed their appreciation to him for speaking to them. Before we left the meeting, one of the faculty leaders said, 'I'm coming to your speech, and I'm going to bring my hat, but I'm not going to wear it.' You know, in the end the university received an unintended benefit from having Larry speak. Students learned that this is the way to handle differences of opinion without being confrontational. If someone throws water on you, what do you do? Instead of getting mad, you ask why they are mad. Dialogue is different from confrontation."

As Gail recalls, the meeting was typical of Larry. "That was the way he did things—head on; let's get it out in the open. A lot of the people stayed afterward and talked with him. Some of them hugged me and thanked me for accompanying my husband. The thing about Larry is that he really didn't put people in cubicles. There were no boundaries with him."

CHAPTER 30

NEVER ON A SUNDAY

D o you know where I was when Michael Jordan stole the ball in Game 6 of the 1998 NBA Finals and then sank a jump shot with five seconds left to win the game, and his sixth and final championship, 87–86?

I was out for a drive in my car.

It was one of the biggest games in the history of our franchise, and I had to watch it later on videotape. It's still difficult for me to watch it. I don't know if I'll ever get over the disappointment.

I also missed Game 4 of the Lakers-Jazz playoff game in 2008. Instead, I went on a long drive in the mountains. Usually Gail rides shotgun with me, but this time an ESPN reporter, Gene Wojciechowski, kept me company and wrote a story about my private boycott of Sunday games.

The reason I missed those games is because they were played on Sunday, and, for religious reasons, I don't attend games on Sunday. In

256

the Mormon faith, we are taught to keep the Sabbath day holy. We attend church, spend time with our families, perform Church duties, visit the sick or elderly, or read scriptures. We don't work and we don't play. It's a day of rest from the things we do throughout the week.

It's a personal decision, and my decision—though certainly not an easy one—to not attend games on Sunday. But a woman in our ward told us a story. She said one Sunday her young son told her he didn't want to attend church because he wanted to watch the Jazz play in a playoff game that day. The mother said, "No, we go to church on Sunday, not watch basketball games on TV." As the mother recalled later, the boy replied, "Yes, we can; Larry Miller will watch it."

"No, he'll be at church," the mother said.

Much to the mother's relief, when they went to church that Sunday there was Larry in his regular seat in the chapel. "See, he's here," she said to the boy.

In the early years of my involvement with the Jazz, I attended games on Sunday. But as my visibility in the community grew, I began to feel a responsibility to set an example. I felt that people were watching me and, in fact, over the years whenever I did miss a game it was reported in the news. I am one of the few owners who actually sit in a floor seat, which increases my visibility.

On the occasions there are Sunday games, I attend church, come home, change clothes, eat a meal, and then go for a long drive, which is something I do to unwind and clear my head, think about things, and be with Gail. No, I don't tune in the game on TV or radio, as I'm often asked, although on rare occasions, if it's an important contest, I might check the score during or after the game or watch the final minute. Sometimes I show up at the arena just as the game is ending to congratulate the team or greet them. Sometimes people would see me there at the end of the game and assume I had attended the whole game.

The league has tried to accommodate my feelings about Sunday as much as possible. They have tried to schedule as few home games on Sunday as possible. During the playoffs, it's more problematic, and scheduling Sunday games can't be avoided as easily.

Over the years, I have received letters from people who said they joined the Church because they began to explore my faith when they saw that I refused to attend games on Sunday. My Sunday boycott has garnered much attention from the media and fans, as evidenced by the ESPN reporter choosing to ride with me instead of watching a playoff game. This is not a bad thing. It educates people about our faith and leads to more understanding. But even if no one noticed, I would choose to miss the Sunday games anyway. It just feels like the right thing to do.

PART VI

How'd You
Do It?

CHAPTER 31

PASSION AND INTENSITY

For whatever reason, I have always had an intensity about the things I do, even when I was a kid practicing for marble tournaments or softball. There's a story called "The Five-Dollar Job" that describes me exactly. (The story is reprinted in the back of this book.) It's about doing a job so meticulously and so in-depth that you really do control the outcome. It's about doing your best work and discovering your own capacities. That passion or intensity drove me to work the long hours. It drove me to find better time-management systems, even as a kid working in a book bindery. It drove me to learn everything I could about whatever I was doing, whether it was perfecting new softball pitches or understanding movie theater design or memorizing the serial numbers of automobile parts and where they were stored.

I did micromanage my company in the early years, but we had better results because of it. For me, the hands-on style with which I worked was not about power or control. It was about doing it right. It was about my passion and intensity for whatever I was doing and the outcomes I sought with that intensity.

A lot of people simply don't bring this intensity to work, although they don't realize it. I try to describe it this way: Let's say there's an intensity level of 10. Some people can work to a certain intensity level and think they worked hard and achieve a 9½. Another person can work at it and do a bad job and believe he or she worked at a 9 or 10, but it would actually be a 4. So many people work at the minimums rather than the maximums. They're going to do as little as they can to get by and get it done; someone else will do a great job and pull together all the loose ends. A bunch of people say, "I wanna have . . ." and "I wanna be . . ." but they're not willing to pay the price. The price is time and effort and being a student of what you're doing.

I have already related the epiphany I had in the early years of my career: I was at work and realized that I had to support a growing family and it scared me. I had nothing to fall back on in the way of an education. All I had was my capacity for hard work. I decided I was going to be the best parts manager in existence. It took many hours, and I had to become a student of everything—ordering systems, controlling parts obsolescence, delivery systems, hiring practices, training practices, retention practices. I decided to become incredible in all facets so that I could control the outcome. And that's what happened. When I took over the parts department in March of 1971, the monthly record for parts sales was $9,091. In 1973, my second full year, we were averaging $83,000 a month. That's what I meant about controlling the outcome. I studied the business and I worked hard.

I often remember that discussion with Grandpa Horne that had such a profound influence on my life and the way I worked. You'll remember that I was discouraged because I was working very hard and had earned great responsibility from my employer, and yet I was paid like everyone else and was refused a raise. I told my grandpa that if they were only going to pay me $1.45 an hour, then I would give them only a $1.45 effort. That was when he told me that no one would know the difference except me. And then he promised me that if I worked as hard as I could and learned all that I could in that business, someday it would pay off many times over. It was not about my employer; it was about me. Everything Grandpa Horne promised has come to pass.

There's another famous story that illustrates the ideal of what an employee or any worker should be. During the Spanish-American War, as the Americans prepared to invade the Spanish colony of Cuba, they needed to contact the leader of the Cuban insurgents to help coordinate the assault—his name was Garcia. No one knew where he was. The mission to deliver the message was given to a soldier named Andrew Summers Rowan. He didn't ask any questions—he didn't ask how or where he could find Garcia, he didn't ask for help, he didn't complain or object to being assigned such a difficult job. He simply did it. He found Garcia in the mountains and delivered the message. This story is often used to illustrate a can-do person, an independent, resourceful worker. That's what I strive to be and strive to find in a worker.

As is often the case, my strength is also my weakness. My passion and intensity sometimes manifested itself in another way. I had to work hard at controlling my temper. I had high expectations for everyone else like I had for myself, and I expected the same dedication, hard work, and results.

POSTSCRIPT

Says Gail, "His temper caused a lot of stress in relationships. He was impatient with others, whether they were employees or the kids or me. He expected perfection and didn't tolerate stupid mistakes or someone not following through. He was such a doer and such a perfectionist. He had a hard time understanding why others were not that way too.

When he needed someone, if they were not there and he couldn't reach them, like on a Saturday, he wondered why they weren't at work. If he was upset, the first person he saw would catch it.

"His temper was something I don't know that he ever got over, but he learned to control it. He confused temper and passion a lot. I told him that, but he had a hard time seeing it. He felt like if he didn't get angry he wasn't true to his passion. One time he said to me, 'You wouldn't understand because you're so milquetoast.' But finally it dawned on him that you don't have to be angry to be passionate or strong-willed. You can still be those things and be a nice person."

Says Greg, "I don't know why he was that way, but he was quick to become angry. He usually tried to fix things afterward. I don't know—he expected more of people than they could deliver in most cases."

Larry's employees did not always match his intensity and business acumen, of course. This was difficult for him to understand, and it tried his patience, which wasn't in great supply anyway. "Was he emotional?" says CFO Clark Whitworth. "Yes. After he shredded someone, he would always come back around and smooth things over. He just couldn't stop himself. He worked hard at it. He was an artistic personality. He was so driven, and almost 100 percent of the time he was driven by something that was right; he was pushing a right principle."

Miller was conflicted about his temper and his tendency to lash out because he also had an intense desire to be liked and was extremely sensitive to others' feelings. As Whitworth notes, when Miller lashed out, "He'd always pick up the collateral damage afterward. He was an incredible, phenomenal businessman. Any criticism bothered him. He wanted all his people to be loyal. We had a guy quit and Larry was baffled. 'Why would anyone leave me?' he asked me. The rest of us wanted this guy to go, but Larry wanted to know why. Even when a Jazz player would leave, he took it personally."

Whitworth likes to tell this story to illustrate Miller's intensity and determination: *The Miller family was driving from Colorado to Salt Lake City one winter when Gail informed Larry from the backseat that the car was on fire. Larry immediately pulled to the side of the road somewhere near Evanston and tossed handfuls of snow onto the fire in the wheel well to put it out. The wheel bearings were burned out. "Most people would just call the tow truck, but not Larry," says Whitworth. Instead, he called someone from Salt Lake City to pick up his family, and then he continued to limp the car the rest of the way to Utah. Every few miles the wheels would get red-hot, and Miller would have to stop the car, dump snow on the wheel bearings to cool them off, and then hammer the wheel back into the axle. The wheel could have come off at any time, but nothing would deter Miller. "That's the drive, the determination," says Whitworth. "He was not going to have that car towed. He was going to conquer the problem. He was going to get the car there, and he did—at about 2:00 A.M." Says Gail, "He was so determined that that car was not going to sit on the freeway and get the best of him. It was like a lot of things for him—he just willed it till he got what he wanted."*

CHAPTER 32

BLOCKING AND TACKLING

How did we do it? I get asked that often. Here is one of the main messages in this whole book: It is not fancy. It is as fundamental as blocking and tackling. I just did it. I just went to work every day and did everything that needed to be done.

I have a three-legged milk stool in my office perched on top of a cabinet. It is a great symbol for how to succeed in business. There are three legs: Take care of the customer, have a little fun, make a little money. If you don't do that, it doesn't work, but if you do, it comes together easily.

Since I had no formal university education and never took a business class, I had to learn along the way and make a conscious decision to do so.

I learned that too many people who become bosses don't understand the market or work as hard as they should.

Here's a classic trap: A businessman is successful with one

business, so he thinks two or three or four would be even better. This changes the equation dramatically. With one operation, you can be there yourself and use the sheer force of your personality to drive it, but as soon as you get two you're dividing your time; you need someone who is strong and good enough to run the other business. It's going to be more difficult to make a profit. Other people don't care about it as much as you do. There are some who work hard, but they are few.

Some business owners try to expand too fast. They grow into a second and third operation before the first one is solid. The first one is almost holy. Protect the base. Hand off to someone you trust, and then you can move on.

Good people are hard to find, but they're there. We've got many really good people in our organization. The trick is to find them jobs that keep them interested and match their talents and what they want to do (and not everyone is a boss). Then you have a happy, motivated work force. In our company, we give our general managers the opportunity to buy 10 percent of the dealerships they manage. We prefer that they do this—obviously, someone who has a financial stake in the business is motivated to work hard and make the business a success.

I learned that when you're in negotiations, you need to go early and inspect what you want; decide what you're willing to pay beforehand; don't want the item too badly; take time to learn what the person on the other side of the table wants; don't assume anything; don't give away things piecemeal; be able to think on your feet; and always negotiate for yourself because no one will negotiate it as well as you.

I learned you must control advertising. We have formulas for it, and even when things are slow we don't break our own rule. We just stay with the formula. In the car business we have three big costs we can control: (1) people—we don't take their jobs lightly, but personnel is a controllable expense; (2) advertising—we advertise at the level of business we're actually doing, not at the level of business we wish we were doing; (3) flooring costs. We don't have enough money to own our inventory, so we finance it, and this is called "flooring." We can control the interest we pay on the inventory by lowering inventory. We might not replace everything we sell. If things are slower, we keep the inventory smaller to control flooring interest.

I learned that when you are creating a pay plan for someone, especially one that involves a commission, and in many other instances involving money, a useful method of analyzing the situation is to look at the equation in its extremes. Specifically, what would happen? How would this pay plan work if things really got difficult? We look at the worst-case scenario. Does it still make sense even if the worst case should occur? Conversely, what happens if it takes off and runs, and suddenly we're paying ten times more than what we anticipated? I have known a lot of people who got sideways with a boss or owner because they had a pay plan that looked reasonable at the beginning; however, the designers of the plan didn't run it out far enough to see what would happen in very good times, so maybe an employee got paid too much occasionally, sometimes even more than the boss or the owner. When I was parts manager in Lakewood, for example, I was making more than the general manager. That didn't sit well with him. You need to examine the best-case and worst-case scenarios. Failing to do that is an easy trap to fall into.

I learned that the worst part of growing a company is that some degree of bureaucracy is inevitable. When a company becomes big, you must create layers to manage it; you can no longer do everything yourself. You must hire others to oversee parts of the whole. I resisted this and never was completely comfortable with it. I missed the personal contact that allowed me to see firsthand how the business was doing and to make sure things were done right. I missed the relationships and interactions and getting to know people. The relationships were important to me; they were very fulfilling and allowed people to get to know me and gain trust in me. That's how I did business—through relationships. As we grew bigger, I lost some of that and missed it.

I micromanaged for years, and that was a great reason for my success. Eventually, I had to rely on others, and I didn't like it because I knew no one would care about it like I do. But I managed it by requiring daily reports so I knew what was happening. The thing I always say is this: I worry a lot about how bad the bureaucracy in our organization would be if I didn't worry about it as much as I do.

One thing I did was minimize bureaucracy wherever possible. I structured the company so that there were as few layers as possible between me and the businesses. I hired two general managers—one to oversee sports and entertainment and one to oversee automotive—and they report directly to me. Each of them has a handful of vice presidents, who represent one more layer, and there is another layer below them. I receive reports from all of them, and I am still the ultimate decision maker. I am not so removed from them that I don't know the people, plus most of them have been with me so long that I already knew them anyway. This helps me to watch over the company.

The following is a list of suggestions and principles—common sense, really—I would offer to anyone who asked for general advice about succeeding in the business world:

- The only stupid question is an unasked question.
- Even more important than the will to win is the will to prepare to win.
- You don't have to blow out the other person's candle to let your own shine.
- Don't make a bad deal just to make a deal.
- Keep money in perspective.
- Be patient.
- Life is a journey, not a destination.

- Play to your own strengths.
- Trust your instincts. You have within you abilities to deal with everything you will need to.
- Manage business at the level of business you're actually doing, not the level you wish you were doing.
- Learn not to confuse the elements of motion and progress. Progress always requires motion, but motion isn't always progress.
- I'd rather be doing stuff than reading reports.
- There is no limit to what a person can accomplish if he doesn't care who gets the credit.
- Risk may cause failure, but success cannot come without it.
- The words "can't be done" are only for the faint of heart.
- If you want extraordinary results, put in extraordinary effort.
- Never assume your people see the problems as clearly as you do.
- More important than the action is the philosophy behind it.
- Let the fires burn all around you and fix one problem at a time.
- The market speaks.
- Always boil things down to their lowest common denominator and then look at the extremes.
- You can't do it if you're not there.

POSTSCRIPT

In January 2007, Larry called his four sons and his wife to a meeting at his home and announced that he was going to start preparing them to take over the company someday. He handed each of his sons a thick notebook and said, "You're going to want to take notes." They met for four hours every Friday for the next two years until Larry's health declined. Shortly after his father's death, Greg said, "It was like a university class. I filled three legal pads plus a thick notebook with notes from those meetings and from management meetings, where he would speak for five or six hours at a time. I have read these notes twice since my dad got sick." He pulled out a large cardboard box filled with files that are crammed with notes from the things he learned at his father's knee. "If the building were on fire," says Greg, "this would be the thing I would run for. It's what I treasure most." Looking back on those meetings with his father, he recalls, "We would have a list of things he was going to discuss. He'd look at his Day-Timer and say, 'This is what I've done for the past week.' And he'd talk about those things: 'I met with the governor,' for instance, and he'd tell us what it was about. These things would lead to philosophical issues, and eventually the discussion would migrate away from the philosophical to the pragmatic."

Some of the notes were remarkably prescient. On March 1, 2007, Greg recorded in his notes these words from his father: "There are major storm clouds out there right now, bigger than I've seen in 15 years. It's not going to be business as usual. . . . I've always gone by feel on these things, and I haven't had the feelings I'm having now for 10 to 15 years." The severe economic downturn that Larry felt was coming arrived in earnest in December 2007, nine months later. Says Greg, "He would preach in these management meetings that we needed to work as if prosperity was going to end and to get our lives in order because we had never lived in a downturn. Everything he did was by feel."

"A Message to Garcia," by Elbert Hubbard, which was reprinted in a pamphlet and a book and sold a reported 40 million copies, was a favorite of Larry's. One of his local Church leaders once called him into his office and said, "I need a message delivered to Garcia." He was being figurative, of course, but Larry knew what he meant. "What's the mission?" he asked. The leader told Miller that he wanted a softball field and athletic complex built in a sagebrush field adjacent to their ward, and he wanted it done in 45 days, and he couldn't use Church funds. Miller rounded up an architect, a general contractor, brick masons, and a sprinkler contractor, and they built the field along

with pavilions, barbecues, and a fire pit in six weeks with donated time and materials.

Larry often referenced the story of "The Five-Dollar Job," along with "A Message to Garcia" and "Starfish," especially in meetings with employees. All three stories were included in a thick three-ring binder in which he collected favorite stories, poems, and quotes; he referred to the notebook when he prepared speeches and Church talks.

Greg believes that his father's "disdain" for bureaucracy was a little stronger than it should have been. "He viewed his role as someone who had spent his whole life planting a garden and now he was going to go around and pull weeds in the garden, dealing with little problems that sprang up," says Greg. "He thought he could deal with everything himself, but he became a bottleneck—a lot of decisions didn't get made or weren't made in a timely fashion. He finally did head in the direction of becoming more bureaucratic, but he didn't go far enough down that path to see its benefits. He was still too hands-on. That was his antidote to bureaucracy. People we had hired were underutilized. He just never felt comfortable with it."

It should be noted that Larry felt a great need to pass on what he had learned and what he had done in his life, as evidenced by many things—this book, the themes of the speeches he made to his managers on frequent occasions, the weekly family meetings with his children, and the fireside he called immediately after being released from the hospital following his heart attack. "He called the fireside because he felt an urgency to explain some of the history of the company and his life to his friends and employees who might not have ever had the chance to hear those stories," says Gail. "He could have gone on for a long time, but he didn't want to keep them too long that night. I'm not really sure he got the message across that he wanted to. He was not really at his full capacity that night."

CHAPTER 33

5 + 0 =

One day in my second-grade class, my teacher, Miss Issacson, posed a math problem for her 30 students to work out on the blackboard. Row by row, we each walked to the board and wrote 5 + 0 = and filled in the answer. I was in the last row, and after completing the problem on the board I returned to my seat. But when I studied the blackboard, I noticed that I was the only kid in the class who had written "5" as the answer.

Reasoning that the rest of the class couldn't all be wrong, I returned to the blackboard and changed my answer to "0" and went back to my seat. "Why did you change your answer?" Miss Issacson asked. I explained, and then she revealed the answer.

That day I learned that it is possible to be a small minority and still be right, and I learned the value of having confidence in your own abilities. Sometimes you have to take risks and follow your convictions. As noted in my list of business suggestions in the previous chapter, risk may cause failure, but success cannot come without it.

I have often found myself in a position in which I was the minority in my opinion, and, unlike that day in Miss Issacson's class, I did not flinch from going it alone because I knew I was right. I had done my homework, and I trusted my feelings. I did many things simply by going with my gut feeling.

Think about this: The things that set this organization apart from other organizations are the things that never should have happened—the arena, keeping the Jazz in Utah, my first car dealerships, the speedway, the novel and expensive way we built the theaters. Nobody believed those things would work.

If I had taken the attitude I did in Miss Issacson's class, I never would have tried to keep the Jazz in town because I could see clearly that nobody else thought it could be done or believed it was worth the financial risk. Remember, I was eager for someone else to step forward; it didn't have to be me, as long as the team remained in Utah.

Sometimes you have to have the courage to take risks. In 1990, as our company continued to grow and grow, one of my top executives grew scared of our growth and didn't think we could make it if we continued this way. He quit. It was an amicable parting—I even helped set him up in another business—but he didn't have the stomach for growth and risk.

I was the only one who believed the basketball arena should be built. The city, county, and state didn't want to finance it; neither did private individuals. That could have scared me off—everybody else can't be wrong, right? I had to go it alone and take on all that debt; I believed it could work. It was the exact same story with buying the basketball team.

The first car dealership I bought was another case of going it alone. I ignored common sense and traditional loan protocol, leveraged myself to the hilt, and did it. Maybe if I had understood debt-to-equity ratios then, I would have talked myself out of the deal. But it was just something I thought I could do. I went with my gut on that one, too.

You're supposed to hire specialists to find the big loans that we used to finance construction of the arena. That's just standard procedure for such large-scale projects. We did it ourselves. We did our homework, learned what it would entail, and found our own financing, saving ourselves millions of dollars.

Similarly, people who construct theaters always hire consultants; we didn't hire any until after the fact. We did our homework and went with our gut and it turned out to be a beautiful project. The experts told us that the things we did would never work, that they were too impractical and expensive. Six months after we opened we were getting calls from theaters around the country asking us to "teach us what you did." We're still getting those calls.

Sometimes everybody else is wrong.

POSTSCRIPT

"Even people here [in the company] didn't want him to buy the Jazz," says Miller's CFO, Clark Whitworth. "He wasn't even that big of a basketball fan. He was just a trout in a stream that eats what comes along. He just loved to solve problems."

Larry lived his life according to the quotation from President Theodore Roosevelt: "Far better it is to dare mighty things, to win glorious triumphs, even though checkered with failure, than to take rank with those poor spirits who neither enjoy much nor suffer much, because they live in the grey twilight that knows no victory nor defeat."

CHAPTER 34

REPUTATION AND TRUST

Once a man representing a group of dealerships in Boise called to ask if I would be interested in buying their eight car dealerships. My first answer was no. The second time he called, I asked him, "Why are you calling me?" The man explained that they wanted to ensure that their 377 employees would be taken care of by whoever bought the business. "We asked around, and you were at the top of the list," the caller explained. "You have a reputation for doing what you say you will do."

I tell this story not to boast, but to make a very clear point, and one about which I feel passionate: A reputation for integrity and honesty is desirable for its own sake, but it also will reap opportunities. I've seen it happen again and again in my life. I can go anywhere in this city and people will say, "Larry will do what he says he will do." My people who have watched me negotiate deals tell others that if I make a deal, even a verbal one, I will keep it. They've seen this.

I can honestly say that in all the times I have bought a dealership, I have never had to avoid the previous owner when I see him. That's not an accident. I keep that in mind when I'm making the deal. I make sure in a negotiation that the seller tells me that he has been treated fairly. I have bought close to 90 businesses, and I never had anyone say I took something away from them at the closing table. The reason I conduct myself with strict honesty and fairness is not to create business opportunities—I do it because it's what I believe in—but it certainly seems to work out that way.

As I mentioned earlier, my first partner in the car business, my Uncle Reid, got himself into serious financial trouble that threatened our entire business. If he had filed bankruptcy, it could have brought us both down. I needed about $700,000 to buy him out, an amount I couldn't come close to paying on my own. I was turned down by a number of lenders and finally went to John Firmage, a fine gentleman and businessman who owned a financial firm. He said he would loan me the money, but he would require me to pay prime plus six. Prime was 16 percent at the time, so that put me at 22 percent! And he was charging me 10 points on the loan, which came to $70,000 a year, renewable each year at the original amount.

"Okay, let me get this straight," I said to him. "You're telling me that at the end of the year, if I have paid the loan down to $1,000, I will still have to pay your $70,000 in points?"

Firmage's lawyer pointed out that it was still cheaper than a partner, which would cost me 50 percent of the business. I agreed to the terms, but at the end of the meeting I told him, "This loan will never see a birthday."

I paid off the loan in 364 days by finding a cheaper loan. I did what I said I would do.

To pay off John Firmage, I arranged to meet with Larry Tunnel of World Service Life, which was our underwriter for our insurance products. I met Tunnel and three other WSL representatives over lunch, and we batted around ideas of financing, including collateral and repayment and rates and so on. This went on for some time and we were getting nowhere. I was getting tired of it, and so was Tunnel. Finally, Tunnel, from the other end of the table, put his arms out and said, "Larry, let me ask you a question. Why are you here?"

"I want to borrow $770,000 to repay a loan I have, plus points."

"Okay, if I loan you the money, will you pay it back?"

"Yes, I will."

Tunnel turned to his guys and said, "Cut him the check." Tunnel knew my track record. He knew he could trust me; he knew I was a man of my word, and he took me at my word. We'd only been in business two and a half years, but Tunnel liked what he saw.

I have said that no one ever can say I didn't treat them fairly in negotiations. Well, in the years after our split, Uncle Reid was telling everyone that I had cheated him when I bought him out of the business. This bothered me; I cared about my reputation, and I felt ill-used. He had gotten himself into so many foolish financial ventures and lost almost everything, and I had loaned him money to help him survive it, and in the end he had come to me to straighten out his financial affairs, which took a week for me to sort through. It was unfair for him to say I had treated him unfairly, so one day I arranged for me and my attorney and accountant to meet with Uncle Reid and his attorney and accountant.

"I want to clear the air in front of these guys," I began. "You have said that I cheated you on this car deal. I have a proposal for you right now. You give me back the $770,000 that I borrowed, plus $700,000 for my half of the partnership, which is what I paid you plus the points, and it's all yours. You can have the same deal I have." All he said was, "You know I can't do that." He knew he didn't have the operational capability.

The way I do business has paid off. I am honest in my dealings, and I'll do what I say I will do, and people know this. This reputation was the only way I was able convince a bunch of conservative bankers to loan me $8 million to buy a professional basketball team that had been bleeding money for more than a decade—when I was worth half that. It's the way I convinced the city to give me a bond to build an arena no one else wanted to finance, and they believed me when I said I wouldn't sell the team to another city.

In the early years of my business I pulled off a lot of deals because people simply trusted me; it wasn't because of my bank account, which wasn't much in those days.

As I explored ways to buy a second car dealership, my reputation paid off again. The dealership was in Spokane, Washington, and the banking community in that state had imposed on itself a moratorium for new financing. We were a new business, and we needed to set up an operating business with a bank. Well, after I met with them, two banks agreed to be my lender despite the moratorium. They knew our track record, even though it was a short one. They knew we paid our bills and ran a good operation.

I was asked to speak to a bunch of junior college professors once, and at the end of the meeting I was asked to name my three greatest attributes. I answered: integrity, reliability, and hard work.

If you treat everyone with dignity, respect, and fairness, you never have to worry about meeting them again. I've always liked to give the other guy what he wanted in negotiations—if you give him what he wants, he'll give you what you want. There's no reason to be greedy. Why not try to make both parties happy? There seems to be this mentality that for us to succeed, someone else has to fail. I like this saying: You don't have to blow out the other fellow's candle to let your own shine.

The final word on this subject is something I have always told my sons and those I work with: The single most valuable asset I have is my reputation.

POSTSCRIPT

"That was how he carried himself all the time," says Clark Whitworth, Miller's longtime right-hand man. "And he was always getting the effect of that. He didn't understand the cause—how truly impeccable his honesty was. Even in the toughest times, he never compromised. Every deal he did, he wanted to be sure that after they were done he wouldn't have to avoid the guy on the street. If anyone questioned him, he caved. He wanted to ensure that on a personal basis he didn't have a problem with anyone. There was never a question about trust or integrity. Every deal had that. He was a perfectionist. He would give in on pay as opposed to trying to crush someone else. Larry would meet with someone to create a deal and list everything he was going to do. An attorney then drafted the agreement, and he'd come back and tell Larry, 'You should have had this and that and the other.' They thought he had shortchanged himself. But Larry would tell them, 'You don't renegotiate anything I do or take anything out.' He'd usually let the other side strike those things.

"Sometimes on deals we felt like Larry was in the huddle with us and then we'd go to the line of scrimmage and he was on the other side. He wanted to make sure everything was fair. He would almost negotiate against himself—he'd say to the guy on the other side of the table, 'What do you need? That may not be enough.' That kind of thing. Imagine if you're on the other side and you see that behavior from someone. That's what people would see, and that's what would drive his reputation for integrity. The bankers who saw that were overwhelmed.

"When Larry was building the arena, everyone knew he was leaving the Salt Palace and building the Delta Center. He really got no help. The RDA was there for everyone, and the property tax more than covered it [the $20 million bond]. Well, someone read the lease agreement with the Salt Palace and discovered it had a breakage fee— $300,000. They invoked it. I went with Larry to pay the $300,000

'extortion.' He never made a stink about it. That's how he was. Public opinion would have gone crazy on it. Everyone in the county was in on the Delta Center, and the county owned the Salt Palace. If Larry had been in their position, he would have let it go. But if he was on the other side, he paid. The sword only cut one way.

"Marriott Corporation was the first food-service provider we hired at the Delta Center. We signed a five-year deal with them. But after a year or so, Marriott said they were losing money, and Larry undid the deal. He didn't force them to honor it. He let them out of the contract. We didn't know going in what was going to happen. We were both taking a chance. It was a win-win for everyone to be fair.

"If a businessman said to Larry, 'This isn't personal,' that would light him up. A banker said that to him once, and Larry said, 'Everything is personal to me!' It was. That was part of the integrity. Part of my job was to tell him he didn't need to sign personal guarantees. I'd tell him, 'You don't need to do that.' And then he'd meet with bankers and the first thing he'd do, of course, was make a personal guarantee. 'I'm going to pay it back, so why not?' he'd say. He would have worked 24 hours a day to pay his debts."

CHAPTER 35

LOYALTY

M any years after I left Colorado, I learned that my old boss and mentor, Gene Osborne, was having financial difficulties. His car dealerships had crashed and burned. He had borrowed $7 million from a bank to recapitalize his dealerships, which left him a monthly payment of $100,000 plus interest. He was struggling even then, but he had money flying out the door. There were expenses for personal family problems, but also he had a penchant for spending money, whether it was on clothes or a big house. He made two payments on the loan and that was it. He couldn't pay anymore. Things got so bad that the bank asked Gene for some protection on the loan, and Gene wrote them a note on the spot assigning all of his business and personal assets as collateral. He called me and told me about his problems. I called the bank and offered them $4.5 million for the note. They refused. They called me back a few days later and asked if there was more there. I said maybe, but I told them I needed to see the books first for Gene's four dealerships. So I sent a three-man team to look at the books of their businesses, both assets and liabilities. They reported their findings to me, and I called the bankers again. This time I told them I would offer $3.5 million for the note; instead of offering more money, as they had hoped, I was offering $1 million less. They were shocked.

"I saw the books," I told them. "They're worse than I thought. You've got four days to accept my offer." The deadline was a Friday. On Friday at 4:58 P.M., they called to say they would accept my offer.

I took over Gene's businesses. We had to get people in there to run them correctly. We kept paying his large house payment out of the Toyota Store, and then after we finished paying off the house we continued paying that money to him. We set him up with an auto finance business to generate some net worth so he could buy back into a dealership. We bought a dealership for him to run—a VW dealership because Gene lived close to it.

Over the years people have asked, "Why did you do that for Gene?" Well, what we really did was create an opportunity for Gene to build some net worth for his retirement. People viewed that as giving it to him. Let me make this simple: If it weren't for Gene Osborne, I wouldn't be sitting here. It surprises people when I tell them that. It's about what he did to teach me in the 1970s.

When I went to work for Gene in the 1970s, I was the parts manager and Gene was part owner and general manager. Gene set me up on a pay plan that consisted of $700 per month plus 25 percent of the gross profit of the parts department, minus 25 percent of the labor of the parts department. I worked there for the first three months and quintupled sales, but every month there I made less money. I went to see Gene about this. I showed him the parts sales and the gross profit and what I was earning, and he said, "Boy, I didn't know we did that to you. We'll have to fix it." And he did. He paid me right on the spot, and he paid me retroactively. I can't tell you how refreshing this was, especially given how many times employers had cheated me previously. It made me want to work even harder for this guy. He was loyal to his people, he lived up to his word, and he rewarded those who did a good job.

Fast-forward two years. We were having dinner to celebrate our status as the number-one parts dealer in the nation. We were at a nice restaurant and Gene was there, along with about 20 people. I said to Gene, "After we became number one in the Denver metro area, you paid us bonuses, and then last year you told us if we were number one in the nation you'd double the bonus for all of us—$500 a person."

"Boy, I don't remember saying that," Gene said.

"Well, you did," I said.

Five or ten minutes later he turned to me and said, "Did I really say that?"

"Yes."

"Then we'll pay it. Tell me what I've got to do."

That's who Gene Osborne is.

A few weeks after that incident, I was in the office talking to Gene and decided to raise an issue that concerned me. We were on such a roll in volume sales and profitability that I was actually making more than Gene, who was my boss. My bonus had escalated to the point that I was nervous about it.

I told Gene, "I've had something on my mind for a while, and I've been nervous to talk to you about it, but I need to do it. I've worked for other employers who, when I started making what they deemed to be too much money on a pay plan because of the way it was structured, they changed my pay plan."

Gene said, "Let me tell you how I look at that. The more you make, the more we make. So go for it."

Gene's statement further cemented what would become my philosophy toward my own employees. It was such a great feeling to know that my employer honored his commitments. I thought, *If I ever get my shot at it, as a general manager or owner, that's how I will treat employees.* It has served me very well. One of the phrases I use when guys come to work for us and have been there a little while is this: "Once you get in here, it's hard to get out." We take care of them. Look at our track record. We don't lose many people. We keep our word to them. We're loyal to our employees, and they're loyal to their employers. I'm tough to work for, and I can be a hard guy sometimes, but if I'm so bad, then why do we have so many longtime employees?

I never forgot how Gene treated me, and when he needed help, I was glad to provide it. That's part of giving back and remembering where you came from and who helped you along the way.

POSTSCRIPT

Larry was loyal in everything he did. As Lee Benson wrote in the Deseret News: "What I admired most about him was his loyalty to friends. And if you met him for any substantive length of time, he was your friend. Every time he opened some new venture—his basketball practice facility, his racetrack, Jordan Commons, a new movie complex, the Silver Jubilee of the Miller conglomerate—he made sure I got an invitation. 'I don't care if you write anything,' he'd say. 'But I thought you might like to come. . . . You were there when we got started.'"

He was like that in every arena of his life. Most NBA owners go through coaches and front-office personnel like office temps; Miller never fired anyone. Jerry Sloan, the Jazz coach, is the longest tenured coach of any coach in American professional sports. Even when the Jazz slumped in the post–Stockton and Malone years, Miller never wavered in his commitment to the coach. Think about it. He stuck with the same girl since junior high. He stuck with the same basketball players—namely Stockton and Malone—and promised them he would never trade them, and never did, and eventually he even set them up in their own car dealership.

He stuck with the same employees and they stuck with him. At the time of Miller's passing, he had 12 employees who had each worked for him for at least 25 years—clerks, executives, parts managers, controllers, office managers, and claims officers, including some who were there when he started his business in 1979. There would be more, except that many have died or retired. Part of it was because Miller hated change, but also he had a deep sense of loyalty and gratitude to those who had helped his company succeed.

He was loyal to his childhood friends from Capitol Hill. "He was fiercely loyal to relationships and helping people," says Greg. "He had a friend named Ron Westerman. He had known him since he was four. Ron had severe health problems. He had a back condition that was so bad he could hardly move. He couldn't work. He owned Grandma's Tires, but his health got so bad that he sold the company. My dad gave him a job at our ranch in Idaho and a free place to live on the property and a small income. His job was to watch for poachers and mow the lawn. His wife wouldn't move up there, and Dad finally told him it wasn't good for him to be up there without her. So Ron moved back to Salt Lake, and Dad gave him a job at the racetrack. He really wanted to take care of him. Ron died shortly after moving back to Salt Lake City, and Dad has really missed him."

After Frank Layden decided to step down as head coach of the Jazz, "they could have easily said good-bye," says Layden. That's the normal procedure in the NBA, but Miller, ever loyal, asked Layden to stay with the team. He named him team president. "It was an honorary position," says Layden. "I didn't do much. I was out front doing a lot of speaking engagements and luncheons, meet-the-public and TV work, sitting in on some meetings, and every now and then I'd be involved in some team decisions. I was a roving ambassador. It was a nice job, and I was paid very well. Larry appreciated what I had done. He was very loyal to me. All those years I was coach and general manager and we were losing, I never worried about my job, and I was paid well and treated with great respect."

Similarly, when Jazz vice president Jay Francis prepared to leave the company to serve three years as an LDS Church mission president in Pennsylvania, Miller promised him that he would have a job when he returned. He is now a member of the advisory board on the automotive side of the operation.

PART VII

THE END

CHAPTER 36

THE LONG GOOD-BYE

I was out for one of my Sunday neighborhood walks on a June afternoon in 2008 when I was suddenly overcome by extreme fatigue. I returned to the house and sat at the counter in our kitchen. I told Gail, "I don't feel good. Something is wrong with me. This is different from anything I've experienced." In retrospect, it was a sign of trouble, but I ignored it, the same way I had ignored my health for years.

I went to work late the next morning, but I continued to feel weak. On Tuesday, Gail had scheduled a doctor's appointment to have her knee checked, and at the last minute she suggested that I accompany her and have my lab work done again since she was going there anyway. When we returned to the house that evening following our visit to the doctor's office, I was so tired that I went straight to bed. A short time later, Gail answered a phone call from Dr. Russell Shields. "Larry's labs don't look good," he told her. "It's changed a lot since the last time he was here." I had had an electro-cardiogram done six months earlier and my heart was fine, but now it was clear that something had happened in the interim. Gail woke me to tell me the doctor wanted me to return for further evaluation that night, but I refused and said I would go the next day.

Gail decided to take my blood pressure—we keep a blood pressure cuff in our room because it's part of insulin treatment for diabetes. Usually, my blood pressure is 160/90—that's high, but that's what it is. Gail strapped the cuff to my arm and the reading was 80/55. We thought it might be a bad reading, so we took it again with the same result. We kept taking it every 20 minutes, and it kept dropping—64/47 with a pulse rate of 37, then 55/37. I knew I was in trouble. At about 9:15, Gail called Dr. Shields and reported my blood pressure readings; he told her to call an ambulance.

During the ambulance ride to the hospital, my condition continued to deteriorate. I learned later that I was having a heart attack right then. I told the ER people that I felt tightness and pain in my jaw, which is one of the classic signs of a heart attack. After several minutes, the EMT who was monitoring my vital signs told the driver to turn on the siren. A team was waiting for me at the hospital. The doctors said that if I had waited longer, I might not have made it. Most of the doctors speculated that I'd had minutes left, not hours, before my heart shut down.

This was the start of a 59-day stay in the hospital, during which one problem after another manifested itself. It was as if all the years of neglect and abuse of my body had caught up with me at once. After about three weeks of hospital life, I told Gail I couldn't do it anymore. I wanted to hire my own team of doctors and have them treat me at home. But I wasn't going home anytime soon.

Late one night—on July 23—I began to suffer severe gastrointestinal bleeding. At about 12:30 I was aware that I was in trouble even though I had been asleep. I called the nurses, and when they entered the room, they weren't prepared for what they saw. The doctor told me later that I lost eight pints of blood that night. (The body only holds eight pints.) It was a mess. I should have been dead. They immediately began an IV to pump saline solution to stabilize me and transported me from Huntsman to the University Hospital ICU by ambulance. During the next few days they gave me at least eight more pints of blood and ten liters of saline solution (about two and a half gallons). The doctor said he almost lost me twice that night. This was the fourth time that I had a near-death experience.

The truth is, my health had been declining for years, and I was paying for it. Looking back now, I realize that when I quit playing softball, I didn't replace it with anything except more work, and that is the biggest reason I got myself into health problems. I just did not exercise, and it put me on a gradual downhill slide for 23 years. I made things worse by eating erratically. There were days when I was so caught up in a project—building the arena or the speedway or buying the Jazz—I would go all day without eating. Other people might get away with that, but not someone with the Type 2 diabetes I had been diagnosed with years earlier. I guess I was in denial. For years I didn't even tell Gail that I had diabetes. I didn't want to admit that I had a problem, so I resisted doing anything about it. I took pills for a while, but inevitably I would stop taking them. I didn't like the way the medicine made me feel. I didn't eat breakfast. I usually had a half sandwich for lunch at midday and then the other half at 3:30. I wouldn't eat again until I got off work at 7:30 or 8:00. My blood sugar crashed. It was not good for my body. Gail would call me at work and ask, "Are you coming home?" I'd say, "Oh, what time is it?" I was so engrossed in my work that I would forget the time and the demands of my body. I'd come home and measure my sugar level and it would be low. With diabetes you want to be as consistent as you can be—you want to avoid the ups and downs. I was putting substantial stress on my whole system. In case you haven't figured this out yet, I'm not exactly an ideal patient.

THE END

The lesson, of course, is to take care of yourself, to make time to eat and sleep and exercise. I learned that lesson too late. Yes, I would do some things differently. Aside from regrets about not spending more time with family, I would enjoy life more. I would spend more time doing the things I love to do. I love the racetrack and the cabin in Idaho.

I was so busy working and handling details. I'd get involved with people and relationships and details of situations and specs on buildings and how much steel was going in them and architects and builders. I had the opportunity to do a lot of neat things. There were a lot of events that other people would consider great, but I was so involved in them that I wasn't able to sit back and enjoy them because there was so much demand and pressure to do them. It was the only way I knew. I took on such loads. I'd go to, say, certain dinners I had to go to, and I was just going to get it done, or maybe I was speaking or just needed to be there. I missed the races at the racetrack, and I rarely went on the road with the team because I felt like there were more important things to do here. It's sad. I'm missing opportunities that other people would die for. I missed the greatest moment in the Jazz's history: John Stockton's last-second shot in Houston that sent us to our first NBA Finals in 1997.

Each year, some advertisers take their top clients on an annual trip. It's a nice international trip with good dinners and tours. I never go. Gail and the kids have gone, and I stayed home to work. The Jazz 100 Club takes a trip with the team each year to a selected city. I never go. The Jazz have an annual golf outing every year. I never go, even just to socialize. The point is, with me being so involved with details, there isn't time to go. My mind is so full of things to do that I don't even regret not going—at least, not at the time. I look back today and realize that's where the fun stuff is. What I would enjoy is being with the people, talking to the 100 Club people, advertisers, sponsors, season ticket holders. I enjoy my work and get a lot of satisfaction out of it, and I just got caught up in it and was very good at it. But I would like to have enjoyed things more along the way.

Gail doesn't believe me. She thinks I'd do it all over again the same way. Maybe she is right.

POSTSCRIPT

"Larry cheated death so many times," says Gail. "He was a little disappointed he didn't go sooner. Even as early as July [2008] he asked, 'Why don't you just let me go?'—as if I had any choice in the matter."

Larry's problems probably began long before the heart attack in the summer of 2008.

About five years earlier, Miller took a serious fall. The day was bitter cold and the parking lot outside Larry's office complex at Jordan Commons was a sheet of ice with a skiff of snow on top—the perfect combination for a slick surface. Larry, who stubbornly had refused the urging of his employees to use one of the company's covered parking spaces, parked in his usual spot and made it only a few steps before he lost his footing and fell hard onto his back, smacking the back of his head on the asphalt. A lady walked over to assist him, but she also fell and slid into Larry. Richard Nelson, one of Larry's VPs, happened to look out the window and saw Larry sprawled on the ice. Nelson called an ambulance and ran downstairs. He found his boss flat on his back, unable to get up, and his head was bleeding. Larry asked for someone to retrieve a blanket from his car. He was eventually taken to Alta View Hospital by ambulance.

As Whitworth recalls, "There was no concussion. But we all said this was going to start a downhill slide, and it did. It was a big fall. He wasn't taking care of himself. From there we noticed little things. He even said to me one time that the fall had taken something off his sharpness."

Everyone noticed the decline and his refusal to watch his health.

That was why Stockton "kidnapped" Miller and took him to his doctor in Pocatello. "That gave Larry another year," says Whitworth.

Seeing his decline as early as four years ago, Gail gave him a decorative board as a gift, with the inscription, "Grow old along with me, the best is yet to be." She placed it in the bathroom where he could see it every day as incentive to take care of himself so that he would remain her partner for as long as he could. Larry told her at the time that he would give her 10,000 more days.

But he grew weaker and weaker. His condition deteriorated so much that Gail resigned from the board of trustees at Salt Lake Community College to be with Larry. He had surgery to remove a large calcium deposit on his leg. "From that point on he became weaker," says Gail. He was sleeping late, he was chronically tired, his diabetes was out of control, walking was difficult. Gail had to help him dress. He could barely make himself go to work, which certainly was unlike Larry.

"I don't fear death," Larry said at the time. "If I die now, I won't feel too bad. I've been able to do so many things on a regular basis that would have been lifetime experiences for most people. What I do worry about is leaving Gail. She's been so good to me. I'm fighting to live out our later years together."

After the heart attack, life became a series of doctor appointments and hospital stays and blood tests and hyperbaric treatments and rehab exercises. Larry, predictably, just wanted to return to work—the Joseph Smith Papers, this book, and his company's 30th anniversary celebration were his latest projects, among other things. He turned for counsel to Elder M. Russell Ballard, a member of the Quorum of the Twelve Apostles of The Church of Jesus Christ of Latter-day Saints, who became a great source of strength in Larry's final weeks, helping him find perspective in his pain and suffering.

In October, Larry was hospitalized with the bone infection and diabetic ulcers in his feet. A few weeks later he had two toes amputated. One night in early December, Gail heard Larry mumble

The Larry and Gail Miller family, December 2005.

Larry, Gail, and grandson Zane.

Larry and his son Greg have always shared a love of cars. It was a special day for both when Larry surprised Greg with the keys and the ownership of a 1966 Shelby Mustang (Greg's birth year).

Larry with his fleet of school Mustangs used in the Driving School at
Miller Motorsports Park in Tooele, Utah.

Larry and family members and MMP employees gather at the Ford factory in Dearborn,
Michigan, to receive the first of seventy-seven FR500S race cars built exclusively in a joint
venture between Ford and Larry for the "Miller Cup" Mustang Challenge, a circuit of
races originating at Miller Motorsports Park.

Larry gives a few instructions at the groundbreaking for the Miller Motorsports Park, April 26, 2005.

Larry looks over plans for the racetrack with designer Alan Wilson (right), architect Ken Louder (left), and contractor Tom Mabey (second from left).

Construction under way at the racetrack.

Larry with his family prior to departing from the track on the first Utah Fast Pass fund-raiser for the Fallen Heroes Foundation.

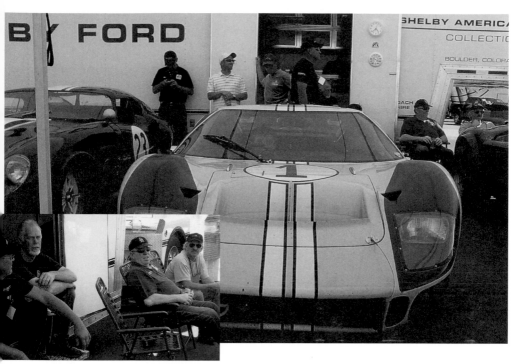

Larry and his Cobra enthusiast friends, relaxing at Miller Motorsports Park during the Shelby American Automobile Club annual meet in 2007.

PHOTO BY ERIC SAWYER

In the lead—Larry races car number 13 at Goodwood, England, in the "Hillclimb" event.

Ribbon-cutting ceremony for the baseball stadium in Salt Lake City, home of the Triple A Salt Lake Bees. Larry oversaw construction of the stadium and later bought the team.

The office tower and restaurants at Jordan Commons theater complex.

Salt Lake Community College Miller Campus; one of several buildings for entrepreneurial study.

Larry with some of the Junior Achievement participants he helped support.

Groundbreaking for the baseball/softball complex at Brigham Young University in Provo, Utah.

Larry provided major funding for the Joseph Smith Papers project, which was very dear to his heart.

Larry and Gail with David M. Brown, who was instrumental in their returning to activity in the LDS Church while living in Colorado.

Larry teaches a Sunday School class in his Salt Lake ward. He loved the youth.

Larry received five honorary doctorate degrees, including
this one from Salt Lake Community College.

Larry accepts an award from the Salt Lake
Chamber of Commerce as "A Giant
in Our City."

Larry's last public appearance—accepting a
plaque acknowledging his induction into the
Utah Auto Dealers Hall of Fame in early 2009.

Jon Huntsman Sr., Larry Miller, Spence Eccles, Sam Battistone, and Greg Miller
at the 25th anniversary celebration of the Larry H. Miller Companies.

Jon Huntsman Jr., then governor
of Utah, visits Miller Motorsports Park
to ride his motorcycle.

With Carroll Shelby, whose name is
synonymous with the classic Shelby Cobra.

British Prime Minister Margaret Thatcher visits with Gail, Larry, and Robert Graham
as Larry is recognized as a distinguished Utahn.

Utah Governor Norm Bangerter and Larry
at a press conference to recognize Karl Malone
of the Utah Jazz.

Larry meets the Dalai Lama.

Talking with President Gordon B. Hinckley.

With Pulitzer-Prize-winning author David McCullough and his wife, Rosalie.

Larry and Gail participate in the torch run for the Salt Lake City 2002 Olympic Winter Games.

Larry greets Juan Samaranch, president of the International Olympic Committee, and presents him with an autographed Jazz basketball.

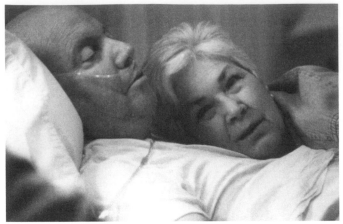

Larry's last days—resting at home with Gail.

Larry's watch and ring, tokens of a simple man.

Grandchildren gather for a last sleepover in Larry's bedroom.

Larry's casket was painted to match his favorite Shelby Cobra.

Gail receives the game ball at the first Jazz game after Larry's death.

Larry H. Miller. His legacy lives on.

something in his sleep, and when she tried to roust him she noticed he was cold and clammy. After measuring his blood sugar at an alarming 47, she gave him apple juice and checked his blood sugar again. This time it was 25, which meant he was nearing coma stage. He was taken to the hospital by ambulance and stayed one night. A couple of days later he ate little and told Gail he didn't feel good enough to attend that night's Jazz game—something he almost never missed.

The next day he could barely move or maintain his balance. Elder Ballard came to the house and gave blessings to both Gail and Larry. Larry continued to be lethargic, and the next day, Sunday, he stayed in bed. Gail called the doctor, and a nurse came to the house to take a blood test. After seeing the test results, Dr. Bill Dunson called to tell Gail to take her husband to the hospital's medical ICU unit. As fate would have it, both Bryan and Roger were visiting babies in the same hospital where Larry was being treated—Bryan's child and Roger's grandchild were both born prematurely. Both sons were there in the NICU when Larry arrived.

The boys visited their father, and, after they left, as Gail and Larry talked, he said, "If this is the end, I want to say good-bye to the children." Then he lost consciousness. Gail told a nurse that Larry wasn't responding, and she continued to call Larry's name to try to revive him. The nurse called out the door for the code team. Larry had gone into cardiac arrest—his heart had stopped. They revived him with CPR while Gail stood in the corner and watched.

So he cheated death again. He recovered and returned home, and he managed to attend the Christmas sing-along in the basketball arena, one of his favorite events and one he had rescued from extinction. It was only a brief respite from his problems.

On January 20, 2009, Gail called Dr. Dunson to report that Larry's temperature had soared to 104.7. He told her to bring him to the hospital immediately, but Larry refused. "I've had enough," he said. The doctor came to the house. He unwrapped the bandages from Larry's foot, and fluid poured out of the bunion incision where the joint of the big toe had been surgically removed. Larry was driven to the hospital again and then later moved to the ICU. The diagnosis: sepsis—blood infection. The doctor told Gail, "You need to call your children. I don't know which way this is going." He recovered again—he had cheated death yet again—but for the first time there was talk about the possibility of amputation.

Larry's health continued to deteriorate. For weeks he underwent hyperbaric treatments and dialysis. His lower legs were turning black, and whenever he stood the increased flow of blood to his legs caused excruciating pain. One morning he told Gail, "I know what I'm in for, and I don't even want to get out of bed because I know it's going to be so painful."

There were daily complications, and his days were filled with more treatments and doctors and hospitals. His strength waned. He complained frequently about his "diminished capacity." There was no time to live his life, no time to work, which was what he loved. "That's why he decided to have his legs amputated," says Gail. On January 23, doctors amputated his legs six inches below the knees.

Larry received a few visitors while he was in the hospital, among them the Jazz players and coaches. They showed up in the surgical ICU with glum faces, but Larry wouldn't have it. "Hey, why the long faces, guys?" he said, and that broke the ice and they had a good visit.

Larry and his family believed the amputation would finally stabilize his health. Larry himself looked forward to learning to use prosthetic legs; for ten days he was shuttled by ambulance between the rehab department of the hospital and the hyperbaric treatment building down the street. His rehab consisted of learning how to get in and out of his wheelchair and bed, how to operate the electric wheelchair, and other activities that would afford him a measure of independence without legs. This was a very difficult time for him. He wondered, "How am I ever going to do this?"

After ten days, doctors removed the casts from the stumps of his legs. "I'm standing there thinking, that does not look good," recalls

Gail. "But I didn't say anything because I didn't know how it should look. The skin looked very fragile; it was not pink and healthy looking. The doctors didn't say anything for a couple of days." Then the skin on his legs started to turn black, and the ends of his legs were so painful that even to put the dressings over them was excruciating.

"We realized then that something was terribly wrong," says Gail. Not only did his legs begin to blacken, but so did his fingers. Three of the fingers actually died.

Tests revealed that he had calciphylaxis and had had it for some time. It's a rare disease in which the blood vessels fill with calcium, preventing oxygen from reaching tissue. That's why his legs were beginning to blacken—they were dying.

Larry received this news on Thursday, February 12. He had months to live if he chose to continue the dialysis, or five to nine days if he chose not to continue it.

"On Friday we spent the day talking about what to do," says Gail. "His biggest concern was how I was going to manage without him. He had a really hard time with that. Once I convinced him I'd be okay, he said we needed to call the kids."

Greg, Roger, and Steve immediately left Phoenix, where they were attending NBA All-Star Game events, to return home. The family met at the hospital on Saturday night and stayed until midnight. Larry explained that he had decided he would no longer undergo dialysis treatments. On Sunday morning the Miller children returned, and they held a church service in Larry's hospital room.

Gail called Elder Ballard and told him that she had convinced Larry she would be all right if he moved on; he was ready. Elder Ballard came to the hospital and visited with Larry and then gave him a blessing. As the family looked on, Elder Ballard told Larry it was time to start preparing for the other side.

On Monday, Larry called members of his advisory board to his hospital room and told them the news. That afternoon, his children arrived. Gail brought photo albums so they could reminiscence. Larry *was tired, but he interacted with the family as much as he could. Later that night, as Gail sat with Larry in his hospital room, she received a call from Karen, their only daughter. Knowing Larry was scheduled to return home the next day, she asked, "What would you think about having a sleepover? What if all the children and grandchildren slept at the house?" Larry returned home Tuesday morning. The Miller children and grandchildren—32 in all—spent the next three nights sleeping on the floor around Larry's bed. They watched old videos—some of them family videos, some of them news clips and documentaries detailing Larry's projects and accomplishments, some of which the grandchildren had never seen. Larry was aware of his surroundings, and every now and then he provided commentary for the gathering. One video clip showed him making polite comments in a TV interview about the negotiations he had completed with a Jazz player. "That's a bunch of baloney," Larry said, referring to the (overly) diplomatic comments he had made for the TV audience.*

On Wednesday, at Larry's request, Gail began calling old friends to invite them to the house to say good-bye. One by one, or in groups, they arrived and climbed the stairs to the master bedroom to see Larry for the last time, some coming from as far away as California. They were old softball teammates, childhood friends from the Capitol Hill gang, friends from the Colorado days, close business associates, relatives, Church leaders. Larry's children and grandchildren also made their way up to the room to talk with him. He gave them advice and admonished them to have a good life.

Larry wanted to ensure that his family was taken care of—and then there was the question of what to do with the bear. Two years earlier, one of his granddaughters, Madelaine, ten at the time, had saved her money to buy a gift for her grandfather on his birthday. The gift she settled on was a Build-A-Bear in a race car and Jazz clothing. Larry kept the gift in his room, and when he could see that his days were numbered, he decided to return it. He called Madelaine to his room and told her how much the bear meant to him and that she should have it now. She cried; he cried. He told her it was one of the best gifts anyone had ever given him.

Seven months earlier, Larry had received a blessing from Elder Ballard and had subsequent discussions in which he was told that he would recover from his heart attack because he still had work to do with his family, to bring them closer to the gospel and unite them. "Sustained close relationships were always difficult for Larry," says Gail, "and also he didn't feel there was that much wrong with his family and that he had done a lot of work and made a lot of progress. The family was closer than they ever had been. He had grown closer to the gospel in his own life. We had been doing monthly family home evenings with our children and grandchildren for years. He didn't think this was something he needed to be saved for. He felt there had to be something else; he wanted it to be something like the Joseph Smith Papers, which he viewed as maybe his life's greatest legacy after his family. But he did come to realize that blessing at the end, because he spent a lot of time talking to Roger and Karen about getting back into the Church. That last week was the fulfillment of it all. It really united the family. His family literally came closer; they came together and were gathered in his room and were united."

Gail and Larry had also been brought closer, literally and figuratively. For all those years that he was preoccupied with work and had left her at home to raise the kids alone for long hours, the last seven months of his life he was forced to retire and remain at home to recover, throwing him and Gail together around the clock. It wasn't always easy. She had her routine, and he had his. She dropped everything to care for him. She wanted no regrets, and this drove her past normal endurance. She drove him around town and lifted him in and out of cars and bed and into the bathroom, and she treated his ulcerated feet. Even after she finally got him in bed at night, she worked on his ravaged feet for another hour. This was difficult for Larry to accept, and he told her this. "I can't do anything for you; all I can do is take," he said. Says Gail, "I told him he had done *everything. There wasn't much left to do. But he was trying to validate what he had done with his life, and now I felt he should be the receiver. He worried about the stress it put on me."*

By Friday, February 20, rumors of Miller's condition were reaching the media. The Millers decided it was time to make an announcement—something they had put off for days to give themselves privacy. They called Linda Luchetti, vice president of communications for the Jazz and Miller Sports and Entertainment, to the house late that afternoon to prepare a press release. Gail, not wanting to leave Larry alone, invited Luchetti to the upstairs room. Gail sat on one side of the bed with her back to her husband, and Karen sat on the other side of the bed facing her father, while Luchetti sat in a chair. Just as they began to decide the wording of the press release, Karen told her mother, "Mom, Dad's changing." Gail, who earlier in the morning had suspected (based on her observations) that this would be Larry's final day, asked Luchetti to leave. The family all gathered around the bed so they could be closer to Larry in his final moments.

"We all stood around him and said our good-byes," says Gail. "He took a deep breath and sighed and then he was gone. A tear fell from his left eye."

Larry Miller shared everything with the public. He wore his feelings openly—he shared his tears, his thoughts, his troubles, his regrets, his weaknesses, his private life. And so his good-bye was public as well. "Larry was just a public man," says Gail, "and to do anything less would not have been the right tribute to him."

The family opened the viewing and the funeral to everyone. After consulting with Church authorities about the setting—they were told the funeral should be held in a building that had been dedicated (blessed through formal prayer)—they settled on EnergySolutions Arena, which had been dedicated upon its completion. "The idea," says Gail, "was that anybody who wanted should be able to pay tribute, in light of the fact that he had touched so many lives. We had no idea how many would attend, but we wanted to make it available to all."

The Miller family arrived at the arena for the viewing at 2:30 on a Friday afternoon—a workday. They didn't leave until after 10:00 that night. Gail and her children and their spouses and the grandchildren stood in line greeting well-wishers nonstop. The line snaked from the main entrance all the way through the concourse, down the stairway, and through the hallways under the bleachers to the viewing room. The first hour was reserved for those closest to Miller—Jazz players and officials, Church leaders, family members. Gail greeted every visitor personally, and there were thousands of them. "It wasn't for them; really it was for me," she says. In a single afternoon and evening, Gail hugged more people than Bob Barker and Richard Dawson combined, most of them perfect strangers. She removed her shoes to relieve her tired feet and greeted the people barefoot, as if she were welcoming guests to her home. The people arrived in T-shirts and jeans, they came in Jazz apparel, some in suits and ties, some in dresses, others in the Larry Miller uniform—khakis, polo shirt, and sneakers. (Greg Miller had suggested to Gail that he and his brothers wear white sneakers with their dark suits at the viewing, in honor of their father's famous casual fashion statement, but she nixed the idea.) Someone gave Gail a Special Olympics medal; another, a white rose dipped in ceramic and etched in 24-carat gold (an allusion to the white rose she had placed on Larry's empty chair during the first Jazz game after his passing). Others pressed notes into her hand that expressed their feelings about her husband. Still others donated money to LHM Charities in lieu of flowers, which added up to more than $85,000.

The Miller family bore up well; they had had time to adjust to the idea of Larry's death. They had had that final week to be together and say good-bye. So the viewing and the funeral were more of a happy celebration of his life than a sad good-bye, although there were still tears.

Gail and Larry—facing a prolonged separation for the first time since that first date 50 years earlier—had planned his funeral together. He had picked the songs and the text for the printed programs. Thomas S.

THE END

Monson, President of The Church of Jesus Christ of Latter-day Saints, and Elder M. Russell Ballard both spoke, along with Larry's children and grandchildren. Larry was buried in the Salt Lake City Cemetery, which sits at the base of the hill on which Larry's mansion stands. Gail picked out a plot that she could see from her bedroom, and every day she looks out to gaze down at Larry's gravesite. There you are and here I am, she finds herself thinking; after all these years together, we're still close.

Now, it's Larry who is waiting for Gail to come home.

Epilogue

By Gail Miller

What is it like to be married to Larry H. Miller?" That is a question I am asked frequently but not an easy question to answer. Over the course of our lives the answer has varied: sometimes easy, sometimes hard, sometimes fun, sometimes stressful, and sometimes all of the above at the same time. One thing it *never* was was boring!

Let me say right at the outset that, to me, Larry was not such an extraordinary person—at least, not in the beginning. That came later, and even I marveled at all he was able to accomplish. But in the beginning, we were just two young kids trying to make a go of life.

We met when we were twelve. Who knows anything about life at twelve? We started dating at fourteen. Who knows anything about life at fourteen? We married at twenty-one. Who knows anything about life at twenty-one? We didn't even know enough about life to plan ahead. We just jumped in with both feet! Our first six weeks of marriage were spent in a motel room with a kitchenette. We were waiting for the apartment building Larry's Uncle Reid was constructing to be finished so we could become his first tenants. His uncle gave us our first month's rent as a wedding gift. We borrowed furniture from him for the living room because all we had were a bedroom set I had bought after I got my first job in high school and the wedding gifts we received for our reception, which were mostly china dishes, not very useful at the time but treasured now. The first piece of furniture we bought was a TV set so we could watch the new TV shows in the fall. The second piece was a kitchen-table-and-chair set that lasted us twenty years.

At first, being married was very romantic. Our honeymoon lasted ten days and covered three thousand miles. We stayed in cheap motels and ate sandwiches in the car, but we loved every minute of it. Everything was bright and new. Like most young couples, we thought we were invincible. We knew we would be just fine. We were ready to conquer the world, and nothing seemed impossible. As we set up our apartment, it didn't take us long to realize that married life was going to be very different from our dating years. We were so busy. We both worked full-time, and the additional responsibility of running a household made it impossible to be as carefree or have as much time together as we were used to. I think that became our biggest adjustment. After all, we had been constant companions for six years before we got married. Now we had to focus on other things.

When the children started coming we realized what REAL responsibility was. Again, we didn't plan ahead, and when I found out I was pregnant I wasn't sure I was ready to become a mother—but, ready or not, it was happening. What a miracle it is to create a new life! What a blessing children are!

Life for us was very much the same as it was for everyone we knew. We had the same hopes and dreams, the same ups and downs, joys and sorrows, lean times and times of plenty. We never turned back and never relied on our parents for help. We were moving forward and learning a lot along the way.

For the first five years, I was the one with the steady job and the insurance, and Larry was trying to find a job that he could love and thrive with. That didn't come until we moved to Colorado. We moved so he could play softball on a world-class team. Actually, at the time, work was secondary. Softball was first. We moved thinking we would be there for one year—and we stayed for eight and a half years. Larry realized he had to be so good at something that no one could deny him employment. That was crucial because we having our third child, and *they* weren't temporary.

That was the beginning of a new era. If we thought we were busy before, we were wrong. This was busy! During the Colorado years we both learned to sacrifice. We defined our roles in our marriage, not by talking about them but by doing what was necessary to make it work. We put our heads down and moved ahead with a vengeance. My role was to take care of the home and children, and his role was to be the breadwinner. Larry learned quickly that it was going to take a lot to keep our family on a sound financial footing. He began to work a lot of overtime. I adjusted. I learned how to organize my life to keep things on an even keel, still take care of Larry, and spend a lot of time with the children to make up for his absence. I also learned everything there was to learn about running a household by myself, including taking care of the yard, doing all the house repairs (broken windows, holes in the walls from rambunctious boys, and such), all the toy repairs (bikes, skateboards, dolls, kites), and everything in between. I became the inventory control clerk, the scheduler, the maintenance supervisor, the chef, the tutor, the sport and recreation manager, the historian, chauffeur, interior decorator, and family counselor. I was also on call for anything that Larry might need, which always took top priority. In order to spend time with him we attended his softball games, and consequently it felt like our children were raised at the ballpark.

He didn't have time to go to their ball games, so we went to his. Softball was serious business to Larry, almost as serious as work—maybe even more at times.

We had three more children while we lived in Colorado, making a total of five. We did more growing during that time than at any time during our marriage. We also became active in the Church again.

It wasn't until we moved back to Salt Lake and started our own business that life really began to get interesting. We had both thought we would be working for Chuck Stevinson forever. We never talked about going into business for ourselves. It just happened. It was very scary to be the "owner" instead of the employee. This wasn't because I lacked faith in Larry—I didn't. I knew he could do anything he set his mind to and I would support him. He had proved himself in Colorado. The scary part to me was that now we were responsible not only for ourselves but also for all of our employees. That was very hard for me to get my head around.

Every day was a new adventure. Sometimes I likened our life to living in an amusement park where some days it was like being on a roller coaster all day long. I never knew what to expect next. But we made it work. There were lots of parts that I didn't like, but there were lots of good things, too. I don't think I would change a thing except for the hours apart. Time apart takes its toll on a marriage. Life is way too short to spend it all at work. When you are apart for great lengths of time you can't build relationships with your children. You can't have the same kinds of bonds with your family that you have when you *live* life together instead of just "reporting in."

In our relationship, Larry was the more "public" person. I was the "safe place" for him to come to and find peace. It took him a lot of years to accept the fact that I was what he called "milquetoast" until one day I said to him, "That is exactly what you like about me—I am the only steady and calm thing in your life." Instantly he knew I was right. He had to go out into the chaotic world and slay dragons every day, and I was able to stay at home and make a place where he could find refuge, comfort, and love when he returned. He appreciated that.

I always appreciated the fact that I did not have to hold down an outside job. He believed that our children needed their mother to stay at home with them and worked long hours to make it possible for me to do so. One day early in our marriage, when I was feeling guilty about leaving them while I worked, I said to my mother, who was tending them for me, "I feel so bad that they are missing out on so much because I am working." She looked at me with a wise look on her face and said, "They're not missing anything; I'm making sure of that. You are the one missing out!" She was right, of course, so when Larry finally made enough money that I could stay at home with them, it was an easy decision and one we have never regretted. I always loved how they called "MOM?" when they walked in the door from school.

Our life went on this way long enough that I wondered if it would ever change. I was always expecting that it would be different when he got over the current hurdle: Different when he got the parts department organized. Different when he got the next project finished. Different next month, next year, and so on. When he started to formulate five-year plans for his goals at work, I knew that it was never going to be different and that I had better learn to be happy planning my life around his. It was a good thing that I was so patient. It was good that I liked my role at home as wife and mother. It was good that I believed in him and shared his core values.

However, this kind of living was not easy. As Larry worked his way up the job ladder, his problems and challenges at work got bigger and he got more stressed. He had a lot of what he called passion. I called it temper. When the children started to become teenagers, their problems started to get bigger too. By this time, Larry was so entrenched in work that taking our problems to him was out of the question. There was no way, with all that he was dealing with at work, that I wanted to burden him with one more thing. If things got so bad that I couldn't handle them alone and I had no alternative, I would bite the bullet and get him involved. It often wasn't pretty. He would let the offending child know in no uncertain terms that he or she was expected to do things right and do them well and not be a problem for me. Because of his iron-fisted rule, they all vowed they would never be in the car business and be "married to their work like Dad is." It wasn't until much later, after they all went to work in our dealerships after all, that I realized a very important fact. Even though they didn't have the close father-son or father-daughter relationship that they so desperately wanted in their childhood, they did get something I believe was every bit as important. They all got a good foundation of respect, ethics, hard work, selflessness, honor, patriotism, faith in God, and sheer drive. In other words, they have the same basic foundation of values that their dad and I have. I will be forever grateful that they chose to internalize the good in their father rather than rebel and become bitter. Because each one had the opportunity to work in one of our businesses, they, as well as he, had a "second chance" to bond and build a good relationship. It didn't take the place of their childhood, but it helped to fill a big void in their lives and they learned that he had always loved them—he just didn't always know how to be a dad.

One of the things that has been a big plus in our relationship and marriage was our common outlook about money and possessions. We both learned at an early age to be self-sufficient; if we couldn't afford something, we didn't need it. Larry had a paper route as a kid, and I earned my spending money by babysitting and cleaning house for a family in the stake. During our dating years we did a lot of walking. Because we lived close to downtown, we could walk wherever we wanted to go. We often went to dinner and a movie. Many times we had to dig into the bottom of my purse to find another penny or two to be able to afford two tickets to the movie.

Years later, when we built the Jordan Commons movie theaters in Sandy, Larry decided to name them after the theaters we frequented as teenagers: the Gem, the Center, the Uptown, and the Utah theaters. I don't think many people know the significance of the names there. Naming the theaters at Jordan Commons after the ones so familiar to us as kids was Larry's way of immortalizing those dating years.

From the very beginning of our marriage, we were careful with our money. We didn't seek material things. We didn't need to spend everything we earned. I think the fact that neither of us had a lot growing up made it easy for us to find the real wealth in life. We both liked being able to help others. We both liked being able to make something out of nothing. We enjoyed spending time together and we loved being with our children. If one of us had coveted money, we would have been in big trouble.

Looking back now, I am thankful for the challenges life brought us. I realize we had many blessings, but it was the challenges that gave us the most growth, and we are better people because of them. I know that most people who don't know us think we have lived a charmed life—we haven't. Our children have had their share of trials and difficulties. Our marriage survived in spite of the ups and downs that put severe strain on it. I have often said I am grateful that there was never an occasion when we both wanted a divorce at the same time. Money doesn't make a person happy, but I am not foolish enough to believe it doesn't make a big difference in making life less difficult. It was very important to both of us to keep money in perspective. Neither of us wanted it to change us. We liked where we came from and who we were and we worked very hard to stay grounded. We believe that money is a tool to do good things with. Doing good things brings a wonderful kind of reward of its own. We have been very blessed in many ways because we didn't let success and money define us.

All in all, life has been very good. Along the way, Larry and I learned a lot from each other. I think I softened him and he made me stronger. I learned a lot about systems and organization from him and he learned to let go and relax from me. I learned to be interested in more people, to come out of my comfort zone, and he learned to cherish our family more. I learned a lot about business and business practices and he learned how to make wonderful soup. I learned to appreciate his Cobra cars and he learned to appreciate scrapbooking. He learned to listen better and I learned to express emotions better. Together we learned to communicate and our lives became richer. Life is a process, and we learned to enjoy the journey not by trying to change each other but by being willing to change ourselves.

When Larry died, I knew it would take some time to learn how to go on by myself. I knew I would have to try to build a life without him after fifty years of togetherness. (We were married forty-four of those fifty years, but we were constant companions for an additional six years before our marriage.) He often told me that I would be just fine without him because I am so self-sufficient, but that wasn't the issue. Fifty years is a long time to spend with someone; we had become a team, a very good team. Our individual roles were clearly defined in our relationship, but we worked together like two parts of a smooth-running machine. Our lives were separate yet meshed together as one. The challenge now becomes learning how to define my life on my own. I will need to decide what my focus will be without the companionship of my life partner and to prioritize the important things that are left to be done before I join him. No matter the course I choose, I will honor the life he led and continue to do the things that he established as his legacy, working to help make Utah a great place to live.

When a loved one dies, it is a stark reminder of what is really important in this life. It's not what you have; it's what you are that matters.

When I think of Larry, I feel his spirit. His spirit is magnificent.

It is pure and kind and uncomplicated. It is good, righteous, and without guile. It has strength unmatched to do as much good for as many as he possibly can. It is selfless and generous. It is loving and sweet and tender. It is strong and valiant. It is untiring and courageous. It is devoted and fiercely protective. It is soft and gentle. I can see his spirit clearly at all times, and that is why I love him. His spirit is intertwined with mine for eternity, and I am grateful for that blessing.

ACKNOWLEDGMENTS

F rom Doug Robinson: Special thanks to the late, great Larry Miller, for asking me to do this project, which was an honor; to Gail, the serene, steady, and wise woman of Larry's life, who provided me with homemade meals, hospitality, and, in the end, wonderfully perceptive interviews in her husband's stead; to Steve Starks, Denny Haslam, Clark Whitworth, Frank Layden, and Greg Miller for helping to fill in some of the blanks left in the story when Larry passed away; to the *Deseret News*—and especially Joe Cannon, Rick Hall, and Ellis Ivory—for providing remarkable support, patience, and encouragement for this project; to Lee Benson, my adviser, sounding board, therapist, fellow *Deseret News* columnist, and great friend for 30 years and simply one of the finest people I have ever met; to my family, my raison d'etre; and to my sweet mother, Joyce, my longtime loyal reader.

ADDENDA

THE COUNTESS AND THE IMPOSSIBLE

(AKA THE FIVE-DOLLAR JOB)

BY RICHARD THURMAN

No one in our Utah town knew where the Countess had come from; her carefully precise English indicated that she was not a native American. From the size of her house and staff we knew that she must be wealthy, but she never entertained and she made it clear that when she was at home she was completely inaccessible. Only when she stepped outdoors did she become at all a public figure—and then chiefly to the small fry of the town, who lived in awe of her.

The Countess always carried a cane, not only for support but as a means of chastising any youngster she thought needed disciplining. And at one time or another most of the kids in our neighborhood seemed to display that need. By running fast and staying alert I had managed to keep out of her reach. But one day when I was 13, as I was shortcutting through her hedge, she got close enough to rap my head with her stick. "Ouch!" I yelled, jumping a couple of feet.

"Young man, I want to talk to you," she said. I was expecting a lecture on the evils of trespassing, but as she looked at me, half smiling, she seemed to change her mind.

"Don't you live in that green house with the willow trees, in the next block?"

"Yes, ma'am."

"Do you take care of your lawn? Water it? Clip it? Mow it?"

"Yes, ma'am."

"Good. I've lost my gardener. Be at my house Thursday morning at seven, and don't tell me you have something else to do; I've seen you slouching around on Thursdays."

When the Countess gave an order, it was carried out. I didn't dare not come on that next Thursday. I went over the whole lawn three times with a mower before she was satisfied, and then she had me down on all fours looking for weeds until my knees were as green as the grass. She finally called me up to the porch.

"Well, young man, how much do you want for your day's work?"

"I don't know. Fifty cents maybe."

"Is that what you figure you're worth?"

"Yes'm. About that."

"Very well. Here's the 50 cents you say you're worth and here's the dollar and a half more that I've earned for you by pushing you. Now I'm going to tell you something about how you and I are going to work together. There are as many ways of mowing a lawn as there are people, and they may be worth anywhere from a penny to five dollars. Let's say that a three-dollar job would be just what you've done today, except that you would do it all by yourself. A four-dollar job would be so perfect that you'd have to be something of a fool to spend that much time on a lawn. A five-dollar lawn is—well, it's impossible, so we'll forget about that. Now then, each week I'm going to pay you according to your own evaluation of your work."

I left with my two dollars, richer than I remembered being in my whole life, and determined that I would get four dollars out of her the next week. But I failed to reach even the three-dollar mark. My will began faltering the second time around her yard.

"Two dollars again, eh? That kind of job puts you right on the edge of being dismissed, young man."

"Yes'm. But I'll do better next week."

And somehow I did. The last time around the lawn I was exhausted, but I found I could spur myself on. In the exhilaration of that new feeling I had no hesitation in asking the Countess for three dollars.

Each Thursday for the next four or five weeks, I varied between a three- and a three-and-a-half-dollar job. The more I became acquainted with her lawn, places where the ground was a little high or a little low, places where it needed to be clipped short or left long on the edges to make a more satisfying curve along the garden, the more aware I became of just what a four-dollar lawn would consist of. And each week I would resolve to do just that kind of a job. But by the time I had made my three- or three-and-a-half-dollar mark I was too tired to remember even having had the ambition to go beyond that point.

"You look like a good, consistent three-fifty man," she would say as she handed me the money.

"I guess so," I would say, too happy at the sight of the money to remember that I had shot for something higher.

"Well, don't feel too bad," she would comfort me. "After all, there are only a handful of people in the world who could do a four-dollar job."

And her words *were* a comfort at first. But then, without my noticing what was happening, her comfort became an irritant that made me resolve to do that four-dollar job, even if it killed me. In the fever of my resolve I could see myself expiring on her lawn, with the Countess leaning over me, handing me the four dollars with a tear in her eye, begging my forgiveness for having thought I couldn't do it.

THE COUNTESS AND THE IMPOSSIBLE

It was in the middle of such a fever, one Thursday night when I was trying to forget that day's defeat and get some sleep, that the truth hit me so hard that I sat upright, half choking in my excitement. It was the *five-dollar* job I had to do, not the four-dollar one! I had to do the job that no one could do because it was impossible.

I was well acquainted with the difficulties ahead. I had the problem, for example, of doing something about the worm mounds in the lawn. The Countess might not even have noticed them yet, they were so small; but in my bare feet I knew about them and had to do something about them. And I *could* go on trimming the garden edges with shears, but I knew that a five-dollar lawn demanded that I line up each edge exactly with a yardstick and then trim it precisely with the edger. And there were other problems that only I and my bare feet knew about.

I started the next Thursday by ironing out the worm mounds with a heavy roller. After two hours of that I was ready to give up for the day. Nine o'clock in the morning and my will was already gone! It was only by accident that I discovered how to regain it. Sitting under a walnut tree for a few minutes after finishing the rolling, I fell asleep. When I woke up minutes later the lawn looked so good and felt so good under my feet, I was anxious to get on with the job.

I followed this secret for the rest of the day, dozing a few minutes every hour to regain my perspective and replenish my strength. Between naps I mowed four times, two times lengthwise, two times across, until the lawn looked like a green velvet checkerboard. Then I dug around every tree, crumbling the big clods and smoothing the soil with my hand, then finished with the edger, meticulously lining up each stroke so the effect would be perfectly symmetrical. And I carefully trimmed the grass between the flagstones of the front walk. The shears wore my fingers raw, but the walk never looked better.

Finally about eight o'clock that evening, after I had run home at five for a bite of supper, it was all completed. I was so proud I didn't even feel tired when I went up to her door.

"Well, what is it today?" she asked.

"Five dollars," I said, trying for a little calm and sophistication.

"Five dollars? You mean four dollars, don't you? I told you that a five-dollar lawn job isn't possible."

"Yes it is. I just did it."

"Well, young man, the first five-dollar lawn in history certainly deserves some looking around."

We walked about the lawn together in the last light of evening, and even I was quite overcome by the impossibility of what I had done.

"Young man," she said, putting her hand on my shoulder, "what on earth made you do such a crazy, wonderful thing?"

I didn't know why, but even if I had, I could not have explained it in the excitement of hearing that I *had* done it.

"I think I know," she continued, "how you felt when this idea came to you of mowing a lawn that I told you was impossible. It made you very happy when it first came, then a little frightened. Am I right?"

She could see she was right by the startled look on my face.

"I know how you felt because the same thing happens to almost everybody. They feel this sudden burst in them of wanting to do some great thing. They feel a wonderful happiness. But then it passes because they have said, 'No, I can't do that. It's impossible.' Whenever something in you says, 'It's impossible,' remember to take a careful look. See if it isn't really God asking you to grow an inch, or a foot, or a mile that you may come to a fuller life."

She folded my hand around the money. "You've been a great man today. It's not often a man gets paid for a thing like greatness. You're getting paid because you're lucky and I like you. Now run along."

Since that time, some 25 years ago, when I have felt myself at an end with nothing before me, suddenly with the appearance of that word "impossible" I have experienced again the unexpected lift, the leap inside me, and known that the only possible way lay through the very middle of the impossible.

POSTSCRIPT

This story, originally printed in Reader's Digest *in June 1958 by Richard Thurman under the title of "The Countess and the Impossible," was one of Miller's favorites. Miller identified himself as the boy in the story, but, as Gail notes, later he became the Countess character in helping others to reach their capacity.*

"The Five-Dollar Job story epitomizes Larry," says Clark Whitworth. "He envisioned himself as that boy. He would have done everything because he wanted to be perfect, and he wanted his work to be worthy of the highest prize. He was able to project that to his employees. It was genuine. It was home. He was a shark. He had to keep moving. He never would have retired. He was going to work and die. It fulfilled him. It vitalized him. He loved it so much. He loved being in that corner office and solving problems. And he was at his best when times were most challenging."

MILESTONES OF LARRY H. MILLER'S CAREER

DATE	MILESTONE
Thursday, April 5, 1979	Made deal with Hugh Gardner and Tony Hernadez to buy Toyota of Murray in Utah
Tuesday, May 1, 1979	Began operating Toyota of Murray in Murray, Utah
Wednesday, September 19, 1979	Bought Sundance Toyota in Spokane, Washington
Wednesday, January 16, 1980	Bought British-Italian Motors in Salt Lake City, Utah
Monday, September 15, 1980	Formed Landcar Agency (Service Contract Company), Salt Lake City, Utah
Monday, September 29, 1980	Bought Westside Toyota in Phoenix, Arizona
Friday, January 2, 1981	Formed Landcar Management Company, Salt Lake City, Utah
Friday, January 16, 1981	Sold British-Italian Motors in Salt Lake City, Utah
March 1981	Converted Landcar Life to Arizona based Re-Insurance Company
Wednesday, April 1, 1981	Bought Toyota of Moscow in Moscow, Idaho.
Friday, October 9, 1981	Bought House of Compacts (Subaru) in Murray, Utah

MILESTONES OF LARRY H. MILLER'S CAREER

DATE	MILESTONE
Friday, October 9, 1981	Bought out partner Reid Horne
Tuesday, March 16, 1982	Formed Larry Miller Leasing in Phoenix, Arizona, with Lou Gehring
Monday, February 7, 1983	Formed Larry H. Miller Leasing in Salt Lake City, Utah, with Curt Kindred
Wednesday, July 13, 1983	Opened new building for Murray Toyota dealership at 5800 So. State, Murray, Utah (first building built by Larry)
Monday, August 1, 1983	Sold Sundance Toyota in Spokane, Washington
Tuesday, September 6, 1983	Bought Gordon Wilson Chevrolet in Murray, Utah
Friday, March 16, 1984	Bought Jim Lanker Chrysler/Plymouth/Mazda in Glendale, Arizona
Monday, October 22, 1984	Bought Cottonwood Chrysler/Plymouth in Murray, Utah
Saturday, January 05, 1985	Landcar Life Insurance Company became a Utah domiciled insurance company
Thursday, April 11, 1985	Bought first half of Utah Jazz basketball team (NBA franchise) in Salt Lake City, Utah
May 1985	Completed Chrysler/Plymouth building at 5780 South State Street in Murray, Utah
Tuesday, June 18, 1985	Utah Jazz selected Karl Malone in first round (13th overall pick) of 1985 NBA Draft
Wednesday, June 26, 1985	Bought Pioneer Dodge in Murray, Utah
Friday, September 6, 1985	Announced the formation of the Jazz 100 Club
Saturday, December 14, 1985	Jazz retired jersey #7 in honor of Pete Maravich
Tuesday, April 1, 1986	Completed Hyundai building at 5601 So. State, Murray, Utah
Monday, June 16, 1986	Bought second half of Utah Jazz basketball team in Salt Lake City, Utah
Tuesday, December 30, 1986	Formed Larry H. Miller Corporation (holding company for five operations)
Wednesday, December 31, 1986	Purchased Owen Wright Oldsmobile/Cadillac in Midvale, Utah
Saturday, January 24, 1987	Formed Performance Automotive Products (formerly named Formation), Salt Lake City, Utah, with son Greg Miller (see 12/19/96)
Saturday, March 28, 1987	Acquired three Pro Image franchises

MILESTONES OF LARRY H. MILLER'S CAREER

DATE	MILESTONE
Friday, April 24, 1987	Purchased BGR Ranch in Franklin and Bannock Counties, Idaho
Monday, June 1, 1987	Bought Tom Lyons Hyundai in Boulder, Colorado, with Darrell Wells and Matt Singrin
March 1988	Opened new Mazda facility at 4600 West Glendale Ave. in Glendale, Arizona
Monday, June 20, 1988	Bought American Toyota in Albuquerque, New Mexico
Monday, August 1, 1988	Bought European Imports in Albuquerque, New Mexico
Monday, August 8, 1988	Bought Gene Osborn Hyundai in Aurora, Colorado
Monday, August 8, 1988	Bought Gene Osborn Hyundai in Colorado Springs, Colorado
Monday, August 8, 1988	Bought Gene Osborn Toyota in Colorado Springs, Colorado
Friday, September 2, 1988	Bought Toyota of Ogden in Ogden, Utah, with Tony Divino
Friday, December 9, 1988	Jazz retired jersey #1 in honor of Frank Layden
Friday, September 29, 1989	Bought Golden Eagles IHL Hockey Team in Salt Lake City, Utah
Tuesday, October 3, 1989	Formed Landcar Insurance Company of Colorado
March 1990	Completed Chevrolet facility at 5650 So. State, Murray, Utah
Tuesday, May 22, 1990	Ceremonial ground breaking for the Delta Center, Salt Lake City, Utah
Monday, June 11, 1990	Began selling Lexus (at Toyota facility in Murray, Utah)
Monday, June 11, 1990	Actual ground breaking (poured first concrete) for Delta Center, Salt Lake City, Utah
Thursday, September 6, 1990	Completed Lexus facility at 5701 So. State, Murray, Utah
Saturday, September 29, 1990	Completed Toyota facility at 4701 W. Glendale Ave., Glendale, Arizona; moved Phoenix Toyota franchise to Glendale, Arizona
Friday, October 4, 1991	Completed Delta Center Arena, Salt Lake City, Utah
Wednesday, October 9, 1991	Delta Center Arena dedication, Salt Lake City, Utah

MILESTONES OF LARRY H. MILLER'S CAREER

DATE	MILESTONE
Wednesday, October 16, 1991	First ticketed event at Delta Center: Utah Golden Eagles vs. Peoria Rivermen (IHL hockey)
Wednesday, October 23, 1991	First NBA game at Delta Center: Utah Jazz vs. New York Knicks
Thursday, October 24, 1991	First concert held at Delta Center: Oingo Boingo
Thursday, November 7, 1991	First NBA regular season game at Delta Center: Utah Jazz vs. Seattle SuperSonics
Wednesday, December 9, 1992	Bought Heritage Honda, Murray, Utah
Tuesday, December 15, 1992	Agreement with Toyota Motor Sales USA to install first-ever U.S. satellite Toyota dealership (Colorado Springs, Colorado)
Tuesday, February 16, 1993	Bought Channel 14 (KXIV) in Salt Lake City, Utah; renamed station KJZZ-TV
Sunday, February 21, 1993	Delta Center hosted 1993 NBA All-Star Game (Malone and Stockton named co-MVPs)
Monday, March 1, 1993	Bought 37.5% of Ken Ellegard Lincoln/Mercury in Colorado Springs, Colorado
Friday, May 14, 1993	Purchased University Lincoln/Mercury/Volvo/Mazda in Boulder, Colorado
Saturday, July 10, 1993	Opened Arrowhead Honda in Peoria, Arizona, with Ken Ellegard
Saturday, December 4, 1993	Jazz retired jersey #35 in honor of Darrell Griffith
Monday, January 10, 1994	Bought Garcia Toyota in Albuquerque, New Mexico. Renamed Karl Malone Toyota
Monday, March 28, 1994	Sold Golden Eagles IHL hockey team
Wednesday, July 6, 1994	Purchased Merrill Motors (Used Car Supermarket), Auto Mall Drive, Sandy, Utah
Thursday, July 7, 1994	Sold Chrysler/Plymouth franchise in Glendale, Arizona
Tuesday, September 13, 1994	Formed Prestige Financial Services in Salt Lake City, Utah
Wednesday, September 28, 1994	Purchased 33 acres from Woodbury Corp. for Utah Auto Mall in Sandy, Utah
Thursday, November 10, 1994	Purchased Utah Thrifty Rental Car Enterprises in Salt Lake City, Utah
Thursday, December 29, 1994	Formed Miller's Willowcreek Development with Preston Miller

MILESTONES OF LARRY H. MILLER'S CAREER

DATE	MILESTONE
Wednesday, January 4, 1995	Opened Larry H. Miller Used Car Supermarket in Sandy, Utah, with Greg Miller as GM
Tuesday, January 31, 1995	Sold Lincoln/Mercury/Mazda in Boulder, Colorado
Wednesday, February 1, 1995	John Stockton became NBA's all-time assist leader, passing Magic Johnson
Monday, February 6, 1995	Bought Don Chalmer's Chevrolet/Oldsmobile in Tulsa, Oklahoma
Saturday, April 1, 1995	Formed LHM Advertising in Salt Lake City, Utah
Tuesday, April 11, 1995	Opened Larry Miller Dodge in Peoria, Arizona
Monday, June 5, 1995	Purchased 24.8 acres in Peoria, Arizona, for Toyota, Dodge, and Hyundai dealerships
Saturday, July 1, 1995	Bought Bob Roberts Chrysler/Plymouth/Jeep in Hillsboro, Oregon, with Tom LaPoint
Thursday, September 14, 1995	Formed Larry H. Miller Charities in Salt Lake City, Utah
Wednesday, September 27, 1995	Formed Landcar Casualty Company in Sandy, Utah
Saturday, October 14, 1995	Formed Larry H. Miller Real Estate LLC in Sandy, Utah
Tuesday, February 20, 1996	John Stockton became NBA's all-time steals leader, passing Maurice Cheeks
Friday, March 1, 1996	Jazz retired jersey #53 in honor of Mark Eaton
May 1996	Completed Larry H. Miller Used Car Supermarket facility in Utah Auto Mall
Friday, June 28, 1996	Formed Larry H. Miller Education Foundation in Sandy, Utah
Thursday, September 12, 1996	Larry Miller Toyota in Phoenix, Arizona, moved to Peoria, Arizona
October 1996	Moved Larry H. Miller Chrysler/Plymouth and Larry H. Miller Dodge from Murray, Utah, to the Utah Auto Mall in Sandy, Utah
Friday, October 18, 1996	Bought out Pro Image contract; converted to Fanzz
Wednesday, October 30, 1996	Began operating WNBA Utah Starzz in Salt Lake City, Utah
Wednesday, December 18, 1996	Purchased 7 acres on Coors Road in Albuquerque, New Mexico
Thursday, December 19, 1996	Formed Performance Automotive (see 1/24/87)

MILESTONES OF LARRY H. MILLER'S CAREER

DATE   MILESTONE

DATE	MILESTONE
Friday, December 27, 1996	Formed Miller Family Real Estate LLC in Sandy, Utah
Monday, March 17, 1997	Opened Larry H's Gas Station, C-Store, Wendy's in Sandy, Utah
Tuesday, April 1, 1997	Bought Wolfe Auto Group (9 dealerships) in Boise and Caldwell, Idaho: Sundance Dodge; Capitol Cadillac/Buick/Pontiac; Honda of Boise; Target Acura/Mitsubishi; Target Subaru/Hyundai; Happy Day Ford; Better Buick/GMC/Nissan; Easy Auto Finance; Happy Day Wholesale Auto
Monday, April 14, 1997	Purchased 21.83 acres from Jordan School District in Sandy, Utah (site of Jordan Commons)
May 1997	Karl Malone was selected as the 1996–97 NBA Most Valuable Player
Thursday, May 29, 1997	Jazz defeated Houston (4–2) to advance to the franchise's first NBA Finals
Friday, June 13, 1997	Opened Larry H's Car Wash/Quick Lube in Sandy, Utah
Saturday, July 12, 1997	Opened Larry H. Miller Used Car Supermarket in Albuquerque, New Mexico (Coors Road)
September 1997	Formed Landcar Life Insurance Co. (Warehousing Agreement) in Fort Worth, Texas
Saturday, November 1, 1997	Opened Stockton to Malone Honda in Sandy, Utah
Friday, November 7, 1997	Broke ground for Jordan Commons in Sandy, Utah
Friday, November 14, 1997	Opened Karl Malone Toyota in Sandy, Utah
Wednesday, November 26, 1997	Completed Stockton to Malone Honda building in Sandy, Utah
Tuesday, February 17, 1998	Moved Larry Miller Dodge in Peoria, Arizona, to new facility at 8665 W. Bell Road
Friday, March 6, 1998	Purchased Hilton Ranch in Bannock County, Idaho
Friday, May 29, 1998	Completed Peoria, Arizona, Hyundai facility
Thursday, June 4, 1998	Opened Landcar Used Cars, Peoria, Arizona
Thursday, September 17, 1998	Broke ground for Larry H. Miller Entrepreneurship Center (Buildings 1 & 2) for Salt Lake Community College at 9800 So. and I-15, west of the frontage road, in Sandy, Utah

MILESTONES OF LARRY H. MILLER'S CAREER

DATE	MILESTONE
Friday, November 20, 1998	Purchased Dan Eastman Chrysler/Plymouth/Jeep with Barry Engle in Bountiful, Utah
Tuesday, March 16, 1999	Purchased Denver Toyota in Denver, Colorado
Friday, April 30, 1999	Sold Utah Thrifty Rental Car Enterprise
May 1999	Karl Malone was selected as the 1998–99 NBA Most Valuable Player
Monday, August 2, 1999	Purchased Scott Toyota in Scottsdale, Arizona, with Ken Ellegard
Tuesday, August 31, 1999	Opened Jordan Commons office building in Sandy, Utah
Friday, November 5, 1999	Opened Megaplex 17 at Jordan Commons in Sandy, Utah
Friday, January 21, 2000	Dedication and donation of Buildings 1 & 2 at Salt Lake Community College—Miller Campus
Wednesday, March 1, 2000	Sold Broken Arrow, Oklahoma, Chevrolet dealership to Sonic Automotive
Wednesday, March 8, 2000	Opened Mayan Restaurant at Jordan Commons in Sandy, Utah
Saturday, March 18, 2000	Opened Larry Miller Hyundai in Peoria, Arizona
Monday, April 24, 2000	Formed Miller Motorsports Park LLC in Tooele, Utah
Monday, June 19, 2000	Sold Boulder, Colorado, Volvo franchise to Ford Motor Company
Saturday, July 8, 2000	Purchased Brad Francis Chevrolet/Oldsmobile, Belen, New Mexico
Saturday, July 8, 2000	Purchased Brad Francis Ford/Mercury facility, Belen, New Mexico
Thursday, August 31, 2000	Sold 5601 So. State, Murray, Utah, property to Mike Hale
Friday, September 1, 2000	Purchased Scott Toyota Body Shop in Scottsdale, Arizona
Tuesday, October 10, 2000	Purchased Mead, Colorado, racetrack
Thursday, October 12, 2000	Purchased Land in Los Lunas, New Mexico, for Brad Francis dealerships
Monday, January 29, 2001	Purchased Gene Osborn Volkswagen/Kia/Isuzu, Lakewood, Colorado
Friday, March 23, 2001	Purchased 160 acres adjacent to Mead, Colorado, racetrack

MILESTONES OF LARRY H. MILLER'S CAREER

DATE	MILESTONE
Tuesday, April 10, 2001	Completed Subaru facility in Sandy, Utah, and began operations
Saturday, May 26, 2001	Completed Miller Ball Park, BYU campus, Provo, Utah
Tuesday, July 3, 2001	Sold Oldsmobile/Cadillac franchises in Midvale, Utah, to General Motors
Monday, July 16, 2001	Opened Utah Auto Credit in Midvale, Utah
Wednesday, September 26, 2001	Dedicated Buildings 3 & 4 at Salt Lake Community College—Miller Campus
Thursday, November 1, 2001	Opened Megaplex 12 at Gateway Mall in downtown Salt Lake City, Utah
Sunday, December 2, 2001	Bought Ford Truckland, Ford Superstore, and Ford Parts Warehouse in Salt Lake City, Utah, from FICO (Ford Motor Co.)
Monday, December 17, 2001	Purchased Atkinson Ranch in Bannock County, Idaho
Friday, March 1, 2002	Completed Brad Francis Chevrolet facility, Los Lunas, New Mexico
Wednesday, March 13, 2002	Completed Sundance Dodge, Boise, Idaho
Friday, May 10, 2002	Purchased Rose Ranch near Snowville, Utah
Wednesday, May 15, 2002	Dedicated and donated Building 5 at Salt Lake Community College—Miller Campus in conjunction with Pacificorp
Saturday, June 1, 2002	Toyota of Colorado Springs, Colorado, began operating as separate corporation
Thursday, June 13, 2002	Completed Sundance Dodge Body Shop, Boise, Idaho
Thursday, June 20, 2002	Sold 172 W. 7200 So., Midvale, Utah, property to Sportsman's Warehouse
Monday, July 15, 2002	Completed Larry Miller Buick/GMC/Pontiac parts and service facility, Caldwell, Idaho
Thursday, August 1, 2002	Completed Brad Francis Ford/Mercury facility, Los Lunas, New Mexico
September 2002	Completed Brad Francis Body Shop, Los Lunas, New Mexico
Sunday, September 1, 2002	Moved into new Larry H. Miller Ford Truckland facility at 1300 So. 500 W., Salt Lake City, Utah
Saturday, November 2, 2002	Moved Prestige Financial Services to 1414 So. 500 W., Salt Lake City, Utah, a 53,000-square-foot facility

MILESTONES OF LARRY H. MILLER'S CAREER

DATE	MILESTONE
Tuesday, November 19, 2002	Jazz retired jersey #14 in honor of Jeff Hornacek
Wednesday, December 4, 2002	WNBA Utah Starzz moved to San Antonio, Texas
Wednesday, February 12, 2003	Moved Glendale Mazda to Peoria, Arizona
Monday, March 3, 2003	Moved Karl Malone Toyota in Albuquerque, New Mexico, to Copper Ave.
Tuesday, March 4, 2003	Opened the Zions Bank Basketball Center in Salt Lake City, Utah (Jazz practice facility)
Monday, March 10, 2003	Purchased Southwest Hyundai, Albuquerque, New Mexico (moved to old Karl Malone Toyota location)
Monday, March 10, 2003	Started Larry Miller Hyundai, Coors Rd. Albuquerque, New Mexico (Added to UCS—Albuquerque)
Monday, March 10, 2003	Sold Denver Toyota to Sonic Automotive
Tuesday, May 13, 2003	Purchased Lower Ranch (addition to BGR Ranch) in Franklin and Bannock Counties, Idaho
Wednesday, July 2, 2003	Purchased Lindon, Utah, real estate (18+ acres for Lexus, Mercedes Benz, etc.)
Wednesday, July 30, 2003	Sold Peoria Mazda to Kemp Biddulph
Thursday, August 28, 2003	Donated Daktronics Electronic Scoreboard to University of Utah
Monday, December 1, 2003	Completed Gene Osborn Volkswagen facility in Lakewood, Colorado
Tuesday, March 30, 2004	Awarded Mercedes-Benz franchise in Lindon, Utah
Saturday, April 10, 2004	Completed Gene Osborn Kia facility in Lakewood, Colorado
Wednesday, April 14, 2004	Completed Lexus building in Lindon, Utah
Monday, April 19, 2004	Opened Larry H. Miller Lexus in Lindon, Utah
May 2004	Formed All-Star Catering in Salt Lake City, Utah
Saturday, May 1, 2004	Opened Larry Miller Volkswagen in Avondale, Arizona
Monday, November 29, 2004	Purchased Butterfield Ford in Sandy, Utah, from Brent Butterfield; renamed Champion Ford
Monday, October 25, 2004	Opened Mercedes-Benz of Lindon in Lindon, Utah

MILESTONES OF LARRY H. MILLER'S CAREER

DATE	MILESTONE
November 21–22, 2004	Jazz retired jersey #12 and dedicated a statue outside Delta Center in honor of John Stockton
Tuesday, January 11, 2005	Entered operating lease at Thanksgiving Point in Lehi, Utah (Megaplex 8)
Wednesday, March 30, 2005	Purchased Salt Lake Stingers (Triple-A baseball team) in Salt Lake City, Utah
Tuesday, April 26, 2005	Broke ground for Miller Motorsports Park in Tooele, Utah
Thursday, September 15, 2005	Opened Miller Kart Track at Miller Motorsports Park
Thursday, October 27, 2005	Changed name of Triple-A baseball team to Salt Lake Bees
Monday, December 12, 2005	Broke ground for Megaplex 13 in Ogden, Utah
Monday, January 30, 2006	Purchased St. Johns Nissan in Denver, Colorado; renamed Larry Miller Nissan
Thursday, March 23, 2006	Jazz retired jersey #32 and dedicated a statue outside Delta Center in honor of Karl Malone
Saturday, April 1, 2006	First track day event at Miller Motorsports Park
Wednesday, April 5, 2006	Opened Miller Performance Training Center at Miller Motorsports Park
Tuesday, April 18, 2006	Purchased Honda of St Johns in Hillsboro, Oregon; renamed Honda of Hillsboro
Tuesday, April 18, 2006	Purchased Portland Honda Motorcyle in Hillsboro, Oregon
Monday, May 15, 2006	Opened Megaplex 20 at The District in South Jordan, Utah
June 17–18, 2006	First AMA Superbike Championship and AMA Supermoto Championship races at Miller Motorsports Park
Monday, June 26, 2006	Purchased property at 175 W. 11400 So., Draper, Utah, from Corvallis
Saturday, July 15, 2006	First American Le Mans Series race at Miller Motorsports Park
Wednesday, August 9, 2006	Signed four-year contract extension keeping the Bees and Angels affiliates through the 2012 season
Tuesday, August 15, 2006	Completed clubhouse at Miller Motorsports Park

MILESTONES OF LARRY H. MILLER'S CAREER

DATE	MILESTONE
Saturday, September 2, 2006	First Grand-Am Rolex Sports Car Series race at Miller Motorsports Park
Wednesday, November 8, 2006	Miller Motorsports Park named "Motorsports Facility of the Year" by the Professional Motorsport World Expo in Cologne, Germany
Monday, November 20, 2006	Announced naming rights deal changing Delta Center to EnergySolutions Arena
Thursday, December 7, 2006	Purchased Scottsdale Nissan in Scottsdale, Arizona; renamed Riverview Nissan
Tuesday, December 12, 2006	Sold Hillsboro Chrysler-Jeep
Monday, January 29, 2007	Purchased Mesa Riverview Autoplex, Mesa, Arizona
Wednesday, April 11, 2007	Jazz retired jersey #4 in honor of Adrian Dantley
Tuesday, May 1, 2007	Opened Lindon Used Cars Supermarket in Lindon, Utah
Friday, June 1, 2007	Larry H. Miller Communications Corporation dba KJZZ-TV took over operation of KFAN radio
Friday, June 15, 2007	Opened Megaplex 13 at The Junction in Ogden, Utah
Saturday, July 14, 2007	First NASCAR Grand National West Series event at Miller Motorsports Park
Wednesday, September 5, 2007	Purchased Avondale Mazda in Avondale, Arizona; renamed Larry Miller Mazda
Saturday, September 29, 2007	Sold the one-millionth car in company history
Wednesday, October 3, 2007	Purchased Dodge franchise from Menlove in Bountiful, Utah
Thursday, February 21, 2008	Added Smart Cars to Mercedes franchise in Lindon, Utah
Friday, April 11, 2008	Purchased property at 551 W. 1700 So., Salt Lake City, Utah, from DSKW
Tuesday, May 13, 2008	Added Chrysler-Jeep to Dodge franchise in Boise, Idaho
Saturday, May 10, 2008	Closed (Larry Miller) Capitol Pontiac-Buick-Cadillac in Boise, Idaho
Monday, May 19, 2008	Karl Malone Toyota moved into Draper location
Sunday, June 1, 2008	First HANNspree FIM Superbike World Championship event at Miller Motorsports Park

MILESTONES OF LARRY H. MILLER'S CAREER

DATE	MILESTONE
Monday, June 30, 2008	Purchased Spaghetti Mama's at Jordan Commons in Sandy, Utah
Wednesday, July 16, 2008	Greg Miller promoted to Chief Executive Officer of the Larry H. Miller Group of Companies
Wednesday, July 16, 2008	Created Larry H. Miller Group of Companies Advisory Board
Monday, August 11, 2008	Closed Lindon Used Cars Supermarket
Monday, September 1, 2008	Changed name of LHM Advertising to Saxton I Horne Advertising I Media Services
Saturday, October 4, 2008	Opened Off-Road Course at Miller Motorsports Park
Monday, December 1, 2008	Saxton I Horne Advertising I Media Services acquired Grizzly Gulch Advertising
Tuesday, December 2, 2008	Miller Motorsports Park named "2008 World Superbike Organizer of the Year" by the HANNspree FIM Superbike World Championship
Tuesday, December 16, 2008	Sold Mayan Adventure and Spaghetti Mama's at Jordan Commons in Sandy, Utah, to Atlantic Restaurant Consultants
Friday, February 20, 2009	Passing of Larry H. Miller

INDEX

INDEX

INDEX